UNDERSTANDING THE MASS

Different Names for the Eucharistic Celebration

UNDERSTANDING
THE
MASS

Historical, Biblical, Theological,
and Liturgical Perspectives

Bishop Joseph Osei-Bonsu

Foreword by Cardinal Peter K. A. Turkson

Paulist Press
New York / Mahwah, NJ

Cover image by 501room/Shutterstock.com
Cover design by Sharyn Banks
Book design by Lynn Else

Library of Congress Cataloging-in-Publication Data
Names: Osei-Bonsu, Joseph, author.
Title: Understanding the Mass : historical, biblical, theological, and liturgical perspectives / Bishop Joseph Osei-Bonsu ; foreword by Cardinal Peter K. A. Turkson.
Description: Mahwah, NJ : Paulist Press, 2016. | Includes bibliographical references and index.
Identifiers: LCCN 2016026450 (print) | LCCN 2016030711 (ebook) | ISBN 9780809153022 (pbk. : alk. paper) | ISBN 9781587686375 (Ebook)
Subjects: LCSH: Mass. | Mass—Celebration.
Classification: LCC BX2230.3 .O84 2016 (print) | LCC BX2230.3 (ebook) | DDC 264/.02036—dc23
LC record available at https://lccn.loc.gov/2016026450

ISBN 978-0-8091-5302-2 (paperback)
ISBN 978-1-58768-637-5 (e-book)

Published by Paulist Press
997 Macarthur Boulevard
Mahwah, New Jersey 07430
www.paulistpress.com

Printed and bound in the
United States of America

To all the people of Ghana

Chapter Two

The Assembly and Its Ministers

HAVING TOUCHED BRIEFLY ON THE THEOLOGY OF the Christian Eucharist as it evolved through the Last Supper, we can proceed to looking at those who gather to celebrate the Mass today. The General Instruction of the Roman Missal repeatedly stresses the communal character of this assembly. In this chapter we will examine the nature and purpose of the Christian assembly, the roles which its members play, and more specifically the role of its ministers.

The Assembly

In order for Mass to be celebrated, it is necessary to have people of God to gather in the name of Christ in this celebration. "Where two or three are gathered together in my name, there am I in the midst of them" (Matt 18:20). According to the General Instruction of the Roman Missal, the faithful always form the holy people of God, in order to give thanks to God and offer the unblemished sacrificial victim not only by the hands of the priest but also together with him, that they may learn to offer themselves. The assembly, religious, the church, the people of God, we all gather to share the life of the Church and to encourage, to thank, and to offer forgiveness, and a sense of community, each of us in the work of God. And through the cooperation between the priest and the faithful, the community itself shares in the offering of the sacrifice through participation. We also may by our brokenness pray for silence. This allows the people to

Contents

Foreword

PREACHING TO HIS FLOCK ON THE IMPORTANCE OF THE Eucharist as Bishop of the North-African Church of Hippo, St. Augustine (+430) stated, "It is your own mystery which is placed on the Lord's table. It is your own mystery that you receive at Communion when the priest says 'The Body of Christ' and you reply 'Amen.' When you say 'Amen,' you are saying yes to what you are" (Sermon 272). In another of his sermons, Augustine states, "If you receive worthily, you are what you have received" (Sermon 227). For Augustine, Christ's Body is both on the altar and gathered around it.

Many centuries later in his *motu proprio* on sacred music, *Tra le sollecitudini* (November 22, 1903), Pope St. Pius X (+1914) spoke of the sacred liturgy as the Church's most important and indispensable source, "that is, active participation in the sacred mysteries and in the public and solemn prayer of the Church."[1] Those words of Pius X became the *magna carta* of the twentieth-century Liturgical Movement that paved the way for the liturgical reforms of the Second Vatican Council (1962–65). Indeed, the Council's Constitution on the Sacred Liturgy, *Sacrosanctum Concilium*, echoed the words of Pope Pius X when it stated that "the liturgy is the summit toward which the activity of the Church is directed; at the same time it is the fount from which all her power flows" (no. 10).

This is a very rich understanding of what happens when we gather to celebrate those sacred mysteries, and what our liturgical participation challenges us to recognize as we live our daily Christian lives. And yet, we know how often this fundamental truth can easily be overlooked. That is why this book by Bishop Osei-Bonsu is so very important. It makes a significant contribution to the ongoing liturgical renewal within the life of the Church in Ghana and beyond.

Just as the Bishop of Hippo addressed his own local church on the centrality of the Eucharist so many centuries ago, the following pages of this book reflect the twenty-first-century concerns of one who is at once a bishop, a pastor, and a chief shepherd seeking to help his flock celebrate the sacrament of the Holy Eucharist meaningfully and with the greatest profit. It is thus an undertaking that expresses a genuine pastoral solicitude for the worthy and fruitful celebration of the Mass. As such, *Understanding the Mass: Historical, Biblical, Theological, and Liturgical Perspectives* is also a useful pastoral resource and a noteworthy addition to the literature that already exists, seeking to help the Church to properly celebrate the one sacrament that is the "source and summit" of her life and mission.

Our catechists and religious education instructors are to be commended for the great sacrifices they make and for the efforts they put into preparing candidates for the sacraments—especially the sacraments of christian initiation. Nevertheless, it is not an overstatement when the author writes, "Many attend Mass regularly but there are many things in the Mass that they may not understand or that may puzzle them." This is not because the Mass is celebrated in some foreign language. For even when it is celebrated in local languages, as the author continues, "it is still the case that many things are unintelligible to many people." Accordingly, his book "attempts to throw light on the Mass by means of historical, biblical, theological, and liturgical insights."

The author does this in seven chapters of essentially two distinct compositional styles: a first chapter of scholarly, critical, and analytical presentation on the origins and evolution of the structure and the form of the Mass, rich in references; and then six subsequent chapters on the celebration of Mass: the various actors, their postures, their dressing, gestures, and so forth, which make up the celebration of the Eucharist. Here, the author draws substantially on the *General Instruction of the Roman Missal*, documenting his text with occasional biblical and canonical references as appropriate. Accordingly, the concluding chapter 8, which includes "Notes on the Celebration of the Mass," offers a helpful survey of the "dos and don'ts" in the celebration of the sacrament of the Eucharist. Such concrete examples enrich the work, calling for greater attention and vigilance on the part of bishops and priests, to guarantee prayerful liturgical celebrations that are based on a solid liturgical theology.

Indeed, this same scope is in keeping with the spirit and goal of the *General Instruction of the Roman Missal* itself, in helping both clergy and laity alike to realize that when they gather together at Mass, they "form a holy people, a people of God's own possession and a royal priesthood, so that they may give thanks to God and offer the unblemished sacrificial Victim not only by means of the hands of the Priest but also together with him and so that they may learn to offer their very selves" (*GIRM 95*). Thus, the aim of this book is ultimately to help the lay faithful and ordained ministers to recognize that in a proper and dignified celebration of the Holy Eucharist, they share in the sacrifice of Christ, offering themselves with him. And this is not mere rhetoric!

Fifty years after the Second Vatican Council, we have barely grasped the full import of those words—how the lay faithful are called to join their own lives, their own sacrifice—with the sacrifice of the priest through their full, active, and conscious participation in the celebration of the sacred mysteries. This is well articulated in the exchange at the Preparation of the Gifts, when the priest says to the liturgical assembly, "Pray brothers and sisters that my sacrifice and yours may be acceptable to God, the almighty Father." It is the one sacrifice of Christ in which priest and people share, and the one Body of Christ that members of the Church receive together for their own sanctification, that they might themselves become a Holy Communion—Christ's Body and Blood, broken and poured out in service of those within God's world who are most in need. Indeed, in the sacrifice of the Mass, we celebrate Jesus' offering of himself to the Father in an atoning sacrifice. The power of this atonement saves us, rendering us capable to also offer ourselves to the Father: to live for the Father. This is the core of the celebration of the Mass as the *sacrament of our salvation*.

The Mass, of course, is never an end in itself. In fact, the very word *Mass* comes from *missio*—mission. From start to finish, Eucharist and mission are intimately linked, and the liturgical assembly is sent forth—transformed by the Body and Blood of Christ that it has received, to become the Body and Blood of Christ in a broken world, so desperately in need of encountering it and being nourished by it. It is therefore most appropriate that the Latin dismissal at the end of the liturgy *Ite missa est*, literally means "Go, you are sent."

As Pope St. John Paul II stated:

> The Eucharist is not merely an expression of communion in the Church's life; it is also a project of solidarity for all of humanity....The Christian who takes part in the Eucharist learns to become a promoter of communion, peace and solidarity in every situation. More than ever, our troubled world, which began the new Millennium with the spectre of terrorism and the tragedy of war, demands that Christians learn to experience the Eucharist as a great school of peace, forming men and women who, at various levels of responsibility in social, cultural and political life, can become promoters of dialogue and communion.[2]

This means that the Eucharist necessarily links us to one another within the mystical Body of Christ with whom we share Communion, but it also calls us forth beyond the walls of our churches and communities to the margins—to the periphery—as instruments of God's justice and peace, embracing the whole of God's world as Christ would have us do.

This work deserves a wide international reading, as both the lay faithful and ordained ministers all over the world seek to improve the quality of their own Eucharistic celebrations, so that God may be worshipped "in spirit and in truth." Thus, I am grateful to Bishop Osei-Bonsu for offering us a helpful resource in our efforts toward a more meaningful celebration of the Mass, as we strive for a deeper understanding of those sacred mysteries that we are so privileged to celebrate.

Cardinal Peter K. A. Turkson
Rome, the Conversion of St. Paul, January 25, 2015

Preface

EVERY GOOD CATHOLIC HAS BEEN RAISED TO ATTEND Mass (especially on Sundays) because the Mass is the center and apex of the liturgical life of the Church. Many Catholics attend Mass regularly, yet there are many things that they may not understand or that may puzzle them. For instance, they may not understand the significance of the sprinkling of water, the use of incense and candles, the many gestures used in the Mass, including the making of the Sign of the Cross, making the Sign of the Cross on the forehead, lips, and the chest before the proclamation of the Gospel, bowing, kneeling, genuflecting, and so on. Many may not know the history behind the prayers said during the celebration or of the vestments and vessels used. Even though the Mass is celebrated in many places using the people's own language, it is probably true to say that the Mass is not fully understood by many people today. This is partly because the Mass is a rite that has over two thousand years of history behind it and contains elements with origins in Jewish, Greek, Roman, and other ancient cultures.

Against this background, this book attempts to throw light on the Mass by means of historical, biblical, theological, and liturgical insights. A summary of the history of the Christian Eucharist from the Last Supper until the present will be given, taking note of Jewish, Greek, Roman, and other influences on it. There is also an overview showing how deeply rooted the Mass is in the Bible and in the theology of the early Church. This book likewise looks at the liturgical norms governing the celebration of Mass. The text of the Mass is given attentive treatment. At times, examples will be given of the many things done by priests and bishops in the celebration of Mass that are not liturgically correct, lacking any basis in the liturgical norms. These correctives are important because these mistaken practices can get passed on to young priests through the example of older priests and bishops.

I owe a debt of gratitude to the following people for reading the manuscript in its entirety and offering invaluable comments and suggestions: Rev. Keith F. Pecklers, SJ, Professor of Liturgy, Pontifical Gregorian University, and Professor of Liturgical History, Pontifical Liturgical Institute, Rome; Rev. Vincent Owusu, SVD, former lecturer in Liturgy at St. Victor's Seminary, Tamale, Ghana; Rev. Dominic Nyamekye Peprah, lecturer in Liturgy, St. Peter's Regional Seminary, Pedu, Cape Coast, Ghana; and Rev. Martin Asiedu-Peprah, former lecturer in New Testament, St. Peter's Regional Seminary, Pedu, Cape Coast, Ghana. I am most grateful to His Eminence, Cardinal Peter Kodwo Appiah Turkson, President, Pontifical Council for Justice and Peace, for writing the Foreword.

Most Rev. Joseph Osei-Bonsu
Mampong, Feast of Epiphany, January 6, 2015

CHAPTER ONE

The Evolution of the Christian Eucharist

IN THIS CHAPTER, WE WILL LOOK BRIEFLY AT THE evolution of the Catholic Mass from the Last Supper to the present. However, given the ecumenical liturgical collaboration that grew in the twentieth century, and especially after the Second Vatican Council, much of what is said about the Catholic Mass is, in fact, also applicable to the Christian Eucharist in a wider ecumenical context. This is especially evident in terms of structure and content, even despite the doctrinal and disciplinary issues that continue to divide Christians at the altar of the Holy Eucharist. We should note that in the period after the Second Vatican Council, many non-Catholic churches have adopted the Catholic structure of the Mass for the revision of their Eucharistic rites, as well as the three-year cycle Roman Lectionary. In revising their liturgical calendars, a number of these churches have even included liturgical texts from post-Reformation Catholic saints, such as Ignatius Loyola, Pope St. John XXIII, and Mother Teresa! Now even some Presbyterian churches distribute ashes on Ash Wednesday!

To that end, we would like to address "The Evolution of the Christian Eucharist" rather than "The Evolution of the Mass," as it would better correspond to the chapter's content, and would be a bit more ecumenically sensitive in the case of Episcopalians (Anglicans), Methodists, and Lutherans who may read the book. Indeed, much of what is said in the book as a whole about the Catholic Mass is, broadly speaking, applicable to the Christian Eucharist.

The Christian Eucharist and the Last Supper

The Christian Eucharist consists of two main parts: the Liturgy of the Word and the Liturgy of the Eucharist. The Liturgy of the Eucharist has its origin in the Last Supper that Jesus had with his disciples (Matt 26:26–29; Mark 14:22–25; Luke 22:15–20; 1 Cor 11:23–26). According to the accounts of the Last Supper in these passages, Jesus took bread, blessed God, broke the bread, and gave it to his disciples, telling them to eat of it because it was his body. In the same way, after they had eaten, he took the cup, gave thanks, and gave it to them, telling them to take it and drink of it, because it was the cup of the covenant in his blood. At the end he said, "Do this in memory of me" (Luke 22:19; 1 Cor 11:24). In performing these actions, Jesus gave a model so that his followers might do what he himself had done. When the Church celebrates the Eucharist, it obeys Christ's command and does what he did at the Last Supper.

How did the Christian Eucharist as we know it today develop from the Last Supper that Jesus shared with his disciples? The first step in answering this question is to try to understand this important meal. What then was the Last Supper?

The Last Supper in the New Testament

There are many references and allusions to the Last Supper in the New Testament (1 Cor 10:1–22; 11:20–22; Luke 24:30; Acts 27:35; Mark 6:41; 8:6; John 6:25–59; 19:34; Acts 2:42, 46; 20:7, 11), but most important are the four accounts in Matthew 26:26–29; Mark 14:22–25; Luke 22:15–20; and 1 Corinthians 11:23–26. We will look at these four accounts starting with 1 Corinthians 11:23–26, which is the oldest among them.

THE LAST SUPPER IN 1 CORINTHIANS 11:23–26

1 Corinthians was written by Paul around AD 54 in response to a letter that he had received from the Christians in Corinth in which they mentioned a number of problems facing their community. After speaking about how they should behave toward

non-Christians, Paul dealt with the issue of how the Corinthian Christians behaved at "liturgical assemblies" (chs. 11–14). He spoke of a church meal called the Lord's Supper (1 Cor 11:20; cf. "the table of the Lord," 1 Cor 10:20) that was celebrated, evidently on a regular basis, in their Church. However, there were problems with the way this meal was celebrated.

The fundamental problem had to do with tensions that existed in the church between the poor and the rich. Since the Christians in those days did not have church buildings, the church meals had to be held in the houses of church members. The size of the house determined the number of people that could meet there. It is likely that the houses of the rich were often selected as they were big enough to accommodate large numbers of people.

Yet, unlike our practice today where the Eucharistic meal is shared with the purpose of expressing love and solidarity within the community, there was another meal that was eaten strictly according to class in line with the practice in wider Greco-Roman society. It is clear from the way Paul speaks that when they met for such meals, some members consumed excessive amounts of food and drink. The rich seem to have brought a lot of food (including meat) for themselves, whereas the poorer members had to be content with the little that they had.[1] Thus, although the rich made their houses available to the church, they did so in a manner that maintained social divisions. It is likely that the rich were guilty of overindulgence, causing feelings of envy among the poor who were made to feel inferior (cf. 1 Cor 12:15). For Paul, this went against the purpose of such meals. Both hunger and drunkenness had no place in a church meal. Disorderly conduct and social distinctions also tainted the celebration. Paul criticized these practices in 1 Corinthians 11, saying that in view of these abuses, the church meal could not be said to be the *Lord's* Supper. In light of such conduct, it was clear to Paul that the Corinthian Christians had "lost any sense that love as the right relation to others is the... necessary expression of their faith as the right relation to God,"[2] Because of this "lack of love...in reality there was no Eucharist."[3]

Paul instructed that if the rich wanted to have a bigger meal or more expensive food, they should have a private meal at home. If this was done, the celebration of the church meal would not be characterized by social divisions. To correct these abuses,

Paul appealed to the tradition that he had received concerning the Lord's Supper and which he had earlier passed on to them by word of mouth. The language that Paul used in citing this tradition makes it clear that we are dealing with "an accepted, authoritative tradition."[4]

Paul says that he received the Eucharistic tradition that he handed on "from the Lord." In the view of some scholars, this was something that he had received in the form of a private vision or was communicated to him directly from the Lord. However, it is more likely that it was a piece of church tradition that had the authority of the Lord behind it (cf. the use of words of the Lord, undoubtedly handed down in church tradition to Paul, in 1 Cor 7:10, 9:14).[5] It has been noted that "by his use of the terms *received* and *delivered* it is clear that he is referring to a tradition which he was taught by the church."[6] It should also be observed that *received* and *delivered* were technical terms used to describe the passing on of oral tradition (cf. Luke 1:2; 1 Cor 15:3).

According to this tradition, Jesus took bread, gave thanks, and broke it with the words "This is my body which is for you. Do this in remembrance of me" (1 Cor 11:24). Next, "after supper," Jesus acted "in the same way" with the cup, saying, "This cup is the new covenant in my blood. Do this, as often as you drink it, in remembrance of me" (1 Cor 11:25).

We should note that whereas Paul and Luke respectively have "This is my body which is for you" and "This is my body which is given for you," in Mark and Matthew, we have simply "This is my body."[7] Protestant interpreters take the phrase "This is my body" as figurative, so that one would translate *is* as "signifies" or "represents." In this view, Jesus was not referring literally to his physical body and blood with this phrase but was indicating that the physical elements are symbols of his life that would be given for them. Roman Catholic scholars, however, find a presence of the Lord in the bread based on "This *is* my body." The Catholic understanding establishes a direct link between the broken bread ("the body given for you") and Jesus' death on the cross and, therefore, maintains that there is a sacrificial dimension to the Eucharistic meal. Grammatically, the present participle ("which is given" [Gk: *didomenon*]) may sometimes be used in place of the future participle to indicate the end in view (cf. Luke 1:35;

13:23; 22:20, 21). In that case, "which is given" may be translated "which is to be given" or "which will be given."

In "This is my body which is for you" (1 Cor 11:24), we should note that the phrase "for you" forms part of a series of statements which teach that Christ died for other people (Rom 5:8; 8:32; 1 Cor 15:3; 2 Cor 5:15 [3x]; Gal 2:20; 3:13; Eph 5:2, 25; 1 Tim 2:6; Titus 2:14) and which are found throughout the New Testament (Mark 10:45 [Gk: *anti*]; John 10:11, 15; 11:52; Heb 2:9; 9:24; 1 Pet 2:21; 3:18; 1 John 3:16). Thus, the death of Jesus is seen as his self-giving in death so that other people might be redeemed from sin and its judgment and be justified.

In Luke, Jesus speaks of his body being "given" for the disciples. Elsewhere the word *give* is sometimes found with the meaning of giving in offering, in sacrifice, and even in death (see Luke 2:24; cf. Mark 10:45; Gal 1:4; 2 Cor 8:5; John 6:51; 1 Tim 2:6; Titus 2:14). Jesus gives himself vicariously for "others."

In the Pauline and Lucan accounts, we have "Do this in remembrance of me" (1 Cor 11:24, 25; Luke 22:19). This instruction to the disciples is not found in either the Marcan or Matthean versions. "Do this in remembrance of me" means "perform this action in remembrance of me." "Do this" is a reinterpretation of "remembrance" that the Passover meal itself is supposed to be: "that you may remember the day of your departure from the land of Egypt all the days of your life" (Deut 16:3). As Jesus in the celebration of the Last Supper replaces the Passover lamb, so the remembrance of him is to replace the remembrance of the Passover itself. This remembrance is further explained by Paul when he says of the celebration of the Lord's Supper, "For as often as you eat this bread and drink the cup, you proclaim the Lord's death until he comes" (1 Cor 11:26). It is not merely a matter of calling to mind what Jesus did, but "a re-presenting of him and his act at the Last Supper to the awareness of the apostles."[8] The disciples are to do this continually in order to bring Jesus to mind.

Next, we have "This cup is the new covenant in my blood" (1 Cor 11:25). The same wording is found in Luke. This form identifies the cup with the new covenant, whereas Mark 14:24 more directly identifies it with the blood itself: "This is my blood of the covenant, which is poured out for many." Matthew 26:28 has a similar wording, "For this is my blood of the covenant." The "new covenant" is an allusion to Jeremiah 31:31, the promise made by Yahweh of a pact that he would make with "the house of Israel and the house of Judah." This new covenant spoken of by Christ reflects the "old covenant" (see 2 Cor 3:14) made by Yahweh and the people of Israel on the mountain when Moses took the blood of twelve sacrificed oxen and sprinkled it, half on the people and half on the altar in token of the pact: "See the blood of the covenant that the Lord has made" (Exod 24:8). In this new form, the covenant is established "in my blood." Jesus' own blood is now involved in the sacrifice.

In conclusion, we can say that what Paul says in 1 Corinthians 11:23–26 gives us an insight into the celebration of the Lord's Supper in Corinth. However, it is important to bear in mind the context in which he makes this statement concerning the celebration of the Lord's Supper. He does not set out with the primary intention of describing *how* the Eucharist should be celebrated. What he says here should not be taken "as an *ordo*, or script: Paul quotes it in order to remind the Corinthians of the meaning that he attaches to their celebration of the Lord's Supper."[9]

THE LAST SUPPER IN THE SYNOPTICS

As mentioned earlier, the other three accounts of the Last Supper are found in Mark 14:22–25; Matthew 26:26–29; and Luke 22:14–20. The earliest of these, the Gospel of Mark, dates from around AD 70. In these Gospels, the Last Supper is presented as being celebrated in the context of a Passover meal, eaten at the time when the Passover was being celebrated. In the discussion of the tradition that Paul received and passed on to the Corinthians, we saw that there were Passover motifs in the institution narratives of 1 Corinthians 11:23–26 and Luke 22:14–20 with their references to "Do this in remembrance of me" (1 Cor 11:24, 25; Luke 22:19). In light of this and of the fact that the Synoptics place the Last Supper in the context of the Passover, it is necessary to look briefly at the Passover.

In the Book of Exodus, God commanded the Israelites to observe the Passover feast (or *Pasch*) in memory of their deliverance from Pharaoh (Exod 12). The eating of the Passover involved the washing of hands, eating bitter herbs (to remind the Israelites of their slavery in Egypt), explanation of the symbolism of the foods being eaten, the blessing and distribution of wine and unleavened bread, the eating of the paschal lamb with joy, and a particularly solemn blessing pronounced over the Cup of Blessing by the father of the family or the one presiding at this meal. In this great prayer of praise and blessing (*berakah*), those eating the meal blessed (i.e., praised) God and thanked him for all the blessings that the Israelites enjoyed, especially their freedom from slavery in Egypt and their Exodus or coming out of Egypt into the Promised Land.

There are many strong arguments that support the view that the Last Supper was associated with a Passover meal. Some of these are:[10]

1. It was required that the Passover meal be eaten inside the walled city of Jerusalem, and the Last Supper was indeed eaten inside the city walls.
2. It was a requirement that the Passover night be spent inside greater Jerusalem, which comprised Jerusalem and the surrounding hills facing it. Jesus and the disciples spent that night, unlike other nights, in Gethsemane, within greater Jerusalem, and not in Bethany.
3. Jesus and his disciples reclined as they ate (John 21:20). It was the custom to sit while eating ordinary meals but to recline at the Passover.
4. People in Israel normally ate two meals a day. The first was a breakfast eaten around 10:00 or 11:00 in the morning, and the second was the main meal eaten in the late afternoon. The Last Supper was eaten in the evening (1 Cor 11:23; Mark 14:17), as demanded by the Law for the Passover (Exod 12:8).
5. The Last Supper was concluded with a hymn (Matt 26:30; Mark 14:26), and it was customary at the end of the Passover to sing the last part of the Hallel Psalms (i.e., Psalms 113—118).
6. It was the custom during the celebration of the Passover to offer an interpretation of the meal's elements (Exod 12:26–27).
7. It was also customary at the Passover to give some money to the poor, a practice that would explain Judas's leaving the gathering (John 13:29).

None of these arguments by itself is conclusive, but when taken together, they strongly suggest that the Last Supper was indeed associated with a Passover meal.

Even though the Synoptic Gospels set the Last Supper in this paschal or Passover setting, John does not. However, by highlighting Jesus' unbroken bones, John alludes to the fact that the death of Jesus resembled a Passover sacrifice (John 19:36), a connection made explicit by Paul in 1 Corinthians 5:7, "For our paschal lamb [lit. "our Passover"], Christ, has been sacrificed."[11] Perhaps John was more interested in portraying Jesus as the paschal Lamb of God (John 1:29), whose death could be compared to those lambs being prepared for slaughter for the Passover that had not yet taken place (John 18:28; 19:31).

If the Last Supper was eaten in the context of a Passover meal, then it would have reminded Jesus and his disciples that they formed part of God's people who had been delivered from bondage in Egypt by God's mighty action.[12] However, Jesus took the Passover meal and gave it a new significance as a meal whose repetition by his followers would enable them to remember him. Instead of reinterpreting the Passover lamb, he used the bread and cup as symbols of his body and blood. He spoke of his own death as a sacrifice that would usher in a new covenant; the bread was to represent his body given in death for the people, and the cup was to represent his blood shed in sacrifice ("which is poured out for you," Matt 26:28; Mark 14:24; Luke 22:20). In this way, Jesus linked the Last Supper with the crucifixion to come the next day and so established the new covenant (cf. Matt 26:28; Mark 14:24; Luke 22:20). Those who partook of the bread and cup thus formed a fellowship through their common participation in the benefits brought about by his sacrificial offering of himself.

THE INSTITUTION NARRATIVES IN THE SYNOPTICS

In discussing the institution narrative as found in the tradition that Paul mentions in 1 Corinthians 11:23–26, we saw that the versions found in Paul and in Luke are very similar but differ in some ways from the Marcan and Matthean versions. In this section, we will look at aspects of the words of institution found in the Synoptics that have not already been treated in the discussion on 1 Corinthians 11:23–26.

1. "The blood of the covenant which is poured out *for many*" (Mark 14:24) or "the blood of the covenant, which is poured out *for many for the forgiveness of sins*" (Matt 26:28). The word *many* here is most likely used in the Semitic sense of "all" (as it is, e.g., in Rom 5:15, 19) and may point to the underlying Hebrew or Aramaic spoken at the meal.[13] Daniel Harrington explains that the phrase "for many" in Mark and in Matthew "means for all, not just for a few." He cites as the basis for Mark and Matthew the words of Isaiah 53:12, that is, the Servant by his suffering "bore the sins of many." *Many* is a collective, not restrictive, word: it means "all."[14] According to Stein, "it is illegitimate to interpret 'many' as denoting a limited atonement, for the expression here means 'transgressors,' i.e. it refers to all, as the synonymous parallelism in Isaiah 53:12b–c clearly indicates."[15]

   Albert Vanhoye points out that the corresponding Hebrew word for "many" (i.e., *rabim*) indicates a great number without specifying whether it includes many or all. According to him, in the Hebrew equivalent, there is no dialectical opposition between *many* and *all*, which is not the case with modern languages like English, where these words are mutually exclusive. He contends that the intention of Jesus at the Last Supper was not directed to a specific group of people, however numerous: his intention as the Savior of the world was universal.[16] Whether or not everyone will welcome Jesus' universal offer of salvation ultimately depends on human freedom.

2. "…for the forgiveness of sins"

   These words are unique to Matthew. They are not found in the other Last Supper accounts. They stress that the death of Jesus has a saving effect; it is a deliverance from slavery to sin. As in Romans 11:26–27; Hebrews 10:16–19; and 11:15, the new covenant is linked to the forgiveness of sins. These words call to mind Matthew 1:21, "And you are to name him Jesus, for he will save his people from their sins." Jesus saves his people from their sins by dying for them and thereby making a new relationship with God possible.

In the foregoing, we have looked at the accounts of the Last Supper as found in 1 Corinthians 11 and in the Synoptics. It should be observed that these accounts of the Last Supper were written twenty-five to sixty years after the event. During this period, what really took place would have been partly lost and each community would have remembered the event in the way it had been passed on to it. In their accounts of the Last Supper, the authors would have been influenced by the way the Eucharist was celebrated by their communities at the time when they wrote.

Indeed, one issue that scholars have to contend with regarding the origin of the Eucharist is the question of how far the accounts of the Last Supper can be taken as reliable accounts of something that actually took place and to what extent they have been influenced by the later liturgical practices of the early Christians. According to many scholars of liturgy, we should avoid interpreting the structure and wording of the institution narratives as actual liturgical texts. They caution us against trying to find in these institution narratives the local Eucharistic practice of the communities in which these Gospels were written. For example, the earliest Gospel, Mark, as has been noted above, was most likely written in Rome around AD 70. As has been indicated above, in Mark and the other Synoptic Gospels, the Last Supper is linked with a Passover meal; however, scholars argue that we should not make too much of this, "since Mark's church is unlikely to have been concerned with the observance of the external details of the Jewish Passover ritual...[since] the entire focus of the meal is on Jesus' death."[17] In this connection, we note Marshall's observation: "The somewhat stylized nature of the accounts suggests that the wording had become 'fixed' as part of a liturgical statement used in church meetings and was incorporated into the Gospels."[18] According to Bradshaw, "The institution narratives were neither liturgical texts to be recited at the celebration nor liturgical instructions to regulate it, but instead catechesis of a liturgical kind. It was their regular repetition for catechetical purposes within some—but apparently not all—early Christian communities that gave them their particular literary style and character."[19]

The Celebration of the Last Supper in the Acts of the Apostles

In the Acts of the Apostles, there are many passages that speak of the "breaking of bread" (Acts 2:42, 46; 20:7, 11; 24:30). While it is uncertain that these passages refer to a celebration that derives its origin from the Last Supper, there is no doubt that this is how Luke understood it.[20] Support for this can be found in Luke's use of the expression "breaking of bread" (Luke 22:19, "And he took bread, and when he had given thanks he broke it and gave it to them, saying, 'This is my body which is given for you. Do this in remembrance of me'"). Further support for it is found in the fact that in Acts 20:7, the breaking of bread occurred in the context of church worship that took place on the first day of the week. Thus, Luke understood these passages that speak of the "breaking of bread" to mean the fulfilment of Jesus' command to "do this in remembrance of me" found in his Gospel. According to Stein,[21] it will not be right to take them simply to be referring to ordinary meals, or even "love feasts," as that would go against Luke's usual practice of showing how the followers of Jesus in Acts carried out his teachings. The breaking of bread may have taken place normally during a love-feast, but in view of the fact that the wording here is similar to that of the Last Supper ("breaking bread"), it would seem that what is most important for Luke is the celebration of the Supper.[22]

It is clear that the early Christians almost immediately separated the celebration of the Supper from the Passover, for the "breaking of bread" was practiced far more often than once a year. There are hints that it was celebrated on a weekly basis (Acts 20:7, 11; 1 Cor 16:2) and even daily (Acts 2:46–47). However, the New Testament does not state how often it should be celebrated. In the very early stages of the Church, the supper was celebrated in the context of a "love feast" (Jude 12; Acts 2:42, 46; 1 Cor 11:20–

22, 33–34). The early Christians did this since Jesus' Last Supper was associated with a meal (Luke 22:20; 1 Cor 11:25).

The Abandonment of the Meal

In the accounts of the Last Supper in Luke 22:15–20 and 1 Corinthians 11:23–26, there is reference to the main meal: the blessing of the wine comes "after supper," an expression that is not found in Mark 14:22–25 and Matthew 26:26–29. This might indicate that the meals ceased to be held during the fifties and early sixties of the first century. When the meal disappeared, the two blessings remained and were brought together into one sequence. The Eucharistic celebration then started to resemble a service rather than a meal. Instead of the celebrant bringing the bread and wine, these were put on the table on which the Eucharist was being celebrated. This marked the beginning of the presentation of the gifts. The time that was formerly used to celebrate the meal was gradually used for an enhanced and expanded prayer of thanksgiving.

Several reasons have been offered to explain why the meal was abandoned. As Christian congregations became bigger, it was not possible any longer to hold the meal every Sunday. Another reason was that the early Christians did not want to attract attention at a time when they were facing persecution and so they changed the time of the Eucharistic celebration from evening to morning. A third reason had to do with the existence of abuses, at least in Corinth, where people formed cliques, ate their own food instead of sharing it, talked loosely, and occasionally even became drunk.

When the Eucharist was no longer celebrated in the context of an actual supper, it developed into an assembly. Those who took part in the Eucharistic celebration did not sit or recline, but stood during the celebration. There was only one table, which was used by the person who presided over the Eucharist. This became the center of attention as the altar is today. The people stopped meeting in a medium-sized dining room and rather met in a hall big enough for a large assembly to gather in front of the altar. The names "breaking of bread" and "the Lord's Supper" slowly went out of use, while the term *Eucharistia* (thanksgiving) remained.

External Influences on the Celebration of the Eucharist

In the foregoing, we have had a look at the institution narratives as found in Matthew, Mark, Luke, and 1 Corinthians. We have also looked at the factors contributing to the abandonment of the meal during the Eucharistic celebration. We shall now look at external factors that may have influenced the celebration of the Eucharist in the early Church.

GRECO-ROMAN MEALS

Modern scholars of liturgy have studied the meal practices in the first century Greco-Roman world to see if they can find any factors that possibly contributed to the way the Eucharist was celebrated in the early Church.[23] For example, from a study of the structure of the Greek *symposium*[24] (or Latin *convivium*), it has been concluded that the celebration of the Eucharist in some places may possibly have started with the meal (what we may call the Liturgy of the Eucharist) and may have concluded with readings and discussion (which may point to the Liturgy of the Word).[25]

OTHER EARLY SOURCES

Other early sources give us some idea of how the Eucharist was celebrated in the early Church.[26] For example, from the writings of the apologists and bishops of the early Church we learn how the Eucharist was celebrated in their local communities. One important example is the *First Apology*[27] of Justin Martyr (Rome), which dates from around AD 150 and was addressed to the Roman Emperor, Antoninus Pius. In this *Apology*, there are two brief accounts of how Christians celebrated the Eucharist. One of these accounts forms part of a longer passage that describes baptism, and the second seems to be "an outline of a normal Sunday gathering."[28] In the section that deals with baptism, Justin mentions (1) common prayers said for the newly baptized and the community; (2) the exchange of a kiss at the end of the prayers; (3) a prayer over bread and cups of water, and wine mixed with water; the prayer ends with an "Amen" said by all the people; and (4) the elements of bread and wine that are distributed by deacons to those present (as well as to those who are absent). Later in the passage, the words of Jesus over the bread and cup are also recited.

The second account of a Eucharist speaks of an "assembly" on the "day called Sunday." During this celebration, readings from "the records of the apostles or writings of the prophets are read as time allows," after which the presider "in a discourse admonishes and exhorts (us) to imitate these good things." The assembly next offers prayers; the "bread and water and wine" are brought and the presider prays over them, after which the people "assent, saying the Amen." Then the elements (over which thanks have been given) are distributed and everyone partakes of them.

In this *Apology*, there are some elements that are found later in the celebration of the Eucharist: (1) prayers of intercession; (2) readings from the "apostles" or the "prophets"; (3) an address (homily?) by the presider in which he explains the readings to the congregation; (4) the "bringing" of the bread and cup; (5) a prayer of "blessing" and "thanksgiving" said over the bread and cup, including a form of the words of institution as found in 1 Corinthians and the Synoptics; and (6) distribution of the blessed elements, with some reserved for those who are absent.

From Justin's *Apology*, we learn about the way in which the Eucharist was celebrated in his time. However, it should be noted that what Justin says about how the Eucharist was celebrated in his time "is also not an *ordo*...; it is a set of descriptions included by Justin in his defense of Christian practice against common rumor and public suspicion."[29]

Another group of texts in the early Church that offer us information on the celebration of the Eucharist are those known as *church orders*. These are documents that date back to early Christian centuries. Principal among these are the *Didache*, the *Apostolic Tradition* of Hippolytus, the *Testament of the Lord*, the *Didascalia*, and the *Apostolic Constitutions*. They are collections containing practical directives for the following of Christ that were intended to regulate the common life of particular churches and were later adopted in part or in whole by others. They include instructions about the right way of celebrating the Church's worship and some texts to be used in it.

These documents differ from the *Apologies* in that they were meant to be used in certain Christian communities as models to structure some elements of their communal celebrations. The earliest of these church orders is the *Didache*, an ancient Christian manual of instruction also called "Teaching of the Twelve Apostles." The place of its composition is most likely Syria, and it dates from either the middle of the first century or the early part of the second century. The *Didache* was "a rule for ecclesiastical praxis, a handbook of Church morals, ritual and discipline."[30] In it, we find two sets of prayers said over bread and wine. One set of blessings is said over cup and bread (9:1–5), while a thanksgiving prayer with three benedictions is said after the meal (10:1–5). This indeed may be regarded as a "Eucharistic prayer."[31]

Later church orders in the same region were influenced for three more centuries by the *Didache*. An example was the *Didascalia Apostolorum*[32] (mid-third century), which in turn influenced the first books of the *Apostolic Constitutions*.[33] Indeed, it is believed that the *Didache* also had an influence on the Roman Missal of 1970.

Another document that was once believed to contain a description of early third-century worship of the city of Rome is the *Apostolic Tradition (ApTrad)*.[34] Until recently, it was thought to be the work of Hippolytus, a third-century Roman presbyter and theologian. This view has been seriously challenged by scholars, who think that the author should not be identified with the early third-century Roman presbyter Hippolytus. It is not at all certain that the document is Roman, nor that every feature of it comes from the third century. In fact, there is a growing consensus that the institution narrative in this prayer was a fourth-century addition.[35] Indeed, many modern scholars are of the view that the *Apostolic Tradition* "represents a complex combination of different rites, from different times and places, compiled later into a single document."[36] Moreover, the *Apostolic Tradition* itself makes it quite clear that the anaphora is an exemplar, not a prayer that must be repeated word for word. If this is the case, then it is not likely that it represents the practice of any single Christian community.

In the *Apostolic Tradition* we find two accounts of Eucharistic Prayers. One is found after the ordination of a bishop (4:1–13) and another is found in the context of the liturgy of baptism (21:25–38). During this liturgy, which clearly refers to the newly baptized, three cups are distributed: one of water, one of mixed milk and honey, and one of wine. There is a third prayer of thanksgiving said at an evening meal (29C), but this does not seem to have been a Eucharistic celebration. However, it should be noted that the meal and the Eucharist are not "so sharply and simply differentiated from one another in the very early period of the Church's history."[37] Like the texts of the *Didache*, the Eucharistic Prayer section of the *Apostolic Tradition* had a major influence on the liturgical reforms of the later twentieth century, including the composition of Eucharistic Prayer II of the Roman Missal of 1970.

OTHER INFLUENCES

Apart from the church orders, other factors that also influenced the manner in which the Eucharist was celebrated included changes made by popes. The most important change was the translation of the liturgy from Greek to Latin in the fourth century during the pontificate of Pope Damasus I (366–84).

It should be noted that when the "Breaking of Bread" was begun in Jerusalem, the disciples of Jesus most likely used the language that Jesus himself had used in his preaching, that is, Aramaic, while Hebrew would have been used when parts of the Old Testament were read to the congregation during the liturgy. Greek-speaking people among them (the Hellenists) would have used Greek. As Christianity spread to Asia Minor and to other Greek-speaking parts of the Roman Empire (including Rome itself), *Koine* Greek, the language of the major cities of the empire, came to be used as the liturgical language of the Church, while the vernacular was used in the rural areas. As Rome in the first century was cosmopolitan in character, *Koine* Greek was used there by both Jews and Christians.

Following the third-century invasion of the "barbarians" who wrote their laws in Latin, the Latin language gradually became common in North Africa and slowly spread to Rome and throughout the West. North African writers who helped to promote the use of Latin included Tertullian (d. after 220), Cyprian of Carthage (d. 258), Arnobius (d. after 305), Lactantius (d. ca. 325), and Augustine (d. 430). By AD 230, much of the Greek version of the Hebrew Scriptures (*Septuagint*) had been translated into Latin together with the Greek New Testament.

As North Africa took the lead in the process of gradually using Latin in the liturgy, it is not surprising that Carthage started using Latin biblical texts before Rome did; the first recognized Latin version of the Bible to be used in the liturgy appeared in Rome around AD 250. Pope Victor I (d. 203), who came from North Africa, tried to introduce Latin into the liturgy during his pontificate. In the third century, as the number of immigrants from the East decreased and the North Africans increased, the use of Latin increased significantly. This made it much easier for Latin to be introduced into the liturgy at Rome, especially as a Latin version of the Bible was already in Rome at this time. Bishops of Rome at first decided to have a bilingual liturgy: Latin was to be used for the readings, while Greek was to be used for the Eucharistic Prayer. The use of these two languages in the liturgy continued until the late fourth century when Pope Damasus I (d. 384) decreed that Latin, which at that time was the vernacular of the Church in Rome, was the language to be used in the liturgy. This change made it possible to use new liturgical texts composed in Latin that reflected the Roman genius rather than Greek liturgical texts translated into Latin. Latin prevailed in the West until the Second Vatican Council (1962–65).

The Responsorial Psalm was most likely introduced into the Roman liturgy by Pope Celestine I (422–32). Certain fifth and sixth century popes were responsible for the composition of Eucharistic Prayers. Pope Gregory I (590–604) changed the wording of the Canon of the Mass. Pope Sergius I (687–701) introduced the *Agnus Dei* to the Eucharistic celebration in Rome.

The Evolution of Different Rites

Even though we have been speaking of the celebration of *the* Eucharist, we need to point out that there were different ways this was done. There existed different particular ways of celebrating the Eucharist; indeed, there were different patterns of worship of particular churches. These came to be referred to as "rites." During the first three centuries of the Christian era, the rite of the Church was somewhat fluid, based on various accounts of the Last Supper. Around the fourth century, the various traditions developed into four liturgies, the Antiochene, or Greek, the Alexandrian, the Roman, and the Gallican. It is from these four that all others have been derived.

In its *Decree on the Eastern Catholic Churches*, the Second Vatican Council recognized that the Catholic Church is comprised of groups of faithful that form particular churches or rites (*Orientalium Ecclesiarum* 2). The emergence of the rites of Eastern and Western Christianity was influenced by various developments and conflicts that took place in the history of the Church. In the East, Antioch and Alexandria were powerful and influential centers for the early Christian communities. Thus, they served as points from which the various Eastern rites developed. Jerusalem also exerted a strong influence and Constantinople eventually became another such center because of its importance as the capital of the empire. The history of the emergence of rites linked with these places is very complex, and it includes theological controversies; geographical, social, and political factors; and the influence of various cultures. This process resulted in a rich diversity of Eastern rites.[38]

The Antiochene Rite, which served as the earliest model for almost all Eastern rites, originated in the patriarchate of Antioch and later gave birth to the Byzantine and Alexandrian rites. The Antiochene family of liturgies includes the Clementine liturgy of the Apostolic Constitutions, which is no longer used; the Syriac liturgy of St. James, used by the Jacobite Church and Syrian Eastern Rite churches; the Greek liturgy of St. James, used once a year at Jerusalem; the Syriac liturgy of the Maronites; the Syriac liturgy used by the Nestorian Church; the Malabar liturgy, used by the St. Thomas Christians of India; the Byzantine liturgy, which came from Constantinople but was a development of the Antiochene tradition as influenced by Jerusalem and which eventually became the most popular of the Eastern rites. It is currently used by all Orthodox churches and by some Eastern Catholics. Also in existence at present are a number of other Eastern rites (e.g., Maronite, Armenian, Coptic) that can trace their origins back to these centers.

The Alexandrian Rite is the system of liturgical practices and discipline in use among Egyptian and Ethiopian Christians of both the Eastern-Rite Catholic and independent Christian churches. It is historically associated with John Mark, a disciple of the Apostles, who traveled to Alexandria, the Greek-speaking capital of the diocese of Egypt and the cultural center of the Eastern Roman Empire. The Alexandrian liturgies include the Greek liturgy of St. Mark, which is no longer used; the Coptic liturgy, which is used by the Copts in Egypt; and the Ethiopian liturgy, used by the Ethiopian Church.

The Gallican liturgy was used in northwestern Europe from the fourth century; it was superseded in France about 800 by the Roman liturgy. From it developed the Ambrosian liturgy, now used principally in the See of Milan; the Mozarabic or Isidorian liturgy, which was the liturgy of the church in Spain from the sixth to the twelfth centuries and is now used only in Toledo and Salamanca; and the Celtic liturgy, which was superseded in the Celtic Church in the seventh century by the Roman liturgy.

The Roman Rite[39] or liturgy is used almost universally by the Roman Catholic Church. From it were derived various medieval liturgies, such as those of Sarum, Paris, Trier, and Cologne, which are no longer in use. The Roman Rite is the way of celebrating the Eucharist and other liturgies that developed in ancient Rome. This style of liturgy, which was later influenced by both Spanish and Gallican liturgical traditions, became the most common form of liturgical worship for the Western Church by the twelfth century. In 1570, Pope Pius V promulgated the Roman Missal that made the Roman Rite the official liturgy of the Western Church, although a few local rites were allowed to continue. A characteristic feature of the Roman Rite (also known as the "Latin Rite") is its simplicity and brevity, unlike liturgies of the Eastern churches, which tend to be much more elaborate and expansive and are fond of repeating words and gestures. Another characteristic feature of the Roman Rite is the fact that it uses unleavened bread at Mass. The Second Vatican Council changed much of the Roman Rite by simplifying many of the rubrics and removing many medieval accretions. Two important changes brought about by the Council were that the vernacular of each local church replaced Latin in the liturgy, and Communion under both species became more common whereas previously it was infrequent or did not even exist.[40] As we continue, we will concentrate on the Mass of the Roman Rite.

Different Names for the Eucharistic Celebration

To conclude this section on the evolution of the Christian Eucharist from the Last Supper, we will look at the different names that have been used of the Eucharist. Several names have been applied to the Eucharist and typically reflected different theological emphases. Some of these names have been used concurrently in Christian history. We begin by looking at the word *Eucharist* itself.

The noun *Eucharist* is derived from the Greek word *eucharistia*, which was in use by the end of the first century. It is first attested in writing in the *Didache*, where the term *Eucharist* appears together with *baptism* and refers to an archaic form of the Eucharistic liturgy (9:1). The noun itself is not found in the New Testament, except as a variant textual reading in 1 Corinthians 10:16. However, the verb from which it is derived (*eucharistein*) is used quite often, especially in the liturgical texts that speak of Jesus' Last Supper, but also in other texts influenced by the early Christian Eucharist. In those contexts, it forms part of a narrative sequence of verbs describing the action of Jesus.

The Greek verb *eucharistein* and the noun *eucharistia* mean "to give thanks" and "thanksgiving," respectively. They entered early Christian vocabulary as translations of the Hebrew verb *barak* and the noun *berakah*, which are also translated into Greek as *eulogein*, "to bless," and *eulogia*, "blessing." For Jews and Judeo-Christians, *berakah*, "blessing-thanksgiving," was an act of praise directed to God and the basic expression of all prayer.

In the New Testament Eucharistic texts, the verbs *eucharistein*, "to give thanks" (1 Cor 11:24; Mark 8:6; 14:23; Matt 15:36; 26:27; Luke 22:17; 24:30; John 6:11) and *eulogein*, "to bless" (Mark 6:41; 14:22; Matt 14:19; 26:26; Luke 9:15; 22:19) can be found without significant distinction. However, the fact that there are two different Greek verbs does indicate a difference in emphasis. The very use of these verbs in reference to the Eucharistic event highlights its importance as a prayer of praise and thanksgiving.

From about the beginning of the second century, the preferred name for the celebration of the Lord's Supper in the Greek writers was *Eucharistia* (thanksgiving). The term *Eucharist* was applied to the meal liturgy of Christians in the letters of Ignatius of Antioch (*Ephesians* 3; *Philadelphians* 4; *Smyrnaeans* 7, 8); in the *Didache* 9, 10; and by Justin Martyr (*Apology* I, 66). From the third century on, it was applied more to the Eucharistic Prayer than to the Eucharistic liturgy. Tertullian, Cyprian, and Augustine applied the term *Eucharist* to the consecrated elements. After Augustine, this name dropped out of use in this sense until it was revived by the medieval theologians. In the twentieth century, the name *Eucharist* has again been used to designate the Eucharistic liturgy as a whole.

The oldest attested name for the Eucharist is the "Lord's Supper" (1 Cor 11:20). This represents the actual term that Paul uses to describe the Church's common meal in 1 Corinthians 11:20 when he criticizes the Corinthians for the way in which they are celebrating it and says, "When you meet together, it is not the Lord's supper that you eat." We may compare how he uses the same kind of language earlier when he speaks of Christians partaking of "the table of the Lord" (1 Cor 10:21). The expression "the Lord's Supper" designates the Eucharist from the point of view of its relationship to the person of Jesus as risen Lord. Those who participate in the Lord's Supper are expected to reach out to all human beings and welcome them in solidarity with Jesus, the Lord of all.

Another name found in the New Testament for the Eucharist is "the breaking of bread" (Luke 24:35; Acts 2:42). The "breaking of bread" was the technical name for the Eucharist in Acts 2:42, 46; 20:7, 11. The corresponding verbal form "to break bread," is used by Paul when referring to the Lord's Supper in 1 Corinthians 10:16 and also by Luke in Acts 2:46; 20:7, 11; 27:35. In Judaism, the breaking of bread was the ritual tearing of the bread at the beginning of the meal. This action has never been merely utilitarian. Already in 1 Corinthians 10:16, the action of breaking the bread received a symbolic interpretation: those who share in the broken bread become one body in Christ. Those who break bread are expected to offer their lives for others in the way Jesus did throughout his life but especially in the passion. The sixteenth-century Reformers favored the term "Lord's Supper" because of its Pauline association. It became the common name for the Eucharist in the Reformed tradition. Again, *Didache* 9:4 regarded the broken loaf as a sign of the gathering into one of the children of God. In the Roman Rite, the fraction occurred after the Lord's Prayer and before the ministration of Holy Communion.

Perhaps the name most commonly used of the Eucharistic celebration is "Holy Communion." This is a term derived from what Paul says in 1 Corinthians 10:16, "The cup of blessing which we bless, is it not a communion of the blood of Christ? The bread which we break, is it not a communion of the body of Christ?" (RSV). The Eucharist has been from the beginning a fellowship (*koinonia, communio*) among Christians and between Christians and their Lord. So important is this aspect of the Eucharist that the name "Holy Communion" has been applied not only to the reception of the sacrament but also to the Eucharistic service itself. Paul develops the idea of communion/fellowship in 1 Corinthians 10:17: "We being many are one bread, one body; for we all partake of the one bread." There is a connection between the sacramental body and the ecclesial body. In Acts 2:42, the term *koinonia* (fellowship) occurs in connection with "the breaking of bread."

The idea of fellowship is also prominent in the *Didache* and in Justin Martyr. In Justin, the Eucharist not only includes and unites all the baptized, but those who are not able to be present at the celebration share in the Eucharistic elements through the ministry of the deacons (*Apology* I, 67). The act of receiving Communion was the chief expression of Christian fellowship from the beginning. Churches which could practice Eucharistic hospitality with one another were in fellowship with one another. The name "Holy Communion" was applied to the Eucharistic liturgy especially in the Anglican and Lutheran traditions. The use of the term "communion" in this verse has rightly been abandoned by modern translations. In its place they use such terms as "participation" (RSV; NIV), "sharing" (TEV), or "means of sharing" (NEB) to bring out the meaning of the Greek word *koinonia* more clearly. Yet people continue to use the term "Communion" as a designation for the sacrament.

"The Mass" is still another term used of the Eucharistic celebration. *Mass* became the name of the Eucharistic liturgy in the Western Church. As Christianity spread from Jerusalem into other lands, the core of the Eucharist, that is, the thanksgiving over the bread and wine, remained, but in different cultures, variations in ritual and language emerged. In Rome, the Eucharistic liturgy was celebrated in Greek until the fourth century. When it was celebrated in Latin, gradually various Roman customs began to be adapted to the liturgy. At the end of a Roman ceremony, all were dismissed with the stylized phrase: *Ite, missa est* (Go, it is finished). The name *missa* derives from the words of dismissal in the Roman Rite: *Ite, missa est.* This phrase, which is probably as old as the Latin Rite itself, was used to conclude every Eucharistic liturgy and finally gave its name to the liturgy as a whole.

The earliest attested use of *missa* with reference to the Eucharist is found in the writing of St. Ambrose, the bishop of Milan, from the year 386 in a letter to his sister Marcellina in which he speaks of celebrating Mass. During a Sunday assembly, someone came to warn the bishop about certain incidents; in spite of this, he celebrated the Eucharist: "As for me, I remained in my office (of celebrant); I began the Eucharist. While I am offering...."[41]

CHAPTER TWO

The Assembly and Its Ministers

HAVING LOOKED BRIEFLY AT THE HISTORY OF THE Christian Eucharist as it evolved from the Last Supper, we will proceed to look at how it is celebrated today as the Mass in the Roman Catholic tradition. Much of what we will say in connection with the Mass will also apply to the celebration of the Christian Eucharist in other traditions. We will start with the assembly and its ministers.

The Assembly

In order for Mass to be celebrated, it is necessary for the people of God to gather in the name of Christ. In this celebration, Christ is really present: "For where two or three are gathered in my name, I am there among them" (Matt 18:20). According to the *General Instruction of the Roman Missal*,[1] the faithful at Mass "form a holy people, a people of God's own possession and a royal Priesthood, so that they may give thanks to God and offer the unblemished sacrificial Victim not only by means of the hands of the Priest but also together with him and so that they may learn to offer their very selves" (*GIRM* 95). The assembly gathers for the celebration, listens to God's Word, prays for the life of the Church and the world, gives thanks, sings, shares Communion, and is sent out at the end of the celebration for the work of loving and serving God. The dialogues between the priest and the assembly as well as the acclamations have the effect of bringing about communion between the priest and the people. The assembly must also have time for silent prayer. This allows the people to engage more deeply in the mystery that is being celebrated. There must also be uniformity in posture and gesture among the people. This expresses and fosters a unity of spirit and purpose.

Roles of the Ordained

In order for Mass to be celebrated, there must be, in addition to the assembly, a bishop or a priest, since only they can consecrate the elements of bread and wine. Deacons also play an important role during the celebration of Mass, though their presence is not necessary in the same way that of a priest or a bishop is.

THE BISHOP

The Mass can be celebrated, in the first place, by the bishop. He is the high priest of his flock. In the early Church, before the system of parishes as we know them today came into existence, it was the bishop who mostly presided at the Eucharist and at all liturgies. It is not possible for the bishop today to preside over every Eucharistic celebration in his diocese. However, he has the role of directing every Eucharistic celebration in his diocese. This is made clear in *Lumen Gentium*:[2] "Every lawful celebration of the Eucharist is regulated by the bishop, to whom is confided the duty of presenting to the divine majesty the worship of the Christian religion and of ordering it in accordance with the Lord's injunctions and the church's regulation" (no. 26).

The bishop is "the first steward of the mysteries of God in the particular Church or diocese entrusted to him. He is the moderator, the promoter, and the guardian of the liturgical life of the Church in his diocese. It is he who offers the Eucharistic Sacrifice, or causes it to be offered, so that the Church continually lives and grows."[3] The *Directory on the Pastoral Ministry of Bishops* states, "To lead those assembled for prayer is the first and primary liturgical role of the bishop."[4] He is expected to maintain high standards of liturgical presidency. "The bishop presiding at worship, both in the cathedral and in the parishes of the dioceses, is the model of all liturgical gatherings of the local Church."[5]

It may happen that the bishop is present at a celebration of the Eucharist but is not the celebrant. In that case, he still presides over the Liturgy of the Word. However, he does not wear the usual vestments for Mass. He wears the pectoral cross, the stole, and cope over the alb. He should also give the blessing at the end of Mass (*GIRM* 92; *Ceremonial of Bishops*[6] 176 and 186).

THE PRIEST

The Mass is also celebrated by a priest, a coworker of the order of bishops. The priest, like the bishop, has received "the sacred power of Orders to offer sacrifice in the person of Christ" (*GIRM* 93). This implicitly makes a theological distinction within the sacrament of holy orders, namely, that bishops and priests are ordained to offer sacrifice, whereas deacons are ordained to minister. Priests share one priesthood (*sacerdotium*) with the diocesan bishop, though they perform different roles.

The idea that the priest acts "in the person of Christ" has been given a more extensive treatment in *Ecclesia de Eucharistia*[7] (nos. 29 and 50), which emphasizes that the congregation cannot provide a priest for itself but is dependent upon the bishop, through the apostolic succession, to provide priests to link their local Eucharistic celebration to Christ's sacrifice on the cross.

The priest is the liturgical president and exercises his responsibility especially in the proclamation of the presidential prayers. These are the Opening Prayer, the Prayer over the Offerings, the Prayer after Communion and, above all, the Eucharistic Prayer. In the celebration of the Eucharist, all those who are not priests—deacons and laypeople—are not allowed to say these presidential prayers, especially the Eucharistic Prayer, with its concluding doxology.[8] The priest is responsible for giving the homily.

THE DEACON

After the priest, "the Deacon, in virtue of the sacred ordination he has received, holds first place among those who minister in the celebration of the Eucharist" (*GIRM* 94). In line with a tradition based on the Acts of the Apostles, the deacon is seen as the servant of the community, and this role as servant is seen in liturgical celebrations. As servant, the deacon is the principal assistant to the presiding bishop or priest at Mass. His role is to facilitate the assembly's worship but not to lead it himself.

The *General Instruction* (nos. 171–86) gives the instructions for the deacon's role at Mass. In the Introductory Rites, the deacon carries the *Book of the Gospels* and places it on the altar. If incense is used, he assists the priest at this point to incense the altar; he also helps the priest to incense the altar at the preparation of the gifts. During the Liturgy of the Word, he incenses the *Book of the Gospels* before proclaiming the Gospel. During the Easter Vigil, it is his duty to proclaim Christ's resurrection by singing the *Exsultet*. He announces intentions of the general intercessions during Mass. Sometimes, after obtaining the necessary permission from the parish priest, he may preach the homily. At the Presentation of the Gifts, he prepares the altar, gives the paten with the bread to be consecrated to the priest, and pours wine and a little water into the chalice and gives it to the priest. At the final doxology at the end of the Eucharistic Prayer, he stands next to the priest holding the chalice until the people have concluded the "Amen." At the sign of peace, he invites the congregation to exchange the sign of peace and helps in distributing Communion. If Communion is given under both species, the deacon is to administer the cup (*GIRM* 182). After Communion, he takes the Communion vessels to the side table and purifies them (either at this point or after Mass). It is his duty to make the announcements following the prayer after Communion and, after the priest's blessing, dismisses the people using one of the four formulas for the dismissal, for example, "Go forth, the Mass is ended."

The Vestments of Bishops, Priests, and Deacons

Having looked at the roles of bishops, priests, and deacons, let us now look at the special clothing, or vestments, that they wear in carrying out their liturgical functions, especially in the celebration of Mass. The wearing of special clothing for ministering at a liturgy can be traced back to the Old Testament. It is mentioned, for example, in Exodus 28, where the Lord tells Moses,

> You shall make sacred vestments for the glorious adornment of your brother Aaron. And you shall speak to all

who have ability, whom I have endowed with skill, that they make Aaron's vestments to consecrate him for my priesthood. (Exod 28:2–3)

This practice is still observed today. The *General Instruction* states,

In the Church, which is the Body of Christ, not all members have the same function. This diversity of offices is shown outwardly in the celebration of the Eucharist by the diversity of sacred vestments, which must therefore be a sign of the function proper to each minister. Moreover, these same sacred vestments should also contribute to the decoration of the sacred action itself. The vestments worn by Priests and Deacons, as well as the attire worn by lay ministers, are blessed before being put into liturgical use according to the rite described in the Roman Ritual. (*GIRM* 335)

VESTMENTS OF BISHOPS AND PRIESTS[9]

For the celebration of the Eucharist, bishops and priests need liturgical vestments. The vestments used today trace their origins to the fashions of the Greco-Roman world. Men's clothing consisted of a long tunic with a rope at the waist (alb and cincture) and a large mantle worn over it (chasuble). In the early Church, the clergy wore this ordinary vesture at liturgies. Even as late as the fourth century, liturgical vesture was of the same type as everyday clothing, though usually of a better quality.

Following the fall of the Roman Empire (487), there were changes in secular dress, but the Church retained the clothing of this earlier period in its liturgy, and thus the vestments acquired symbolic value. Between the tenth and thirteenth centuries, other vesture was introduced such as the use of the surplice by priests in place of the alb at some liturgies, and the use of the miter and gloves by bishops. In the Middle Ages, many of the vestments became more ornate and made of heavier materials. Because of their cumbersomeness, they were designed to be tapered and tight fitting. This style prevailed until the nineteenth century when there was a movement back to the earlier type of vestments, thus introducing the distinction between "Roman" (close-fitting) and "Gothic" (flowing) vestments.

Following the major liturgical reforms initiated by the Second Vatican Council many of the liturgical vestments have been simplified and some are no longer used. Priests today usually wear an alb, stole, and a chasuble at Mass, while deacons wear an alb, a stole, and a dalmatic. The bishop wears these same vestments along with his miter. Other nonordained ministers at a liturgy wear either an alb or a surplice (over a cassock), depending on the local customs. Copes and humeral veils are still worn at certain liturgies. The color of vestments is still regulated by the Church to mark the various seasons and feasts of the liturgical year.[10]

We now examine in some detail the vestments used by bishops and priests in the celebration of the Eucharist.

The Alb

The alb is a common garment for liturgical ministry that identifies any instituted or ordained minister of any rank (*GIRM* 336). The alb (from the Latin *albus*, or "white") is the full-length white linen robe worn by ministers during liturgical functions. Derived from the Greco-Roman undertunic, albs are often adorned with colored bands (orphreys) and embroidered with lace extending from the waist to the ankles. This ornamentation, however, should not detract from the simplicity and modesty of the garment, which symbolizes purity of heart. The alb may be secured at the waist by a cord or belt called a cincture.

For the celebration of Mass, priests are required to wear the alb, over which they wear the chasuble. The practice of wearing the chasuble over the cassock is not liturgically correct, since the cassock is not a liturgical dress but the street wear of the priest.[11]

Stole

The stole is a long strip of cloth, several inches wide, which is worn by deacons, priests, and bishops; a deacon wears it over his left shoulder (like a sash) with ends joined under the right arm and underneath his dalmatic, while a priest or bishop wears it around his neck (allowing it to hang straight down in the front) and under his chasuble. The stole is generally regarded as the unique badge of the ordained ministry and is conferred at ordination. Its origins are obscure, but it probably derived from a handkerchief or a secular scarf used as a symbol of rank.

Even though some priests wear the stole over the chasuble, there are clear instructions that the celebrant is to wear the stole *under* his chasuble. The *General Instruction* says that the vestment proper to the priest celebrant at Mass and other sacred actions directly connected with Mass is, unless otherwise indicated, "the chasuble...worn over the alb and stole" (*GIRM* 337).[12] It should also be observed that *Redemptionis Sacramentum*[13] (no. 123) notes that the stole underneath the chasuble should not be omitted. From the point of view of symbolism, wearing the stole over the chasuble attributes more importance to the stole and reduces the chasuble to a mere background vestment or a setting for an ornamental stole.

The Chasuble[14]

The chasuble is "the vestment that marks both the office of the priest (or bishop) and his ministry... It also signifies the dignity and holiness of the entire liturgical action over which he is presiding."[15] The chasuble is the outermost liturgical vestment worn by clergy for the celebration of the Eucharist in Western-tradition Christian churches that use full vestments, primarily in the Roman Catholic, Anglican, and Lutheran churches. The chasuble originated as a sort of conical cloak, called in Latin a *casula* or "little house," which was the common outer travelling garment in the late Roman Empire. It was simply a roughly oval piece of cloth, with a round hole in the middle through which to pass the head that fell below the knees on all sides. It had to be gathered up on the arms to allow the arms to be used freely. It was especially designed for travelers, since its form as a kind of cloak with hood also provided warmth and protection for those who had to sleep outdoors.

The earliest evidence of its use in the context of Christian liturgy is to be found in a letter of Germanus of Paris (+576) and then in the twenty-eighth Council of Toledo (633). The ample cut of the chasuble was originally designed to symbolize the fullness of charity on behalf of the bishop or priest wearing it—ultimately on behalf of Christ and the Church toward those most in need.[16]

Isidore of Seville (+636) spoke of the significance of the chasuble, around the year 600, describing it as similar to a small cottage or hut that covers the entire person. Thus, even as the chasuble was increasingly used in liturgical celebrations, it continued to be used as a standard item of clerical clothing also outside of the liturgy. It was only in the eleventh century when the cope was established as a liturgical vestment that the chasuble came to be reserved for the celebration of Mass—ample and bell-shaped in its design.

In the thirteenth century, there was a major change in the chasuble's shape and design. It became a more restricted garment in order to use less material and be less cumbersome for the celebrant. Its style and measure were further reduced in the period after the Council of Trent and especially in the eighteenth century, as its sides were cut off, creating what came to be popularly called the "fiddle-back." Thus, the Gothic oval-shaped chasuble gave way to the simpler baroque vestment without sleeves that tended to use heavier, stiff brocades.

Today, the chasuble remains the vestment proper to the bishop and priest celebrant at Mass and at other rites immediately connected with the Mass. However, concelebrating priests may, for sufficient reason, wear only an alb and a stole. The chasuble reflects the liturgical color of the day or season.

Amice

The amice is a rectangular piece of linen with two long strips attached to two of its corners. It is worn under the alb and is optional if the alb is made in such a way as to cover the wearer's street clothing (e.g., the cassock or clerical suit) at the neck.

Cincture

This is a cord used to gather the alb at the waist. It may be white or the liturgical color of the day. It is used especially if the alb is too long.

VESTMENTS FOR CONCELEBRATION

At a concelebrated Mass, the principal celebrant must always wear the alb, stole, and chasuble in the color of the day. Concelebrants wear the same vestments, in white if a set in the appropriate color is not available. They may wear only an alb and a stole, if a good reason should arise, for example, a large number of concelebrants or a lack of vestments (*GIRM* 209). In such a case, the modern broad and "picturesque" stoles, which may seem out of place under the chasuble, may be worn over the alb, since the concelebrants will not be wearing chasubles.

VESTMENTS OF DEACONS

In addition to the alb, amice, stole, and cincture, the deacon may wear the dalmatic. As the chasuble visually defines the liturgical role of the priest, the dalmatic visually defines the liturgical role that the deacon plays. The dalmatic is a long, full, closed gown with long, full sleeves. Worn without a girdle, it was made of linen, cotton, wool, or silk. It varies in length and has various decorative styles. Like the chasuble, the dalmatic is also worn over the alb and stole; therefore, deacons should not wear a stole on the outside of a dalmatic.

The origins of the dalmatic can be traced to the liturgical practices of the early Church and, along with the stole, the dalmatic identifies the deacon and his liturgical ministry. It probably originated in Dalmatia in Greece and was a commonly worn outer garment in the Roman world in the third century and later. Gradually, it became the distinctive garment of deacons. It reflects the liturgical color of the day.

The Colors of Vestments

Liturgical colors are important, as they have a specific purpose in the life of the Church. The *General Instruction* explains,

> Diversity of color in the sacred vestments has as its purpose to give more effective expression even outwardly whether to the specific character of the mysteries of faith to be celebrated or to a sense of Christian life's passage through the course of the liturgical year (*GIRM* 345).

Four colors are used, namely white, red, green, and violet or purple.

WHITE

White is associated with purity, joy, life, and light and thus is used in the Offices and Masses during the Easter and Christmas seasons; also in celebrations of the Lord other than of his Passion, of the Blessed Virgin Mary, of the Holy Angels, and of saints who were not martyrs; on the Solemnities of All Saints (November 1) and of the Nativity of St. John the Baptist (June 24); and on the Feasts of St. John the Evangelist (December 27), of the Chair of St. Peter (February 22), and of the Conversion of St. Paul (January 25).

RED

Red is associated with fire and blood and thus is used on Palm Sunday (or Passion Sunday) and on Good Friday, on Pentecost Sunday, on celebrations of the Lord's Passion, on the feasts of the apostles and evangelists, and on celebrations of martyr saints.

GREEN

Green reminds people of growth, latent life, and hope. It recalls how the same Christ through whom the outer green world was created (Col 1:16) is also the source of the Church's inner life and growth throughout the year. It is used in the Offices and Masses of Ordinary Time.

VIOLET OR PURPLE

Violet is associated with penance, sadness, and royalty and is used during Advent and Lent. It may also be worn in Offices and Masses for the Dead.

Two other colors may be used at choice: black (associated with mourning) for Masses of the Dead and rose (a lighter shade of violet) marking the midpoints of Advent (on the Third Sunday) and Lent (on the Fourth Sunday). The reforms of the Second Vatican Council allow local episcopal conferences in principle to adapt liturgical colors to the traditions of their national cultures.

Insignia of Bishops

In addition to the vestments worn by bishops for the celebration of Mass (described above), bishops wear certain insignia that are distinctive of the Order of Bishop—the pectoral cross, ring, skullcap, miter, crozier (pastoral staff), and for archbishops, the pallium. The regular insignia, which identify a bishop, are the pectoral cross and the ring. The pectoral cross is worn by the pope, cardinals, archbishops, bishops, and abbots. The word *pectoral* comes from the Latin *pectus*, which means "breast." This cross is attached to a chain or cord and is worn on the chest, near the heart. The pectoral cross is to be worn under the chasuble.[17]

Bishops also wear a ring. The ring is "the symbol of the bishop's fidelity to and nuptial bond with the Church, his spouse, and he is to wear it always."[18] During the ordination of a bishop, the principal consecrator places the ring on the finger of the new bishop's right hand and says, "Take this ring, the seal of your fidelity. With faith and love protect the bride of God, his holy Church."

The skullcap or *zucchetto* is a small silk cap worn by bishops. Developed from the *pileus*, a close-fitting, brimless hat commonly worn by the Romans, the skullcap has probably been worn by ecclesiastics since the thirteenth century. It was worn under the miter and biretta to preserve them and is still worn under these head coverings at services. The original use of the skullcap was purely practical. When clerics received the tonsure,[19] they had a ring of hair removed off the top of their head. The skullcap was meant to cover it and retain body heat, which was absolutely necessary in the unheated churches and monasteries of the past. From this practical use, it acquired the role of identifying ecclesiastical rank by the color of the skullcap. The color depends on the wearer's rank. The color white is reserved for the pope. Religious orders whose habit is white, like the Dominicans and Norbertines, may also wear a white skullcap. The color red is reserved for cardinals. Violet is reserved for bishops and archbishops, and black for others. When worn in church, the skullcap is removed after the Prayer over the Gifts and is worn again after Communion just before the Post-Communion Prayer.

The miter has been the traditional headdress of bishops in Western churches since the tenth century. The miter originated in the *camelaucum* (cap or bonnet) worn by the pope. Its use, first granted as a privilege to certain bishops, was gradually extended to all bishops and some abbots. It is worn on the head and has two shield-shaped stiffened halves that face the front and back. Two fringed streamers, known as lappets, hang from the back.

In his hand, the bishop carries the pastoral staff, or crozier (crosier). This is received by bishops and abbots at their installation as a symbol of their authority. The bishop, like a good shepherd, must lead his faithful flock along the path of salvation, disciplining and protecting them as needed. The shepherd's staff is, therefore, a most appropriate symbol for the office of bishop. During the ordination ceremony, after the miter has been placed on the head of the new bishop, the principal consecrator gives the pastoral staff to him, and says, "Take this staff as a sign of your pastoral office: keep watch over the whole flock in which the Holy Spirit has appointed you to shepherd the Church of God."

In the Western Church, the top of the crozier is curved like a shepherd's crook to symbolize that the authority is that of a shepherd who looks after the flock. The curved part of the crozier turns outward toward the community over which the bishop or abbot has authority. Other individuals who may have the privilege of carrying a crozier turn the curved part inward to indicate that they make no claims to authority over the community.[20] From the eleventh century, popes no longer used a crozier, until Paul VI (1963–78) reintroduced its use in the form of a staff with a crucifix on top. Croziers used to be very ornate and costly until the Second Vatican Council, when many bishops started using very simple wooden staffs.

Finally, the Holy Father, metropolitan archbishops, and the patriarch of Jerusalem also wear a pallium, which is made of a circular strip of white lamb's wool about two inches wide and is placed over the shoulders. Two vertical bands, extending from the circular strip in the front and back, give the pallium a Y-shaped appearance. Six crosses, one each on the chest and back and on each shoulder and band, adorn the vestment. By ancient custom, the pope wears it as a symbol of the plenitude of his episcopal power, which he shares with archbishops and bishops having metropolitan jurisdiction, each of whom receives a pallium. (On very rare occasions, the pope bestows a pallium on a bishop as a special honor.) The pallium is made from the wool of lambs and is blessed on the Feast of St. Agnes at the basilica of St. Agnes Outside the Walls. It rests for a night on the tomb of St. Peter before it is sent to a new archbishop.

The use of the pallium by church officials developed from the secular tradition of emperors and other high officials wearing a special scarf as a badge of office. By the fourth and fifth centuries, many bishops wore the pallium; by the sixth century, it was conferred by the pope as a symbol of distinction. Since the ninth century, an archbishop cannot exercise his metropolitan jurisdiction until he has received the pallium from the pope. The archbishop can wear it only within his own province; only the pope can wear it anywhere.

Isidore of Pelusium (ca. 412) explained the wool pallium on the shoulders of the bishop as the lost sheep carried by "a type of Christ." From this symbolism arose the tradition that *pallia* be woven by the nuns of St. Cecilia's convent in Rome from pure white wool taken from blessed lambs.

Liturgically Appropriate Vestments

Having looked at the various vestments worn by bishops, priests, and deacons, we shall now address the issue of liturgically appropriate vestments. Not all vestments are suitable, and so attention should be paid to their design and to the materials of which they are made. According to the *General Instruction*,

> As regards the form of sacred vestments, Conferences of Bishops may determine and propose to the Apostolic See adaptations that correspond to the needs and the usages of the individual regions.
>
> For making sacred vestments, in addition to traditional materials, natural fabrics proper to each region may be used, and also artificial fabrics that are in keeping with the dignity of the sacred action and the sacred person. The Conference of Bishops will be the judge of this matter.
>
> It is fitting that the beauty and nobility of each vestment not be sought in an abundance of overlaid ornamentation,

but rather in the material used and in the design. Ornamentation on vestments should, moreover, consist of figures, that is, of images or symbols, that denote sacred use, avoiding anything unbecoming to this. (*GIRM* 342–44)

Lay Ministers

Below the level of deacon, there are a number of roles that nonordained people play during the celebration of Mass. These nonordained people are chosen by the "pastor or rector of the church" and receive their ministry through a liturgical blessing or a temporary deputation (*GIRM* 107). They are to wear the alb or other vestment that is approved by the Conference of Bishops (*GIRM* 339).

THE MINISTRY OF THE INSTITUTED ACOLYTE

The role of the acolyte is an ancient one in the Church. His ministry is especially oriented to the "service of the altar," a service in "sincere love for the Mystical Body of Christ, the People of God."[21] In the procession to the altar, the acolyte may carry the cross, walking between two servers with lighted candles. On reaching the altar, he places the cross near it and takes his own place in the sanctuary. The acolyte is instituted to serve at the altar and to assist the priest and deacon. The instituted acolyte has "special duties" that he alone should carry out; ideally, these should be distributed among several acolytes. Many of these "special duties" are exercised only when there is no deacon. During Mass, it is the duty of the acolyte to go to the priest or deacon, whenever necessary, in order to present the book to them and to assist them in any way required. In particular, it is his duty to prepare the altar and the vessels and, as an extraordinary minister of Holy Communion, to give Communion to the faithful. He may also incense the priest and the people at the Preparation of the Gifts. Unlike other extraordinary ministers of Holy Communion, the instituted acolyte may help the priest or deacon to cleanse the vessels at a side table. The acolyte can be expected, when necessary, to instruct others (laymen and women) deputed for similar service.[22]

THE MINISTRY OF THE INSTITUTED READER (LECTOR)

The office of lector, referred to in some translations as "reader," is an ancient one in the Church and has been part of Christian worship since apostolic times (cf. Col 4:16; 1 Thess 5:27, 1 Tim 4:13).

It is the duty of the reader to proclaim the Word of God. The duties of the instituted reader are described as specific to him, and he alone should carry them out, even if there are ordained ministers. In the absence of an instituted reader, other well-qualified people may proclaim the Scriptures (with the exception of the Gospel), provided that they have been carefully prepared. Because the office of reading the Scriptures is a ministerial, not a presidential function, "the readings are to be read by a reader, but the Gospel by the Deacon or, in his absence, by another Priest" (*GIRM* 59).

In the absence of a deacon, the reader can carry the *Book of the Gospels* in the entrance procession. When he reaches the sanctuary, he places it on the altar. Then, he takes up his position in the sanctuary with the other ministers. When there is no psalmist, the reader may sing or read the Responsorial Psalm. In the absence of a deacon, the reader announces the intentions of the Prayer of the Faithful.[23] If there is no entrance song or Communion song and the antiphons in the missal are said by the faithful, the reader recites them at the proper time (*GIRM* 198).

MINISTERS OF MUSIC

Music has an important role to play in the celebration of Mass. A psalmist, a cantor, an organist, other instrumentalists, a choir, and a director of music assist the assembly's full participation in singing the songs, responses, and acclamation. These ministers of music exercise a liturgical function within the assembly and by their role help to add beauty and solemnity to the celebration.

The organ and other "lawfully approved musical instruments" are to be situated so as to sustain the singing of choir and assembly (*GIRM* 313). In Advent, the organ and other instruments are to be used with "moderation"; in Lent, they are used "only to support the singing," with some exceptions (e.g., solemnities, feasts, *Laetare* Sunday).

EXTRAORDINARY MINISTERS OF HOLY COMMUNION

The ordinary ministers of Holy Communion are bishops, priests, and deacons. Instituted acolytes are by law extraordinary ministers of Holy Communion. Other laypersons are authorized to act as extraordinary ministers of Holy Communion by the Holy See's 1973 instruction *Immensae Caritatis*.[24] According to this instruction, local ordinaries (normally bishops) can permit some laypersons to assist with the distribution of Holy Communion. Such people are called "extraordinary ministers of Holy Communion" (not "extraordinary ministers of the Eucharist" or "Eucharistic ministers," as some people often call them). The *Instruction* prohibits three specific practices: (1) extraordinary ministers giving Communion to themselves or receiving it "apart from the faithful"; (2) receiving their blessing for this ministry during the Chrism Mass on Holy Thursday; (3) a "habitual use of extraordinary ministers of Holy Communion at Mass, thus arbitrarily extending the concept of a great number of the faithful [approaching the altar]" (*Immensae Caritatis* 8).

Laywomen can also be authorized to act as extraordinary ministers of Holy Communion. According to the instruction on extraordinary ministers of Holy Communion, *Fidei Custos*, "A woman of outstanding piety may be chosen in cases of necessity, that is, whenever another fit person cannot be found" (no. 5). Such laypeople, men and women, who are appointed extraordinary ministers of Holy Communion "must be persons whose good qualities of Christian life, faith, and morals recommend them... No one is to be chosen whose appointment the faithful might find disquieting" (*Immensae Caritatis* 1). Likewise, according to *Fidei Custos*, "A lay Christian who is to be chosen as [an extraordinary] minister of Communion should be outstanding in Christian life, in faith, and in morals, and one whose mature age warrants the choice and who is properly trained to carry out so exalted a function" (no. 5).

These ministers carry out this duty under the following conditions: (1) whenever no priest, deacon, or acolyte is available; (2) whenever the same ministers are impeded from administering Communion because of another pastoral ministry, ill-health, or old age; (3) whenever the number of faithful wishing to receive

Communion is so great that the celebration of Mass or the giving of Communion outside Mass would take too long.[25] This assistance will regularly be needed especially when Communion is given under both kinds. Thus, at a concelebrated Mass at which there are many priests, use of extraordinary ministers of Holy Communion is not permitted.

At Mass, such ministers assist only with the distribution of Holy Communion. They come up to the altar only after the priest has received Communion and always receive Communion from the priest. They also receive from the priest the vessel that contains the Body and the Blood of Christ that they will distribute. The distribution of consecrated hosts and the Precious Blood to sacred vessels is reserved to the priest or deacon.

After Communion, the remaining consecrated wine is consumed by the deacon, or in his absence, by the priest. The deacon, priest, or instituted acolyte is likewise charged with the purification of sacred vessels immediately after Mass. No provision is made for the purification of vessels by an extraordinary minister of Holy Communion, a practice found in some places.

ALTAR SERVERS

In addition to the service of instituted acolytes, there is a long liturgical tradition of other ministers serving at the altar. These servers take part in processions and ensure that whatever is necessary for the celebration is available at the appropriate moments, thus giving the priest freedom to make liturgical gestures.

The server's duties include holding the book while the presiding priest says the presidential prayers with outstretched arms, bringing and holding such things as books, censers (thuribles), water pitcher and towel, plates and dishes, and microphones. They lead the entrance and concluding processions with the cross and candles; they accompany the deacon (or priest) to the ambo and stand while he proclaims the Gospel. On more solemn occasions, they may accompany the procession with the gifts. They take care of the censer, prepare it for the priest or deacon, and incense the assembly and other ministers.

It was customary to reserve all service at the altar to males. It was strictly forbidden to have women serving near the altar within the sanctuary, that is, they were prohibited from entering the area behind the altar rails during the liturgy. In his encyclical *Allatae Sunt* of July 26, 1755, Pope Benedict XIV explicitly condemned females serving the priest at the altar with the following words:

> Pope Gelasius in his ninth letter (chap. 26) to the bishops of Lucania condemned the evil practice which had been introduced of women serving the priest at the celebration of Mass. Since this abuse had spread to the Greeks, Innocent IV strictly forbade it in his letter to the bishop of Tusculum: "Women should not dare to serve at the altar; they should be altogether refused this ministry." We too have forbidden this practice in the same words in our oft-repeated constitution *Etsi Pastoralis*, sect. 6, no. 21.[26]

After the Second Vatican Council, some dioceses allowed girls to act as altar servers. This practice started as early as 1965 in Germany. The Vatican sought to end such experimentation with the 1970 instruction *Liturgicae Instaurationes*,[27] which affirmed that only males could serve the priest at the altar: "In conformity with norms traditional in the Church, women (single, married, religious), whether in churches, homes, convents, schools, or institutions for women, are barred from serving the priest at the altar" (no. 7). However, the practice continued in some places, and the Vatican reaffirmed the prohibition against female altar servers in the 1980 instruction *Inaestimabile Donum*, which says, "There are, of course, various roles that women can perform in the liturgical assembly: these include reading the Word of God and proclaiming the intentions of the Prayer of the Faithful. Women are not, however, permitted to act as altar servers" (no. 18).

With the promulgation of the 1983 Code of Canon Law, some argued that this reservation to males no longer held, based on the inclusion of both males and females in canon 230 §2: "Lay persons can fulfill the function of lector in liturgical actions by temporary designation. All lay persons can also perform the functions of commentator or cantor, or other functions, according to the norm of law." In some dioceses, girls were allowed to act as altar servers under the new canon law, without any explicit decision on the matter from the Holy See.

The decision came in the form of a circular letter from the Congregation for Divine Worship and the Discipline of the Sacraments to presidents of episcopal conferences on March 15, 1994, which announced a June 30, 1992, authentic interpretation (confirmed on July 11, 1992, by Pope John Paul II) from the Pontifical Council for the Interpretation of Legislative Texts. According to this authentic interpretation, canon 230 §2 states that service at the altar is one of the liturgical functions that can be performed by both lay men and women. The circular letter, written by the cardinal-prefect of the Congregation, also clarified that canon 230 §2 has a permissive and not a preceptive character; that is, it allows, but does not require, the use of female altar servers. Thus, it was for each diocesan bishop to decide whether to allow them in his diocese.

A later document made clear that, even if a bishop decided to permit girl altar servers, a priest in charge of a church in that diocese was not obliged to accept them, since there was no question of anyone, male or female, having a *right* to become an altar server. According to *Redemptionis Sacramentum*, "Girls or women may also be admitted to this service of the altar, at the discretion of the diocesan Bishop and in observance of the established norms" (no. 47).

USHERS

During the celebration of Mass and other liturgical functions, use is made of ushers. St. Paul instructed the worshipping community to "welcome one another as Christ has welcomed you, to the glory of God" (Rom 15:7). Ushers exercise this ministry of welcoming people when they greet people at the door and help them to find their places. Such people come as table guests of the Eucharistic meal. Thus, it is important for them to be welcomed by representatives of the worshipping community. In small and stable communities, there may not be the need for a formal ministry of welcome. However, in larger communities whose church attendance may not be stable, it may be necessary to make special arrangements for visitors and those unfamiliar with the community and its worship so that they may be put at ease and drawn into the celebration.

There is also need for ushers when members of the assembly become ill or otherwise need assistance during the celebration. They may also help with the collection and with processions.

CHAPTER THREE

Liturgical Furnishings

HAVING LOOKED AT THE VARIOUS ROLES OF BISHOPS, priests, and deacons and all those who assist them in the celebration of Mass, we now turn to the place where Mass is celebrated.

Every church should have three focal points: the altar, the ambo, and the chair for the presider. These should be distinct and should not be near to each other. This is because each is used for a different part of the Mass. Each of these should be used only for its proper function at the appropriate time during the Eucharistic celebration. It is good liturgical practice for the priest to be seen to go from one to the other, thus drawing attention to the different parts of the Mass. All other parts of the church—the seating, the organ, the space for the choir, and so on—should be arranged with these three focal points in mind.

The Altar

The altar occupies an important place in the church because it is the place where the Eucharistic sacrifice takes place. An altar, in ancient times, was a platform on which sacrifices were offered. In ancient Hebrew religion, altars were used both for animal sacrifice and for offerings of grain, wine, and incense. The altars used in ancient Israel were made of a rectangular stone with a basin hollowed out on its top. The four corners of the basin had horn-like projections, which came to be regarded as the altar's holiest part, so that anyone clinging to them was immune from molestation.

Throughout the history of the Church, the altar can be described as the table on which the Eucharist is celebrated. The earliest Christians did not use either temples or altars in their worship, which was usually conducted in private houses. The earliest

Christian altars would have been the wooden tables in the homes of worshippers. Later, the Eucharist was usually celebrated at the gravesites of the martyrs, which gave rise to the tradition of placing relics of the saints in or near the altar. By the third century AD, however, the table on which the Eucharist was celebrated was regarded as an altar.

In the fourth century, as the Christian communities got bigger, it became impractical to have the communal meal of the Eucharistic celebration, and the sacrificial character of the Eucharist became more pronounced. During this period, churches—with "fixed" or stationary altars made of stone or metal—began to be built over the tombs of martyrs. Since the Church had emphasized for centuries the singularity of the Eucharistic celebration—one bread for the one Body of the Church—tradition demanded that each church should have only one altar. In the seventh century, however, when the practice of offering private Masses for special intentions became more prevalent, other altars were added.

From the fifth century until recently, Western churches were often built with their altars facing east—a practice that it adopted from the Eastern Church. Relics of the saints were exhibited either on or above the altar and, beginning in the tenth century, churches that did not have relics hung paintings of saints behind the altar.

The altar of the modern era, in many ways, resembles that of the early Church. Following the liturgical changes put in place by the Second Vatican Council and the subsequent decrees instituted by the Holy See, altars once again face the congregation, are freestanding, and are situated in such a way that they are the natural focus of attention. Minor altars are now set in separate chapels so as not to detract from the main altar.[1]

The altar should not be used as a general-purpose table or counter. It should be freestanding, with enough space around it so that incensation can be done easily, for concelebration, for special occasions such as visits by the bishop, and for the Easter Vigil. The altar should be made of materials that befit the sacrament of the Eucharist. Ideally, it should be made of stone or marble, good quality wood, or another robust material that has the approval of the bishop.

The altar should be in a central position in the church and should not be too distant from the congregation. The altar is reserved for the celebration of the Liturgy of the Eucharist. Although the priest kisses the altar as part of the entry rite, he should not go to it until the beginning of the Liturgy of the Eucharist.

Fixed and immoveable altars are ritually "dedicated," but moveable altars either may be dedicated or simply be blessed (*GIRM* 300). During such a dedication, the relics of saints may be put under the altar. This is a tradition going back many centuries. According to the current *General Instruction*, the relics should be placed only under the altar: "The practice of the deposition of relics of Saints, even those not Martyrs, *under the altar* to be dedicated is fittingly retained. However, care should be taken to ensure the authenticity of such relics" (*GIRM* 302; my italics). The same idea is found in canon 1237, §2: "The ancient tradition of placing relics of martyrs or other saints *under a fixed altar* is to be preserved, according to the norms given in the liturgical books" (my italics). It should be observed that the previous (1975) *General Instruction* (no. 266) allowed the practice of placing relics *in* the altar as well as *under* it.

What is the origin of this practice? As we have seen above, it was the practice for Christians to build altars and, later, basilicas over the tombs of the saints. It later became the practice in fifth-century Africa that for an altar to be considered authentic, it had to contain some of the relics of the martyrs. This practice in Africa gave rise to the general practice of linking the altar with the relics of martyrs, even in basilicas lacking crypts.[2] After Helena of Constantinople, small pieces of the "true cross" were also incorporated into the altar. Eventually, the relics were made more aesthetically presentable; they were implanted into the altar itself, in more recent centuries, in a small square "altar stone," whose blessed presence would "consecrate" the altar. According to canon 1239 §2, "A body is not to be buried beneath an altar; otherwise, it is not permitted to celebrate Mass on the altar."

The altar has an important place in the church and its dignity must be ensured. The altar is the symbol of Christ as the foundation of the Church, as the spiritual rock (1 Cor 10:4). Since the time of St. Ambrose, the altar has been considered a symbol of Christ. The Second Vatican Council has stressed the importance of the single altar, which represents the place where Christ himself steps into time and space among us. Having many altars in the church obscures the recognition of the one Christ and the one Eucharist in the life of the Church. The *General Instruction* (no. 298) points out the ancient tradition of the altar representing Christ, the Living Stone (1 Pet 2:4; cf. Eph 2:20).

However, in some old churches, there are altars whose placement makes it difficult for the people to participate well in the Eucharistic celebration, and moving them can affect their artistic value. In such cases, other fixed altars should be erected on which Mass will be celebrated. To ensure that the old altar does not distract the attention of the faithful, it should not be decorated in any special way. The old altar could become the place for reserving the Blessed Sacrament.

It is a good idea for the assembly to be able to see the altar as an altar table. It is better to use altar cloths that cover only the top of the altar (*mensa*), and if decorative cloths that hang down are used, these should not cover any symbols or artwork that are part of the design of the altar.

When an altar is dedicated, the bishop anoints its entire surface with chrism, the very oil used to consecrate new Christians at baptism and confirmation, and priests and bishops at their ordination. Indeed, the anointing with chrism "makes the altar a symbol of Christ...; for the Father anointed him with the Holy Spirit and constituted him the High Priest so that on the altar of his body he might offer the sacrifice of his life for the salvation of all."[3]

The reason why the priest and deacon kiss the altar at the beginning and end of Mass (as well as other solemn rites, such as Evening Prayer) is that it is the architectural symbol of Christ in a church. Because of this symbolism, only those things that are necessary for the celebration of Mass should be put on the altar, and only when needed. It should also be noted that during Mass, one bows to the altar, not the cross.

Only what is required for Mass may be placed on the altar. The *Book of the Gospels* can be placed there from the beginning of Mass until the proclamation of the Gospel. From the Presentation of the Gifts until the purification of the vessels, the following are put on the altar: chalice with paten, ciborium, corporal, purificators, pall, and missal (*GIRM* 306). The *General Instruction* 305 states that it is better for flowers to be placed around the altar than upon it—but this is not observed in some countries like Italy and Spain. In addition, the *General Instruction* recognizes that there may be a need to use microphones and says that these should be "arranged discreetly" (*GIRM* 306). This seems to imply that flat microphones that can be placed unobtrusively on the altar may be preferable to those that stand vertically on the altar.

The *General Instruction* also says that candles may be placed on or around the altar (*GIRM* 117, 307). It further prescribes that a white cloth should be used on the altar where "the memorial of the Lord" is celebrated (*GIRM* 304). Other cloths may be used in addition to the altar cloth. However, the uppermost cloth that covers the top of the altar should always be white in color. This directive connects the symbolism of the altar to Christ, as the color white, for example, calls to mind Christ's transfiguration (Matt 17:2), in which the clothes of the glorified Christ are transformed into dazzling white.

The *General Instruction* speaks of the need for moderation in decorating the altar, stating that "during Advent the floral decoration of the altar should be marked by a moderation suited to the character of this time of year" and that "during Lent it is forbidden for the altar to be decorated with flowers" (*GIRM* 305).[4]

The Altar Cross

According to the *General Instruction*, "Either on the altar or near it, there is to be a cross, with the figure of Christ crucified upon it, a cross clearly visible to the assembled people" (*GIRM* 308). Since the recent postconciliar liturgical reform, the American bishops have issued a guideline stating that the cross is to be positioned in a prominent place near the altar, but not on it.[5] It is important to have a cross on or near the altar. The cross of Jesus reminds the believer that God *saves* through the cross (1 Cor 1:17; Eph 2:16; Col 1:20; Gal 6:14). As a constant reminder of the cost of salvation and the symbol of Christian hope, the cross should be visible to the entire assembly during the Eucharist.

The cross on or near the altar is required to have a corpus (body of Christ crucified) on it. In recent times, some churches do not have a cross or have an image of the risen Christ instead of a cross. This is not allowed. As Peter J. Elliot says, "A figure of the risen Christ behind an altar cannot be regarded as a substitute for the cross."[6] In this connection, the *Book of Blessings* says,

> The image of the cross should preferably be a crucifix, that is, have the corpus attached, especially in the case of a cross that is erected in a place of honor inside a church. The cross may be carried in procession, or there may be a fixed cross on or near the altar. The cross has historically been associated with the altar "because of its preeminence as a Christian symbol and because it represents or depicts the sacrifice of the cross which is made sacramentally present on the altar." (no. 1235)[7]

According to the *Ceremonial of Bishops,*

> Of all the sacred images, the "figure of the precious, life-giving cross of Christ" is preeminent, because it is the symbol of the entire paschal mystery. The cross is the image most cherished by the Christian people and the most ancient; it represents Christ's suffering and victory, and at the same time, as the Fathers of the Church have taught, it points to his Second Coming. (no. 1011)

In fifth-century Syria, it was stipulated that a cross was to be placed on the altar during the Eucharistic celebration. In the thirteenth century, the presence of a cross on the altar was required everywhere in the world. Soon after, the crucifix was to be used in place of the cross. Yet it was not until the 1570 edition of the Roman Missal that it became mandatory to use a crucifix on the altar. This cross should be clearly visible not only during Mass, but at all times, recalling "for the faithful the saving passion of the Lord." This cross should "remain near the altar even outside of liturgical celebrations" (*GIRM* 308).

Should there be one or more crosses on the altar? In this connection, Mark E. Wedig and Richard S. Vosko say, "The singularity of the altar corresponds to the one cross. The crucifix correlates the altar with the one sacrifice of Jesus Christ and addresses the need for the faithful to continually see the correspondence between the cross and the altar as Body of the Lord."[8] We should also note that the *Ceremonial of Bishops* presumes that the altar cross has a figure of Christ when it specifies that the figure is to be facing front and that "the recommended practice" is that the processional cross should serve as the altar cross (no. 128).

The *General Instruction* does not specify the number of crosses that should be on the altar, but a clue may be found in what it says about the processional cross: "The cross adorned with a figure of Christ crucified, and carried in procession, may be placed next to the altar to serve as the altar cross, *in which case it must be the only cross used*; otherwise it is put away in a dignified place" (*GIRM* 122; my italics). If there is already another cross with the figure of Christ crucified in the sanctuary, for example, hanging on the wall behind the altar or hanging over the altar, the processional cross is put away in a dignified place. In this case "the processional cross should not be visible to the assembly, so as not to duplicate the cross already in the sanctuary" (cf. *GIRM* 122).[9]

Altar Candles

Candles play an important role in churches. The *General Instruction* states, "On or next to the altar are to be placed candlesticks with lighted candles" (*GIRM* 117). Lighted candles are richly symbolic, both of Christ who said that he was "the light of the world" (John 8:12; 9:5), as well as of his followers who are called to be "the light of the world" (Matt 5:14) and are presented with a lighted candle at baptism. They should be authentic, made of a substance that gives a living flame and is seen to be consumed in giving its light. The candles are to be placed on the altar or, better still, near or around it, in order that "the faithful may not be impeded from a clear view of what takes place at the altar or what is placed upon it" (*GIRM* 307). Candles were first used by Christians of the early Church to provide light during predawn services, and in the catacombs. Then as now, they symbolized the divine light of Christ's presence. Today we use electric lighting, but candles are still used as a sign of reverence and festivity.

The number of candles to be used depends on the type of celebration. At least two can be used in any celebration, four or six for a Sunday Mass or holy day, and seven candles for celebrations at which the bishop presides (*GIRM* 117). The use of seven candles may have come about when people reflected on the theology of the Book of Revelation, particularly Revelation 4:5 ("Coming from the throne are flashes of lightning, and rumblings and peals of thunder, and in front of the throne burn seven flaming torches, which are the seven spirits of God").[10]

It is not good to use one or three candles. This practice seems to have come about when flowers replace candles on one side of the altar. The *General Instruction* does not specify how the candles are to be arranged, but the practice of putting two candles at one end of the altar and a bowl of flowers at the other end is not good liturgical practice, as it is not symmetrical.

The change in the number of candles "does not imply a more efficacious celebration but the uniqueness of festival days over ordinary ferial Masses, and the sign of the Church's unity in the presence of the bishop."[11]

The Paschal Candle

During the Easter season, the paschal candle is in the sanctuary. Blessed on Holy Saturday and lit from the "new fire" at the beginning of the Paschal Vigil, it is a centuries-old symbol of our risen Savior. At the vigil, it is carried through the darkened church by a deacon, who solemnly stops three times before he reaches the altar—each time singing *Lumen Christi* (Light of Christ). It is then used by the celebrant when he blesses the baptismal water. During the paschal season, it remains in the sanctuary and is lit during liturgical services and is incensed. It is also lit during baptisms, and is traditionally placed near the baptismal font. Five grains of incense—representing Christ's wounds—are inserted in the paschal candle during the Easter Vigil.

The Ambo

An important part of the celebration of Mass is the proclamation of the Word of God. In Catholic tradition, this is normally done from the ambo. The ambo is a raised platform in a church, used for chanting scriptural parts of the Mass, preaching lessons of the divine office, and chanting the *Exsultet*. Originally, the ambo was a portable lectern. It was clearly in evidence by the fourth century. By the sixth century, it had evolved into a stationary church furnishing, which reflected the development and codification of the Christian liturgy. It differs from a lectern in structure and decor. The lectern was originally a pedestal-based reading desk with a slanted top used for supporting liturgical books—such as Bibles, missals, and breviaries at religious services—and later, a stand that supports a speaker's books and notes.

There should be only one ambo from which only the Word of God is proclaimed and nothing else. According to the *General Instruction*, "In the celebration of the Mass with the people, the readings are always read from the ambo" (*GIRM* 58). Moreover, "The dignity of the ambo requires that only a minister of the word should stand at it" (*GIRM* 309). If another bookstand is used (by musicians or commentators or even the one presiding), it should be significantly different. This is clear from the *General Instruction*: "The commentator stands in a suitable place within sight of the faithful, but not at the ambo" (*GIRM* 105b).

On the ambo is put the lectionary, exemplifying Christ present in his Word, as the lector proclaims the Word of Scripture. The ambo is to be used primarily for the proclamation of the readings, Responsorial Psalm, and the singing of the *Exsultet*. Secondarily, the ambo may also be used for the homily and the Prayer of the Faithful, which may be done elsewhere. The Introductory Rites, Concluding Rites, and the announcements by the priest should not be done at the ambo but at the presidential chair.

The ambo should be in a place where it can be seen as the focal point of the proclamation of the Word. Preferably, it should be a permanent structure of some dignity, symbolizing the importance of God's Word. Moreover, "It should not be made in such a way that it is far removed from the print of the human hand and craft, and all furnishings taken together should possess a unity and harmony with each other and the architecture of the place." [12] According to the *Book of Blessings*, the ambo is to be blessed before it is used by the local Church (nos. 1173–91).

Chairs

THE PRESIDENTIAL CHAIR

During parts of the Mass, the priest celebrating Mass is required to sit. Accordingly, the *General Instruction* says,

> The chair of the Priest Celebrant must signify his function of presiding over the gathering and of directing the prayer. Thus the more suitable place for the chair is facing the people at the head of the sanctuary, unless the design of the building or other features prevent this: as, for example, if on account of too great a distance, communication between the Priest and the congregation would be difficult, or if the tabernacle were to be positioned in the center behind the altar. (*GIRM* 310)

The chair on which the priest sits during Mass should be in a place where he can be seen to be presiding at the assembly, but it should not be more prominent than the altar or the ambo. It should not look like a throne (*GIRM* 310). If there is enough space in the sanctuary, it should be put to one side of the altar to balance the ambo. It may be behind the altar, but not in a place where it is too far from the people. It should not be put directly in front of the altar or in front of the tabernacle.

The presidential chair is an important place from which the priest presides at Mass. This idea originates from the *cathedra* or the bishop's chair in his diocese. The *cathedra* or chair symbolizes both the teaching authority of the bishop and his communion with the pope and all bishops in the Church. The priest may give the homily standing at the chair. However, it is the normal practice for priests to stand and preach from the ambo. The priest is required to be at the chair when he leads the Introductory and Concluding Rites of the Mass. He returns to the chair after giving the homily to lead the profession of faith and introduce and conclude the Prayer of the Faithful.

OTHER CHAIRS

The seat for the deacon should be placed near that of the celebrant. During concelebrated Masses, seats should be put in the sanctuary for concelebrating priests and for priests who are present for the celebration in choir dress but who are not concelebrating. If, however, there are many of them, seats should be arranged in another part of the church, but near the altar.

Seats for the other ministers are to be arranged so that they are clearly distinguishable from those for the clergy and so that the ministers are easily able to fulfill the function entrusted to them.

The faithful are directed to sit during parts of the Mass, and so the *General Instruction* makes mention of their seating accommodation as well:

> Places for the faithful should be arranged with appropriate care so that they are able to participate in the sacred celebrations, duly following them with their eyes and their attention. It is desirable that benches or seating usually should be provided for their use. However, the custom of reserving seats for private persons is to be reprobated. Moreover, benches or seating should be so arranged, especially in newly built churches, that the faithful can easily take up the bodily postures required for the different parts of the celebration and can have easy access for the reception of Holy Communion.
>
> Care should be taken to ensure that the faithful be able not only to see the Priest, the Deacon, and the readers but also, with the aid of modern technical means, to hear them without difficulty. (*GIRM* 311)

The Roman Missal

The Roman Missal[13] is the liturgical book that contains the prayers, chants, and instructions (rubrics) used to celebrate Mass in the Roman Rite of the Catholic Church. The missal developed from various books used in the early Church, and by the fifth century, separate Mass books had been developed for the use of each participant in the liturgy. For example, the priest who was celebrating Mass at the altar used the sacramentary, a book containing the orations and prefaces that vary from feast to feast. The fixed prayers that form the ordinary of the Mass were also contained in the sacramentary. For Scripture readings, a Bible with marked passages was used. However, after about 1000, a special book called the *lectionary* was developed. This contained only the epistles and Gospels to be read at each feast. The soloist who led the singing of the Responsorial Psalms used a book called the *cantatorium*. The chants to be sung by the choir were to be found in a book called the antiphonary. Finally, a separate book, the *ordo* (*Ordines Romani*), provided instructions for the proper carrying out of the liturgical functions. All these books were gradually combined into one volume, the *Missale plenum* (full missal), which by the thirteenth century, had replaced the older books.

To ensure uniformity, in the sixteenth century, the Council of Trent prepared a uniform liturgy, the *Roman Missal*, and ordered its use by all Roman Catholic churches that had not followed their own liturgy for two centuries or more. The Roman Missal has since been revised three times, in the reigns of Popes Clement VIII in 1604, Urban VIII in 1634, and Leo XIII in 1884. The influential Liturgical Movement in the twentieth century led to the revision of the liturgy of Holy Week under Pius XII in 1955 and culminated in *Sacrosanctum Concilium*, the decree of the Second Vatican Council that allowed the introduction of the vernacular in the liturgy and ordered a complete revision of the missal to be carried out by a postconciliar commission. The revised missal, issued in 1970, consists of two volumes: one containing the Order of the Mass and the other a lectionary of Scripture readings covering a three-year cycle. A fourth revision of the missal was begun in the late 1960s, and in 1975, the English translation of this version was published in the United States. On April 10, 2000, Pope John Paul II approved the Third Typical Edition of the Roman Missal, which appeared in 2002. The English-language version of this edition was subsequently approved and appeared in 2010.

The Lectionary and the *Book of the Gospels*

The Lectionary contains all the readings selected for the celebration of Mass according to the order of the calendar for the liturgical year. Readings for the celebration of some other rites are also contained in this book. The Lectionary for the *Roman Missal* was created after the Second Vatican Council "with a definite pastoral purpose in mind, and the arrangement of the readings is intended to provide the faithful with as wide a knowledge as possible of the depth and richness of God's Word in a pattern consonant with the liturgical year."[14] It is not allowed to replace the biblical texts (readings and Responsorial Psalm) with non-biblical texts.

The *General Instruction* (no. 60) also makes provision for the *Book of the Gospels* (*evangeliary*), which may be carried in the entrance procession and placed on the altar until the gospel acclamation, when the deacon or the priest who will proclaim the Gospel brings it to the ambo. "Because of its rich and ancient symbolism, the Book of the Gospels is the only liturgical article allowed on the altar before the preparation of the gifts, symbolically uniting the table of the Word and the table of the Eucharist."[15]

The Lectionary and the *Book of the Gospels* are the primary ritual objects within the celebration of the Liturgy of the Word. Great care and attention should be devoted to their visual presentation and their ritual treatment.

The *Book of the Gospels* ranks first after the Eucharistic vessels. Every church should have one because its use is a normal part of our Roman Rite. If there is no *Book of the Gospels*, the Lectionary or a Bible should not be carried in the entrance procession. According to the *General Instruction*, the Lectionary should be in the ambo before Mass begins (*GIRM* 118). This means that it should not be carried in the entrance procession, even if there is no *Book of the Gospels*.

The *Book of the Gospels* may be used at any celebration of the Mass. The priorities are as follows: (1) It should always be used during a Solemn Mass when there is a deacon and/or concelebrants, especially when the bishop is the principal celebrant. (2) It should be used at any Mass when there is a deacon. (3) It may be used at Mass, for example, on Sundays, when a reader and servers assist the celebrant, in which case the reader carries it in the procession to the altar. (4) It must be used at the ordinations of bishops and deacons.

It is not good liturgical practice to proclaim the Word of God from disposable worship aids or typewritten pages. According to the *Introduction to the Lectionary*, "Because of the dignity of the word of God, the books of readings used in the celebration are not to be replaced by other pastoral aids, for example, by leaflets printed for the preparation of the readings by the faithful or for their personal meditation" (no. 37).

The Tabernacle

The tabernacle (from the Latin *tabernaculum*, "tent") is the receptacle in which hosts for Holy Communion are reserved in churches and chapels. They are usually constructed of wood, stone, or metal, and are cylindrical or rectangular in shape. A tabernacle normally contains a ciborium for consecrated hosts, a lunette (or luna)—which holds a large consecrated host for use in exposition and Benediction—and a corporal. It is located in the middle of the sanctuary or in a side chapel, and a sanctuary lamp is kept nearby to call attention to the presence of the Blessed Sacrament.

The tabernacle derives from the portable shrine built by the Israelites (under the direction of Moses) to house the Ark of the Covenant (Exod 25—31; 35—40), which they considered the manifestation of God's presence during their years in the desert. The Jewish people continue to honor God's faithfulness to them during this period by celebrating the eight-day Feast of Tabernacles each year.

The term *tabernacle* was introduced by Bishop Matthew Giberti of Verona in 1525 and was ratified by the Council of Trent. Reserving some of the Eucharist for those who could not attend the actual celebration of the Eucharist, for example, the sick and the imprisoned, was customary since the time of the early Church.

Even though reception of Communion became infrequent during the Middle Ages, devotion to the Eucharist grew. Reverence for the Eucharist culminated in the establishment in the Latin Rite of the solemnity of Corpus Christi in the fourteenth century. By the sixteenth century, reservation of previously consecrated hosts in a fixed tabernacle on the main altar became customary. The general prescription appeared in the 1614 Roman Ritual.

Today the Church teaches that the tabernacle should rest upon a pillar or in a niche, but not upon the altar where the Eucharistic action takes place. The tabernacle should be dignified and properly ornamented, but no specific materials are required for its construction. According to the *General Instruction*, the tabernacle requires a special lamp nearby that is "fueled by oil or wax" which should be kept lit to indicate and honor the presence of Christ (*GIRM* 316). This implies that the use of an electronic candle for this purpose is inappropriate.[16]

Sacred Vessels Used in the Celebration of Mass

Receptacles that contain elements used in Christian worship can be called sacred vessels.[17] They are considered sacred because they are set aside for the worship of God. Some of the many vessels used in the celebration of the Eucharist are the ciborium, chalice, paten, censer, cruets, and aspergillum.

According to the *General Instruction*, sacred vessels are to be made "from precious metal" (*GIRM* 328). If they are made from metal that rusts or from a metal less precious than gold, "they should generally be gilded on the inside" (*GIRM* 328). "The inside" is the part that is exposed to the bread and wine. Episcopal conferences, with the recognition from the Apostolic See, can allow the sacred vessels to be made from other materials that are solid and precious according to the "common estimation" of the local region. Such materials should be "suited to sacred use" and should "not easily break or deteriorate" (*GIRM* 329). This applies to other vessels like the paten or the pyx. Vessels that hold the Blood of the Lord are required to have a cup that is nonabsorbent (*GIRM* 330). Vessels intended for liturgical use must be blessed (not consecrated) in accordance with the prescribed rites (*GIRM* 333).

Having looked at sacred vessels in general, we now look at each of them in some detail.

CIBORIUM

This is the vessel in which the bread that is consecrated during Mass, or bread already consecrated from a previous Mass, is kept. In the celebration of Mass, we have the symbolism of the many sharing in the one bread and cup. This symbolism becomes more evident when all the bread is contained in one vessel and all the wine in one cup.

The origin of the word *ciborium* is debated. According to some, the word comes from a Greek word (*kiborion*) that means "cup." The same Greek word can also refer to a dome-shaped canopy over an altar (otherwise known as a *baldachino*).[18] According to others, it comes from the Latin *cibus*, meaning "food." The ciborium developed from the pyx in the thirteenth century. In the past, it was used in addition to a paten if the amount of Communion bread needed for a service was more than the paten could hold. This is the way ciboria are used today. In addition to its original purpose, the ciborium was used to reserve some of the Eucharistic bread for use outside the Eucharistic celebration. At first, this reserved consecrated bread was used to bring Communion to those who could not take part in the Mass, for example, the dying and seriously ill. Later, the reserved sacrament in the ciborium became an object of veneration.

CHALICE

The word *chalice* comes from the Latin word *calix*, which means "cup." The chalice (cup) is the only vessel explicitly mentioned in all the four Gospels in their account of the Last Supper.

In the beginning, chalices were made from various materials: wood, glass, horn, gold, copper, silver. During the first Christian millennium, several efforts were made to retain the use of common substances in making chalices. It was necessary to take the situation of poor people into account. There was also a desire not to give the impression of luxury. For example, St. Clement of Alexandria (third century) was strongly against the use of precious stones, gold, and silver. Sts. John Chrysostom and Ambrose (fourth century) and Boniface (eighth century) also spoke out in this regard. Many saints are reported to have melted their chalices and given the proceeds to the poor, for instance, Sts. Lawrence, Augustine, Gregory, Hilary of Arles, and Exuperius.

While materials of mediocre quality were often used in the making of chalices, people tended from the beginning to use precious substances for vessels in which the Body and Blood of Christ would be put. This tendency received a great boost when Emperor Constantine recognized Christianity, giving it legal backing. Following this recognition, Christians continued the use of precious metals such as gold and silver and the use of precious gems and other substances for ornamentation. From the eighth and ninth centuries, the Church did not permit the use of substances other than the precious metals of gold or at least silver.

Today, even though it is required that the chalice should be made of high quality material and precious metals are often used in making chalices, it is not necessary to use such precious metals (not even gold-plated lining for the cup).

PATEN

The word *paten* comes from the Greek word *patane*, meaning "dish" or "plate." This is the vessel in which the bread is put for the celebration of Mass. It is likely that the ordinary domestic vessel of the time was used at the Last Supper for the bread. Christians in the early Church used patens of different shapes and sizes, but many were large and deep so that the loaves of bread brought by believers who came for the Eucharistic celebration could be put in them.

After the conversion of Constantine, people tended to use precious metals and other precious materials in making the paten. Medieval patens had various designs and decorations in different regions. By the ninth century, the reception of Communion by the whole congregation became infrequent. Moreover, by the end of the ninth century, the rule in the Western Church was that the wafer bread should be used instead of leavened bread. These factors influenced the size of the paten to be used. The circular shape with a wide rim and a depression in the center was customary and eventually became the norm.

CENSER

The censer is a vessel used to incense people, places, and things. It is sometimes called a thurible, from the Latin *thus*, meaning "incense." This is a metal bowl with a perforated cover that hangs from chains. The use of incense in worship predates Christianity.

When it was introduced into Christian worship in the fourth century, Christians used the same kind of vessel, usually clay pots or metal pots with perforated lids (by the Middle Ages), and sometimes with a chain for swinging. Since the twelfth century, an accompanying vessel shaped something like a boat was called by the Latin terms *navis* or *navicula*, meaning "ship" or "skiff."

It is the normal liturgical practice to burn incense in a censer or thurible. However, this is not always the case. When an altar is dedicated, after it has been anointed with chrism, a brazier with burning incense or aromatic gums may be put on it. This is a sign of the sacrifice of Christ that will be celebrated here and the sweetness of the prayers of Christ's faithful, rising with that one acceptable sacrifice.

If used in the celebration of Mass, incense is used in the entrance procession, at the beginning of Mass to incense the altar, at the proclamation of the Gospel, at the preparation of the gifts to incense the offerings, the ministers, and the assembly, and at the elevation of the consecrated bread and cup. It may also be used in the rite of the dedication of a church or altar and in the rite of blessing of oils and consecrating the chrism, as the blessed oils and consecrated chrism are being taken away, and at funerals. The paschal candle is incensed before the singing of the song of joy or the *Exsultet* during the Easter vigil. During the celebration of the dedication of a church, incense is used to consecrate the altar. In addition, incense is used at the celebration of Eucharistic devotions and at the rites of Christian burial, during the Rite of Commendation, and at the cemetery.

The word *incense* comes from the Latin *incendere*, which means "to burn" or "to kindle." Most of the substances used as incense come from trees and plants. Among these, the most used has been frankincense. The use of incense was a common practice in the Jewish religion, as we see in the Old Testament, especially in the Books of Exodus, Leviticus, and Numbers. The meaning of incense is given in the psalms. Psalm 141, for example, compares the use of incense to an oblation offered to obtain the protection and the blessing of God. The use of incense is also mentioned in Revelation 5:8, "...the twenty-four elders....each holding a harp and golden bowls full of incense, which are the prayers of the saints." In Revelation 8:3–4, we read, "Another angel with a golden censer came and stood at the altar; he was given a great quantity of incense to offer with the prayers of all the saints on the golden altar that is before the throne. And the smoke of the incense, with the prayers of the saints, rose before God from the hand of the angel." It is clear from these passages that the rite of incensation is a sign of reverence and prayer.

In the early Church, Christians were unwilling to use incense in their worship. In fact, Christian writers of the first four centuries condemned the use of incense. Undoubtedly, this unwillingness was due to the association of incense with emperor worship, the ceremonies of the pagan world, and the test of loyalty to the emperor, which Christians were forced to endure.[19]

The earliest instance of Christians using incense is in the funeral procession of St. Peter of Alexandria in 311. Christian writers of the fourth century slowly began to change their views on the use of incense. Initially, incense was used honorifically to venerate the relics of saints, altars, holy places, and persons. The introduction of incense into the offices of matins, lauds (morning prayer), and vespers (evening prayer) pointed to a sacrificial use of incense. In his *Commentary on Psalm 140*, John Chrysostom claimed that the vesper service (or evening prayer) was a penitential rite. Thus, the use of incense during vespers was given a propitiatory meaning. It expressed the human self-offering of repentance.

By the Middle Ages, complex rubrics were linked to the many uses of incense that had become part of the Western liturgy. From these usages, three meanings of incense were identified in the medieval world. First, incense was regarded as an honorific, by which persons, places, and things were given veneration and honor. Second, it was regarded as a propitiatory offering for forgiveness and repentance. Third, the use of incense was understood as a form of exorcism. This third meaning is attested to in the texts of the blessing of the censer, which prayed that the incense would dispel demons and protect persons and places from evil.

The liturgical reforms of the Second Vatican Council have modified the uses of incense. In the Roman Rite, incense continues to be used in various liturgical ceremonies at the choice and discretion of the ministers.

Incense can be used at any Mass. However, it seems preferable to use it only when there is music at Mass, because the incensation of the altar and the gifts is best carried out during singing or music. It should be used at the principal Mass on all Sundays and solemnities.

CRUETS

These two vessels contain the wine and water to be used in the celebration of a Mass. The term comes from the medieval French term *cruette*, meaning "little jug." They are made of many materials, such as glass, metal, and clay. During the High Middle Ages and well into the seventeenth and eighteenth centuries, the design of some cruets was richly ornamented. Nevertheless, the intention was not to compete in importance with the chalice and paten. Some of the Reformers did not want cruets used in the celebration of the Christian Eucharist, and some wanted their design simplified. In the recent reform of the liturgy after the Second Vatican Council, not much is said about this, just that their quality and appropriate design should convey the importance of the ritual action being celebrated.

ASPERGILLUM

Derived from the Latin word *aspergere*, meaning "to spray" or "to sprinkle," this vessel is used during the Mass to sprinkle the assembly with water to remind all of their baptism. This container is either filled from the baptismal font or filled before Mass and then blessed at the beginning of Mass.

The origins of an *asperges* rite are uncertain. Psalm 50 and Ezekiel 47 seem to point to a pre-Christian ritual sprinkling. The early Christian writings about the celebration of the paschal vigil contain a blessing of the baptismal waters and contact with the water that took place later. It is probable that the custom of a Sunday *asperges* rite owes its origin to the medieval practice of blessing a monastery on that day. The sprinkling of the assembly, which recalls baptism, helps the assembly to gather and to prepare them to hear the Word of God and celebrate the Eucharist.

The Eucharistic Elements: Bread and Wine

According to canon 924 §1, "The most holy eucharistic sacrifice must be offered with bread and with wine in which a little water must be mixed." The offering of bread and wine in the Mass has strong biblical support. Bread and wine were offered regularly in Israel's sacrificial rites. Bread formed part of the regular offerings and sacrifices (Exod 29:2; Lev 2:4–7; 7:13) and the annual Feast of Weeks ceremony (Lev 23:15–20). Wine was also offered in Israel's sacrifices. It was one of the first fruits presented in the Temple as a tithe (Neh 10:36–39), and was poured out as drink offering (libation) in Israel's thanksgiving and expiatory sacrifices (Exod 29:38–41; Num 15:2–15).

Regarding the type of bread that must be used, canon 924 §2 says, "The bread must be only wheat and recently made so that there is no danger of spoiling." The bread to be used for the celebration "must be unleavened, according to the ancient tradition of the Latin Church" (*GIRM* 320), that is, bread made without yeast or other rising agent. The same idea is found in *Inaestimabile Donum* 8.

The use of unleavened bread, already practiced by the Armenians, became general in the West in the eleventh century. Since the faithful received Communion only infrequently, there were practical problems relating to the reservation of the species. In addition to this, there was the evidence from the Gospels: the Last Supper took place in the Jewish week of unleavened bread. From this time on, Latin theologians condemned the use of leavened bread. The Byzantine Church, which uses leavened bread, took serious offense at this. At the Council of Florence in 1439, both sides agreed that the Body of Christ is present both in unleavened and in leavened bread; however, each priest must conform to the rites of his own Church.

According to the *General Instruction*, "By reason of the sign, it is required that the material for the Eucharistic Celebration truly have the appearance of food" (*GIRM* 321). Ideally, home-baked bread should be used. The bread used must smell, taste, and look like real food. In time, thin white wafers, on which were imprinted religious symbols were used more and more. The unfortunate result of all this is that the symbolism of the hosts was lost, as people could hardly recognize them as bread. Every effort should be made to move from wafer bread (that is, hosts) toward more substantial forms of bread. This is in line with the stipulation of the *General Instruction*, which says, "It is desirable that the Eucharistic Bread...be fashioned in such a way that the Priest at Mass with the people is truly able to break it into parts and distribute these to at least some of the faithful" (*GIRM* 321). This stresses the importance of the union of those present through their sharing in the one bread.

WINE

In the celebration of Mass, the wine that is used must be from the fruit of the grapevine (cf. Luke 22:18). It should be natural and unadulterated, that is, without admixture of extraneous substances (*GIRM* 322). Nicholas Halligan elaborates:

> To be valid material, wine must be made from ripe grapes of the vine and not substantially corrupted; it cannot come from any other fruits or from unripe grapes or from the stems and any skins of the grapes after all the juice has been pressed out. In regions where fresh grapes cannot be obtained, it is lawful to use raisin wine, i.e., wine made by adding water to raisins.[20]

The wine used for Mass must not have any artificial additives (that is, additives other than those made from grapes). One cannot use wine from which all alcohol has been removed or, conversely, which has more than 20 percent alcohol or to which foreign ingredients such as water have been added in equal or greater quantities.[21] Thus, care should be taken when using regular commercial wines.[22]

Although the Eastern churches prefer red wine, the Western Church has used white wine since the sixteenth century. The reason for this is completely practical: at that time, purificators, the small cloths used to cleanse the cup, came into use, and white wine left fewer stains on them. There is no restriction now in the Western Church on whether red or white, dry or sweet wine is used, but some have noted the visual impact of red wine with regard to blood symbolism.[23]

Non-Alcoholic Wine

As stated above, the use of alcoholic wine (less than 20 percent) is the norm for the celebration of Mass. However, the Church makes provision for priests who suffer from alcoholism or other conditions that prevent the ingestion of even the smallest quantity of alcohol. It is recommended that such priests receive Communion by intinction, or in a concelebrated Mass, under the species of bread alone. Such priests can also obtain permission from their bishops, after presenting a medical certificate, to use *mustum*, fresh juice from grapes or juice preserved by suspending fermentation (by means of freezing and other methods that do not alter its nature). In general, priests who obtain this kind of permission are not allowed to preside at concelebrated Masses. However, if it is necessary for such a priest to preside, he must receive Communion under both the species of bread and that of *mustum*. In the very rare case of laypersons requesting this permission, the Holy See must be petitioned.

CHAPTER FOUR

Liturgical Postures and Actions

IN THE CELEBRATION OF THE MASS, A NUMBER OF gestures and postures are used. We examine these in this chapter.[1]

Standing

In the Church's liturgy today, standing is the main posture of Christian prayer. During Mass, "the faithful should stand from the beginning of the Entrance Chant, or while the Priest approaches the altar, until the end of the Collect; for the *Alleluia* Chant before the Gospel; while the Gospel itself is proclaimed; during the Profession of Faith and the Universal Prayer; from the invitation, *Orate, fratres* (*Pray, brethren*), before the Prayer over the Offerings until the end of Mass" (*GIRM* 43).

Generally, standing expresses an attitude of respect. It also shows the relationship between persons: one stands in the presence of an authority or one of greater rank. As it primarily expresses respect, standing has been the main posture used in Judeo-Christian prayer.

This tradition is rooted in the Scriptures. In the story of the reading of the Law from the prophet Nehemiah, there is an example of the standing posture in the liturgical assembly: "And Ezra opened the book in the sight of all the people, for he was standing above all the people; and when he opened it, all the people *stood up*. And Ezra blessed the LORD, the great God and all the people answered, 'Amen, Amen,' lifting up their hands. Then they bowed their heads and worshipped the LORD with their faces to the ground" (Neh 8:5–7). Other passages that show the standing posture for prayer and receiving the Word of God include Exodus 20:21; 33:10; Nehemiah 9:5; and Daniel 10:11. Standing also expresses "readiness," and it is the posture for the celebration of the Passover meal (Exod 12:11). "During Mass, the people stand to welcome the Lord Jesus who is about to be proclaimed in the Gospel reading. As we prepare to hear Jesus speak to us in the Gospel, it is fitting that we welcome him in this way, expressing our reverence and our readiness to listen to him."[2]

Standing for prayer is the model in the Gospels. In Mark 11:25, Jesus says, "Whenever you *stand* praying...." Both the Pharisee and the publican *stand* in prayer even though there is a difference in attitude (Luke 18:11–13).

This conventional posture of prayer whose roots can be traced to the Old Testament is given a new symbolic meaning in the light of the resurrection and the expectation of Christ's second coming. Paul uses the standing posture as a symbol of a slavery that has ended (Gal 5:1; Eph 6:14). In Revelation, there is the element of "worthiness" to stand in God's presence, and the "readiness" in waiting for Christ's coming again in glory (Rev 7:9).

The posture of standing for prayer with hands uplifted continues to be the usual posture of Christian prayer in the earliest times. According to Tertullian,[3] Christians stand on Sundays and during Easter time as a sign of the joy of the resurrection. They are not permitted to fast and to kneel during these times.[4] Jerome says something similar when he says, "It is a time of joy and of victory when we do not kneel or bow to the earth, but risen with Christ, we are raised to the heavens."[5] Justin says that "we do not kneel on Sundays as a sign of the resurrection through which we are freed from our sin by the grace of Christ."[6] The early Christians understood the standing posture to mean that, as a paschal people made worthy to stand in God's presence through their participation in Christ's resurrection, they stand ready to greet him when he comes again.

Sitting

In our liturgy today, we sit during times of reflection, meditation, and reception of instruction. During Mass, the people should "sit...during the readings before the Gospel and the Responsorial Psalm and for the Homily and during the Preparation of the Gifts at the Offertory; and, if appropriate, they may sit or kneel during the period of sacred silence after Communion" (*GIRM* 43).

The sitting posture signifies presence and repose and as such is used by the one who presides with authority over a group as well as by those to whom instruction is given. The person with power and authority sits on a special seat or throne to judge, rule, or preside. "You will see the Son of Man *seated* at the right hand of the Power" (Mark 14:62). Jesus often teaches his disciples from a seated position, as in the Sermon on the Mount (Matt 5:1), or after he has read from the Scriptures, he sits before he begins to interpret them (Luke 4:20). The person who listens with attention also assumes the seated position: "Mary...*sat* at the Lord's feet and listened to what he was saying" (Luke 10:39).

Kneeling

Kneeling in the Roman Rite is a gesture borrowed from the Roman ceremonial before the emperor. During Mass, people kneel for the consecration. The kneeling posture can signify supplication and adoration. It can also have a penitential meaning or it can be a posture for private prayer. The idea of kneeling as symbolizing supplication comes from the clear difference in status between the one who is imploring and the one being implored, as in Matthew 18:26: "So the slave fell on his knees before him, saying, 'Have patience with me, and I will pay you everything.'" Its power as a posture of adoration can be found in Psalm 95: "Come, let us worship and bow down, let us kneel before the LORD, our Maker," and in Ephesians 3:14: "For this reason I bow my knees before the Father."

The sense of "awe" before the Creator moves the person "to the knees." This same sense of "awe" is linked with a sense of unworthiness in the example of Peter falling to his knees in Luke 5:8: "But when Simon Peter saw it, he fell down at Jesus' knees, saying, 'Go away from me, Lord, for I am a sinful man!'" Jesus himself uses this posture of private prayer as he prays in the garden before his passion in Luke 22:41: "Then he withdrew from them about a stone's throw, *knelt* down, and prayed." Stephen kneels to pray before his martyrdom (Acts 7:60).

In the earliest centuries, it was not considered proper to kneel during the celebration of the Sunday Eucharist and during the Easter season because of its penitential and private character. It was forbidden during the Easter season by canon 20 of the Council of Nicaea. St. Irenaeus gives the reason for the prohibition: "The practice of not kneeling on the Lord's Day is a symbol of the resurrection by which, thanks to Christ, we have been delivered from sin and from the death which he put to death."[7]

Although many of the Church Fathers were of the view that it was appropriate to stand for prayer on Sundays and during the Easter season, they also believed that kneeling for prayer as an expression of penitence and humility was in order. For example, Tertullian said, "As for other times, who would hesitate to bow before God, at least for the first prayer by which we begin the day? And on the days of fasting, all the prayers are made kneeling."[8] Origen expresses a similar sentiment in his treatise *On Prayer* when he says that "one ought to kneel when one accuses oneself before God of his own sins and supplicating God to be healed and pardoned."[9]

Prostration

Prostration does not normally form part of the Mass. However, it is used at the beginning of the Good Friday service, although kneeling can be used as well. It is also used during ordination and consecration rites as a posture of intense prayer during the singing of the litany of the saints. This spectacular posture symbolizes total submission to a greater power and a sense of unworthiness. In Scripture, it is used to show intensity of feeling before God, for example, when Abraham falls on his face when God tells him that he will make a covenant with him (Gen 17:3). Jesus falls prostrate on the ground in the intensity of his prayer in the garden (Matt 26:39). This posture can be seen as a more dramatic supplication than kneeling and has been used in this way in liturgical worship, especially for penitents and catechumens in the first centuries.

There are two kinds of prostrations: on both knees with the face to the ground, and the full prostration with the whole body extended lengthwise. The present environment in most churches with pews or seating arrangements renders this ancient posture impracticable, although it is still used in monasteries and in some churches that have open spaces for prayer.

Bowing

During Mass, the presider makes a bow of the body as he reverences the altar, and the whole assembly makes a profound bow at the words of the Creed "by the Holy Spirit…became man" (*GIRM* 137). Those who do not kneel during the Eucharistic Prayer make a profound bow when the priest genuflects after the consecration. According to the *Ceremonial of Bishops*,

> There are two kinds of bows, a bow of the head and a bow of the body:
>
> a. a bow of the head is made at the name of Jesus, the Blessed Virgin Mary, and the saint in whose honor the Mass or the liturgy of hours is being celebrated;
> b. a bow of the body, or deep bow, is made: to the altar if there is no tabernacle with the blessed sacrament on the altar; to the bishop, before and after incensation, as indicated in no. 91; whenever it is expressly called for by the rubrics of the various liturgical books.[10]

This action of inclining the head or torso (upper body) expresses the interior attitude of respect and reverence toward a person or object. Bowing is an abbreviated form of prostration. In the Old Testament, bowing symbolizes a people's recognition of the power of a deity: "You shall not bow down to their gods" (Exod 23:24). In the Psalms, it signifies the adoration due to the sovereign God:

> There is none like you among the gods, O LORD,
>   nor are there any works like yours.
> All the nations you have made shall come
>   and bow down before you, O LORD,
>   and shall glorify your name. (Ps 86:8–9)

Bowing is traditionally the action associated with receiving a blessing. A more profound bow from the waist is required at moments that call for a momentary expression of adoration, that is, the doxology. This action of respect and adoration has always played an important role in the liturgy of the Eastern churches.

Genuflection

A genuflection is made by bending only one knee to the ground. It is a way of showing reverence that has been an important part of Christian ritual for centuries. In today's liturgy, genuflection is prescribed as an act of adoration for the presider after the elevation of the host and chalice and before Communion. It is also the action of adoration before the tabernacle. In the Creed, on the solemnities of the Annunciation and of Christmas, genuflection replaces the bow at the words, "he...became man."

This action, which is a "bow or bend of the knee," is a shortened version of the posture of kneeling and as such, it expresses respect or veneration. In the early Church, it was rejected because of its association with emperor worship and in some places with the mockery of Jesus in his passion (Matt 27:29; Mark 15:19).

An exception to the requirement to genuflect is made for those who are carrying articles, especially if they are in procession:

> Neither a genuflection nor a deep bow is made by those who are carrying articles used in a celebration, for example, the cross, candlesticks, the *Book of the Gospels*.[11]

Elevation of Hands

Normally in the Church, a bishop or a priest addresses prayers to God while standing and with hands slightly raised and outstretched. The classic posture of prayer, the *orans* position for early Christians, includes the raising of eyes and hands. This is the posture of the praying figures (*orantes*) depicted in the frescoes in the Roman catacombs. This tradition is found already in the Old Testament. Exodus 9:29 speaks of Moses stretching out his hands in prayer to the Lord. A similar idea is found in Psalm 28:2, 63 and Isaiah 1:15. In the New Testament, Jesus in his prayer would often "look upward" (John 11:41). Paul urges the community to pray, "lifting up holy hands" (1 Tim 2:8).

For early Christians, raising the arms and extending the hands during prayer was a reminder of the posture of the crucified Lord. This symbolic posture during prayer reminds Christians that Christ, during the celebration of the Mass, prays with them and for them as their High Priest.

Origen says, "As there are many dispositions of the body, it is incontestable that those which consist in raising hands and eyes should be preferred above all, for the body brings to prayer the image of the qualities of the soul."[12] Tertullian sees the image of the crucified Christ in this position. "Not only do we raise our hands, but we raise them in a cross like our Lord in his passion, and by this attitude we confess Christ."[13]

Although this gesture was without a doubt the favorite way of praying for early Christians, later developments that stressed the kneeling position for the assembly diminished its use. It was replaced by the *folding of the hands together*, a gesture that was more suitable to private prayer and the kneeling position. The *orans* position was left to the presider alone.

In the Church today, some communities pray the "Our Father" with open and extended hands. In general, however, this classic position of prayer has not yet recovered its rightful place.

Folded Hands

In this context, the custom of praying with folded hands should be discussed, as many of the faithful do this during Mass and at other times. This custom was derived from the Frankish feudal custom of a vassal presenting himself to his lord. At one time, knights and feudal vassals placed their folded hands in the hands of their king or other feudal lord when they swore their oaths of fidelity or feudal obligation. This symbolic action showed that they stood ready to serve their lord with heart and hands. It is not difficult to transfer the symbolic nature of this action to our stance before God. We should also note that during priestly ordinations, those being ordained put their folded hands into the hands of the ordaining bishop as they take the vow of obedience.

Striking the Breast

In the celebration of Mass, striking the breast is used in the confession of sins. This dramatic gesture expresses an interior attitude of repentance, humility, and extreme sorrow. In the Gospel of Luke, it is used by the tax collector, who "standing far off, would not even lift up his eyes to heaven, but beat his breast, saying, 'God, be merciful to me, a sinner!'" (Luke 18:13). Likewise, this is the gesture used by the witnesses of the crucifixion (Luke 23:48).

Kiss

A kiss is a traditional sign of greeting and reverence that goes back in Christian history to the days of the apostles. Thus Paul tells his readers, "Greet one another with a holy kiss" (Rom 16:16; 1 Cor 16:20; 2 Cor 13:12) or to "Greet all the brethren with a holy kiss" (1 Thess 5:26), and in 1 Peter 5:14, we read, "Greet one another with a kiss of love."

This is the basis of the sign of peace during Mass, but since kissing is not as universally used as a greeting in all cultures, other, more common greetings, such as handshakes, are typically used instead. However, kissing as a sign of reverence does still have a place in the Mass, as priests and deacons are directed to kiss the altar and the *Book of the Gospels*.

KISSING THE ALTAR, GOSPEL BOOK, AND CROSS

During Mass, the altar is reverenced at the beginning and end of the Eucharistic celebration. This same attitude of reverence expressed through a kiss is found in the veneration of the cross on Good Friday.

This gesture expresses a reverence and respect for sacred objects, especially those that symbolize Christ. The kiss as a gesture of honor and respect was taken over from the ancient custom of kissing the threshold of the temple and the images of the gods.

The beginning of the fourth century witnessed the appearance of the popular practice of saluting the altar with a kiss. In the Middle Ages, the priest was required by the rubrics to kiss the altar frequently throughout the ritual, and the gospel book before the proclamation.

KISS OF PEACE

This gesture, which expresses an attitude of interior peace, was used by early Christians as a seal of the prayer that had preceded it. As Tertullian says, "What prayer is complete without the holy kiss?"[14]

Originally, the actual place of the kiss of peace was at the end of the service of readings and prayers. It formed the seal and pledge of the prayers that preceded it. But after the service of readings and prayers had been joined to the celebration of the Eucharist, regard for our Lord's admonition (Matt 5:23ff.) about the proper dispositions in one who wishes to make an offering would probably have led to placing the kiss of peace (as guarantee of fraternal sentiment) closer to the moment when one is "bringing his gift before the altar."

Sign of the Cross

During the celebration of Mass, the assembly makes the Sign of the Cross twice: at the beginning of Mass and at the blessing at the end of Mass. In addition, the "little Sign of the Cross" is made at the beginning of the Gospel, on the forehead, on the lips, and over the heart.[15]

In making the Sign of the Cross, we join a tradition that goes back to the early Church. The gesture of signing someone or something or some place with the cross is a way of designating a Christian relationship with God and praying for the growing significance of this relationship. According to some evidence from as early as the second century, marking one's body with the Sign of the Cross was a form of Christian devotion.

The significance of making the Sign of the Cross was known to Tertullian who says,

In all our travels and movements, in all our coming in and going out, in putting on our shoes, at the bath, at the table, in lighting our candles, in lying down, in sitting down, whatever employment occupies us, we mark our foreheads with the sign of the cross.[16]

A similar sentiment is found in St. John Chrysostom (AD 347–407) who says,

Never leave your house without making the sign of the cross. It will be to you a staff, a weapon, an impregnable fortress. Neither man nor demon will dare to attack you, seeing you covered with such powerful armor.[17]

Sometimes a Christian signed the forehead (St. Basil mentions this); other times a Christian signed the breast or the eyes and later the entire upper body (fifth century). In the West, it was not until the directive of Innocent III (thirteenth century) that the prescription of signing the body with three fingers and touching the right and then the left shoulder emerged. Later the directive was changed to open the entire hand and move from the left to the right shoulder.

The practice of making the Sign of the Cross at the beginning of Mass comes from late medieval usage and became part of the Mass in 1570 (Council of Trent). In making the Sign of the Cross, we call to mind the significance of the cross in our lives as Christians, that is, Christ died for us on the cross. In doing this, we also recall what Paul says in Galatians, "May I never boast of anything except the cross of our Lord Jesus Christ" (Gal 6:14).

While making the Sign of the Cross, we call on God's name, saying, "In the name of the Father and of the Son and of the Holy Spirit." In the Bible, a name is not just a convenient means of distinguishing people. In a mysterious way, a name stands for the essence of a person and carries the power of that person. Therefore, when we call upon God's name, we invoke his presence and his power. The Sign of the Cross made in the name of the triune God also becomes a way of remembering our baptism. We were born again in baptism in the name of the Trinity and made members of the people of God.

It is clear that this tangible Sign of the Cross was linked with the administration of the sacraments, especially those of initiation.

Extension of the Hands in Blessing

This gesture of outstretched arms and hands is the primary one associated with blessing at the end of the Eucharist and other liturgies. This gesture symbolizes the transmission of power from one person to another or to the assembly. In the Old Testament, there are many references to the extension of one's hands as an expression of power. Moses "stretched out his hand over the sea… and the waters were divided" (Exod 14:21). When his hands grew weary in the Israelites' battle with the Amalekites, Aaron and Hur held his hands up until the victory was accomplished (Exod 17:11–12). The Lord God "with a mighty hand and outstretched arm" brought back his people (Ezek 20:33).

The imposition of hands in the rites of initiation, ordination, reconciliation, and healing derives its meaning from this gesture. In these cases, however, there is the added dimension of human touch as it communicates power and grace to another person.

CHAPTER FIVE

The Introductory Rites

THE MASS HAS BEEN REFERRED TO AS TWO LITURGIES, the Liturgy of the Word and the Liturgy of the Eucharist. The former is preceded by the Introductory Rites (unless these are replaced by another rite) and the latter is followed by the Concluding Rite. However, according to the Church, we should not see the two liturgies as completely separate: "The Mass consists in some sense of two parts, namely the Liturgy of the Word and the Liturgy of the Eucharist, these being so closely interconnected that they form but one single act of worship. For in the Mass is spread the table both of God's Word and of the Body of Christ, and from it the faithful are to be instructed and refreshed" (*GIRM* 28).

The Introductory Rites

The Introductory Rites are those that come before the Liturgy of the Word, namely the Entrance, Greeting, Act of Penitence, *Kyrie*, *Gloria*, and the Collect (or Opening Prayer). These rites are led from the chair and not from the altar or the ambo. The purpose of these rites "is to ensure that the faithful, who come together as one, establish communion and dispose themselves properly to listen to the Word of God and to celebrate the Eucharist worthily" (*GIRM* 46). During the Introductory Rites and the Liturgy of the Word, the priest is more properly referred to as the *presider*, whereas he acts as the priest during the Liturgy of the Eucharist.

ENTRANCE PROCESSION

The Mass begins with the entrance song and the procession. As liturgical music, the Entrance Chant "functions in several ways: it opens the celebration, it fosters the unity of the assembly, it introduces the liturgical time of year or feast, and it accompanies and supports the movement of the procession."[1] As DeGrocco correctly says, it is important "to note that the purpose of the Entrance Chant has nothing to do with welcoming the Priest; therefore, announcements such as 'Please stand and greet our celebrant by singing' are inappropriate."[2]

The entrance song was originally functional; that is, it was meant to accompany the procession. Thus, it began when the ministers started their entrance and ended when the procession ended. The entrance song should be such that everyone can join in some way in singing it. It may consist of an antiphon and psalm or another appropriate song. The entrance chant may be sung alternately by the choir and the people, or by the cantor and the people, entirely by the people, or entirely by the choir alone.

If there are concelebrating priests, they should be ready and join in the entrance procession. A priest is not to enter into a concelebration or to be admitted as a concelebrant once the Mass has already begun (*GIRM* 206).

Depending on the occasion, the procession is led by ministers carrying the censer with burning incense, the cross, and two candles. They are followed by acolytes and other ministers, reader, deacon, and priest. If a bishop is the main celebrant, he walks alone, following the priests, but going ahead of his assistants (i.e., those who carry the miter and the crozier). The *Book of the Gospels*, if used, is carried by a deacon. If there is no deacon, a concelebrant, or in the absence of these, a reader, carries the book in the entrance procession. A deacon or a concelebrant carrying the book comes immediately before the concelebrants or the celebrant, walking alone. The book should be carried in both hands in a slightly raised way, but without being held too high, and it is never moved from side to side.

It is not proper for the priest and the other ministers to take the shortest route from the sacristy to the sanctuary. It is better for the procession to go through the main aisle to reach the sanctuary area, if the architecture of the church makes that possible. This was the plan of the old Roman basilicas, in which the sacristy was located next to the main entrance. Procession through the aisle signifies the priest's link with the people and the unity of priest and people in celebrating the liturgy. It could also symbolize the worshippers' journey to God.[3] When the priest comes to the sanctuary by a "short" route, especially if he enters through a door near the altar, this may give the impression that he is like an actor coming on to the stage from the wings.[4] During the entrance procession, music may be played or a piece may be sung by the choir or any group of singers.

The priest and deacon, together with concelebrants and other ministers in the procession, bow to the altar on arrival as a sign of reverence. If the principal celebrant is a bishop, he disposes of the crozier and removes his miter before bowing.[5] If a tabernacle containing the Blessed Sacrament is in the vicinity, they genuflect. Those who carry articles used in the celebration, for example, the cross, candlesticks, the *Book of the Gospels*, are not required to make a deep bow or to genuflect.[6] Anyone carrying the *Book of the Gospels* does not genuflect or bow on arriving at the sanctuary, as this sacred object is a symbol of Christ.

The one carrying the book goes directly to the altar and places it at the center of the *mensa* (surface of the altar), if necessary, closer to the side from which it will later be taken for the procession to the ambo. There are two reasons for placing the *Book of the Gospels* on the altar. First, placing the book on the altar shows the inseparable unity that exists between the proclamation of the Word and the Eucharistic action (*GIRM* 28). Second, when the *Book of the Gospels* is later taken from the altar and carried to the ambo where it is proclaimed, it will become clear that Christ is the source of the proclamation.[7]

The *General Instruction* does not indicate whether the *Book of the Gospels* should be placed lying flat or standing up. It may be better for it to lie flat since there is no special reason why the congregation must see it, and having it stand could prevent the assembly and the priest-celebrant from seeing and interacting with each other.[8]

The functional purpose of the entrance procession is to have the ministers in place for Mass. But the theological reason for the entrance procession and the procession at the end of Mass (recessional) is to signify what all of us do when we celebrate Mass—we gather for worship and are sent forth from worship. We gather in order to disperse to live what we have celebrated.

The entrance procession has a bit of a history. In the oldest Roman tradition, the Mass began with the first reading and without any other preliminaries. Sometime in the fifth century, an entrance chant, later called the *Introit*, with a procession was added to the rite. Its origin seems to have been twofold. Under Constantine, bishops were accorded senatorial rank, and in pre-Christian Rome, when senators went to conduct official business, lighted torches and burning incense contained in a great vessel were carried ahead of them. On their arrival at the senate house, they were greeted formally with chants. Therefore, when the Bishop of Rome went to celebrate the Eucharist in one of the Roman basilicas, a similar ceremony was used. It seems that, like the senators, he was greeted with chants. However, there were differences, if we may judge by rather later evidence. A litany may have been sung during the procession to the church, and the official song to welcome the bishop was sung inside the basilica. This provides the second reason for the chant. Long processions through a big church unaccompanied by any song can be boring, and so a psalm was sung to accompany the procession of the bishop from the sacristy.

VENERATION OF THE ALTAR

The main gestures in the veneration of the altar are the profound bow, the kissing, and incensation of the altar. The celebrant and concelebrants at the beginning of Mass kiss the altar as a sign of reverence. Before this, the concelebrants and deacons would also have reverenced the altar by kissing it. As we have seen already, the altar is a symbol of Christ. Thus, the priest kisses the altar as "a way of greeting and honoring Christ as the high priest and host of this feast. The priest carries out this greeting as the representative of the community, and the whole congregation should join inwardly in this act of greeting."[9]

INCENSATION OF THE ALTAR

How should incensation of the altar be done during Mass? According to the *General Instruction*, "The priest, having put incense into the thurible, blesses it with the Sign of the Cross, without saying anything" (*GIRM* 277). The altar is incensed with single swings of the thurible in this way: (1) If the altar is freestanding, the priest incenses walking around it; (2) If the altar is not free-standing, the priest incenses it while walking first to the right-hand side, then to the left. The cross, if situated on or near the altar, is incensed by the priest before he incenses the altar; otherwise, he incenses it when he passes in front of it.

The altar cross is incensed with three swings of the thurible. As the *General Instruction* says, "Three swings of the thurible are used to incense: the Most Blessed Sacrament, a relic of the Holy Cross and images of the Lord exposed for public veneration, the offerings for the Sacrifice of the Mass, the altar cross, the *Book of the Gospels*, the paschal candle, the Priest, and the people" (*GIRM* 277).

As we have indicated above in chapter 3 on liturgical furnishings, the preference of the *General Instruction* is for the processional cross to be used: "The cross adorned with a figure of Christ crucified, and carried in procession, may be placed next to the altar to serve as the altar cross, *in which case it must be the only cross used*; otherwise it is put away in a dignified place" (*GIRM* 122).[10] In the event that the processional cross is placed near the altar after the procession, it is that cross that is incensed. It is not correct to incense both the processional cross and the altar cross, as some celebrants sometimes do. If the processional cross is placed near the altar, it is preferable that it is placed either on the right or left hand corner of the altar. It should not be placed too far away so that it can easily be incensed by the celebrant as he goes round incensing the altar.

During the Easter season, the paschal candle is incensed. It is appropriate that this is done throughout the Easter season, as a further way of stressing the importance of the great fifty days of Easter. This is standard practice in Rome.

It is not good liturgical practice during a funeral Mass for the celebrant to incense the coffin/casket at this point in the Mass. Incensation of the coffin/casket is done at the Presentation of the Gifts (when the faithful are also incensed) and during the Rite of Commendation.

After kissing and incensing the altar, the priest should go to the presidential chair and remain there throughout the Introductory Rites and the Liturgy of the Word, except when he goes to the ambo for the Gospel and the homily. Indeed, the homily can be given from the chair.

The Introductory Rites should not be conducted from the ambo (which is used for the readings, Gospel, and homily) and certainly not from the altar. If necessary, a small stand can be placed near the chair for the use of the presider (for books and other items).

THE ENTRANCE ANTIPHON

After the incensation, the presider goes to the presidential chair. If there was no singing during the entrance procession, the antiphon in the Missal is recited either by the faithful, or by some of them, or by a lector; "otherwise, it is recited by the Priest himself, who may even adapt it as an introductory explanation" (*GIRM* 48). The foreword to the 1975 U.S. edition of the *Sacramentary* suggests,

> Since these [Introit] antiphons are too abrupt for communal recitation, it is preferable when there is no singing that the priest (or the deacon, other minister, or commentator) adapt the antiphon and incorporate it in the presentation of the Mass of the day.[11]

It is better to sing a song than to recite the entrance antiphon. If this cannot be done, the celebrant should incorporate the antiphon in his remarks in a creative manner. He could reformulate the antiphon and use it to introduce the feast or celebration and go on to the Penitential Rite. Here is an example: "My friends, the psalm reminds us to praise our God with all of our lives and not put our trust in mere human rulers [Psalm 146]. As we gather to praise our God, let us acknowledge that we have sometimes relied on human strength more than God's grace and let us now ask for forgiveness."[12]

THE GREETING

Next, the presider makes the Sign of the Cross while saying, "In the name of the Father and of the Son and of the Holy Spirit." The practice of the priest and the people making the Sign of the

Cross and saying the trinitarian formula together with the people responding "Amen" was an innovation that was introduced into the Missal of Pope Paul VI (1970). The making of the Sign of the Cross is not a formality and the celebrant should not forget to make it. Even when some other liturgical activity takes the place of the Penitential Act (such as the blessing and procession with palms on Palm Sunday), the Sign of the Cross should still precede the initial greeting. It is significant that the Trinity is invoked at the beginning of worship. This trinitarian formula embodies the whole thrust of the Eucharist as an offering to the Father, through the Son, and in the Holy Spirit. After making the Sign of the Cross, the presider should not say "Amen." That is the response of the people and not of the presider.

The word *Amen* was an expression of agreement, confirmation, or desire used in worship by the Jews. The basic meaning of the Semitic root from which it is derived is "firm," "fixed," or "sure," and the related Hebrew verb means "to be reliable" and "to be trusted." The Greek Old Testament usually translates *Amen* as "so be it"; in English Bibles it has frequently been rendered as "verily," or "truly."

In its earliest use in the Bible, the *Amen* occurred initially and referred back to the words of another speaker with whom there was agreement. It usually introduced an affirmative statement. For emphasis, as in solemn oaths, the *Amen* was sometimes repeated. The use of the initial *Amen*, single or double in form, to introduce solemn statements of Jesus in the Gospels (fifty-two times in the Synoptic Gospels—Matthew, Mark, and Luke—and twenty-five times in the Gospel of John) was unparalleled in Jewish practice. Such *Amen*s expressed the certainty and truthfulness of the statement that followed.

Use of the *Amen* in Jewish temple liturgy as a response by the people at the close of a doxology or other prayer uttered by a priest seems to have been common as early as the time of the fourth century BC. This Jewish liturgical use of *Amen* was adopted by the Christians. Justin Martyr (AD second century) indicated that *Amen* was used in the liturgy of the Eucharist and was later introduced into the baptismal service.

A final *Amen*, added by a speaker who offered thanksgiving or prayers, public or private, to sum up and confirm what he himself had said, developed naturally from the earlier usage in which others responded with *Amen*. Use of the final *Amen* is found in the Psalms and is common in the New Testament. Jews used *Amen* to conclude prayers in ancient times, and Christians closed every prayer with it. As hymns became more popular, the use of the final *Amen* was extended.

The Sign of the Cross at the beginning of Mass is followed by the greeting. By means of this greeting, the priest "signifies the presence of the Lord to the assembled community. By this Greeting and the people's response, the mystery of the Church gathered together is made manifest" (*GIRM* 50). This greeting is spoken by the priest with extended hands. Since this gesture accompanies a greeting directed to the assembly and is not a prayer that is addressed to God, "it would be best if this extension of the Priest's hands were not exactly the same gesture used in the *orans* position for the orations; the slight difference in gesture will highlight the different genres of utterances being made."[13]

There are four forms of the greeting. One form runs thus: "The grace of our Lord Jesus Christ, and the love of God, and the communion of the Holy Spirit be with you all." This greeting comes from 2 Corinthians 13:14. The passage from 2 Corinthians 13:14 has "the grace of *the* Lord Jesus Christ," whereas here we have "the grace of *our* Lord Jesus Christ." This greeting conveys the meaning of "wishing the faithful 'the grace of the Lord Jesus Christ', but so as to direct the eye to God the Father as the source of all grace and to the Holy Spirit as the active principle of its unfolding."[14]

A second greeting is "Grace to you and peace from God our Father and the Lord Jesus Christ." Several passages from Paul's letters provided the inspiration of this greeting. Quite often in his letters, Paul wished his congregation grace and peace from God the Father and the Lord Jesus Christ. In many instances, the Father is explicitly referred to as "our Father," in this way echoing the teaching in the Lord's Prayer. Among such passages are the following: Romans 1:7; 1 Corinthians 1:3; 2 Corinthians 1:2; 2 Thessalonians 1:2; Philemon 3. "Grace" here is the favor that God shows and the gift he gives to those whom he saves in Christ, while "peace" is the fruit of the salvation that God gives in Christ.

The presider therefore wishes the congregation God's gift of peace, which includes reconciliation and harmony.

A third greeting is "The Lord be with you." This is the most ancient of the liturgical greetings and is found in most rites. It featured in the Mass in fourth-century Africa. The greeting of the angel to Mary in Luke 1:28 contains the formula "The Lord is with you."[15] The expression is frequent in the Old Testament, in particular in passages where the faithful were being entrusted with a mission by God (Gen 26:24; 28:15; 39:2, 3, 21, 23; Exod 3:12; Deut 20:1; Judg 6:12–14; Ruth 2:4; Isa 41:10; 53:5; 7:14). In this connection, mention can be made of Jesus' promise in Matthew 28:20 ("I am with you").

In connection with the last greeting, one sometimes hears some priests saying, "The Lord *is* with you" instead of "The Lord *be* with you." The two are not the same. The greeting "The Lord be with you" is the shortened form of "May the Lord be with you," and expresses the desire that the Lord may be with the assembly. The form "The Lord is with you" expresses no such desire but states the fact that the Lord is already with the gathered assembly. It is no longer a prayer asking the Lord to be present with the assembly but a declaration that the Lord is there. The two are not the same. In connection with the expression "The Lord be with you," Peter C. Finn and James M. Schellman state, "Since functionally it serves as a greeting, it is not to be interpreted as a statement of fact (e.g., 'the Lord is [*est*] with you') but a prayerful acclamation or salutation (*Dominus sit vobiscum*)."[16] Indeed, Bernard Botte argues convincingly that, if it were a declarative statement or proclamation, the proper response on the part of the congregation would not be "And with your spirit" (*Et cum spiritu tuo*), but the *Amen* of assent.[17]

A fourth greeting, which is reserved for bishops, is "Peace be with you." This greeting has biblical antecedents in both the Old and New Testaments. In the Old Testament, reference can be made to Judges 19:20; 1 Chronicles 12:18; Daniel 10:19; Psalm 122:8, and the like. In the New Testament, we can find examples in John 20:19, 21, 26; Luke 24:36. The use of this form does not mean that bishops cannot use any of the three forms mentioned above. The exclusive use of this greeting by bishops is attested to, for example, by John Chrysostom who notes that the bishop saluted the congregation as he entered the church with the expression "Peace be with you."[18]

Sometimes some priests, in addition to the official liturgical greeting, say "Good morning." They do this in order to create a relaxed, friendly atmosphere. Even though the intention is good, it amounts to greeting the congregation twice! The real greeting of the people is already contained in a sacred liturgical formula, one of the Christian greetings drawn from the Scriptures or Tradition. This greeting is also a kind of blessing, a mutual recognition of the presence of the Holy Spirit in both celebrant and people and the wish that this divine presence would abide forever. To add "Good morning" to these great Christian greetings is to add an unnecessary repetition. It also shows that those who do this lack understanding of the deeper meaning of the sacred greetings in the liturgy. In this connection, we need to note that when we celebrate the liturgy, the forms of language and expressions that we use are different from those we normally use in daily life. We do this precisely to distinguish the liturgical assembly from other gatherings or meetings. We should therefore note that the function of the greeting in this context

> is not one of welcome or casual recognition as "Good Morning" is when said as when one meets another in the street. Rather, the specific function of the liturgical greeting is to mutually declare, affirm, and confess that the community has taken a dimension bigger than itself. The eucharistic assembly is not simply a sociological grouping of individuals as at a purely nonreligious affair. The act of gathering to worship is not the result of purely human initiative; it is the result of grace calling individuals to become the ecclesial Body. Having been gathered to worship, it has become Church, engaged in a cultic act with the active presence of Christ in its midst.[19]

In this connection, DeGrocco observes, "It is not a mere human exchange that is being communicated in the greeting, but rather an exchange taking place in the mystery of Christ's presence, and so the styles of the language used should reflect that mystery."[20]

The response to any form of the greeting is "And with your spirit." This is also the answer in both Greek and Latin liturgies. This response corresponds to the salutations of Paul's letters (Gal 6:18; Phil 4:23; 2 Tim 4:22; Phlm 25). This translation in the new Missal marks a departure from the previous translation, "And also with you." More recent scholarship has moved away from the understanding that *Et cum spiritu tuo* (And with your spirit) means "your person," or simply "you."

The Church Fathers often interpreted the word *spirit* (Greek *pneuma*) in a theological sense to refer to priestly ordination: "It is not the soul that they mean by these words *Et cum spiritu tuo*. But it is the grace of the Holy Spirit through which those who are entrusted to his care believe that he entered the ranks of the priesthood."[21] Similarly, Narsai of Nisibis says, "He gives the name 'spirit' not to the soul of the priest but to the Spirit he has received through the laying on of hands."[22]

In this connection, Henry Ashworth comments,

> The people's response *Et cum spiritu tuo* (i.e., "and with your spirit") is also a prayer for God's accredited minister. It is a prayer which asks that the creative activity and power of the Holy Spirit may fill his *pneuma* (i.e., "spirit") and enable him to obey Christ's command "Do this in remembrance of me."[23]

In the response of the worshipping community, it is argued that there is a reference to that "spirit" given through the imposition of hands in the sacrament of ordination.

However, Anscar J. Chupungco holds a different view.[24] He contends that the influence of Hellenistic anthropology may be present here. According to him, this type of anthropology recognizes three ascending levels in the human person: the body, the soul, and the spirit, with the spirit representing the highest and noblest level in the human person. He says that Hellenism most likely influenced the formula "And with your spirit." In such a case, according to him, it is a courteous way of returning the greeting "The Lord be with you." He suggests that another way of understanding the response is by looking at the use of "spirit" in the *Magnificat* in Luke 1:47, "My spirit rejoices in God my Savior."

He points out that the response, "And with your Spirit," is meant to address the priest-presider in the fullness of his being. He says, "The interpretation that wishes to associate the Holy Spirit or the spirit of the priesthood with this liturgical formula has no solid theological or liturgical basis."[25] As Dominic E. Serra[26] says, it will be important in catechesis to point out that the greeting to the priest's "spirit" does not establish a kind of dualism that may suggest that the spirit rather than the body is honored in the greeting. "Spirit" here, according to him, has the opposite sense as the fullness of humanity.

After the greeting, the celebrant (or another person) introduces the Mass of the day in his own words. The presiding priest (or deacon or another minister) may give a brief introduction after the initial greeting and before the Penitential Rite. This introduction should come *after* the initial greeting and not before the Sign of the Cross, as is done in some parishes. The introduction should be brief. It is not an occasion for one to give a short homily at this point. At this stage, strangers, guests, and special groups may briefly be welcomed to the celebration. Though the priest normally does the introduction, on occasion it may be fitting for the deacon or some other member of the assembly to do this. However, such a welcome should be brief.

Opening Rite

After the introduction comes the Opening Rite. One of the following opening rites is selected. The choice may be made based on the liturgical season, the feast, the particular occasion, for example, a particular ritual Mass, or on the circumstances of the assembly that meets for the celebration. Each of the forms of the Opening Rite begins with an invitation by the priest.

PENITENTIAL RITE

This rite begins with the priest's invitation, "Brethren (brothers and sisters), let us acknowledge our sins, and so prepare ourselves to celebrate the sacred mysteries." According to Dominic E. Serra, these words "were chosen with great care to avoid being misconstrued to be an invitation to an examination of conscience.

We are invited instead to acknowledge our sins so that we may be properly prepared to enter into the celebration of the mysteries."[27]

Silence is required after the introduction to the Penitential Act, as this provides time for the congregation to call to mind their sins. Thus, the celebrant should not rush immediately into the next part of this rite, but must leave a noticeable pause for silent reflection.

The rite may take any of three forms. The first is the *Confiteor*, "I confess," which all say in unison:

> I confess to almighty God
> and to you, my brothers and sisters,
> that I have greatly sinned,
> in my thoughts and in my words,
> in what I have done and in what I have failed to do,
> through my fault, through my fault,
> through my most grievous fault;
> therefore I ask blessed Mary ever-Virgin,
> all the Angels and Saints,
> and you, my brothers and sisters,
> to pray for me to the Lord our God.

This prayer of repentance has its origin in medieval times, when prayers of unworthiness (*apologiae*) were recited by the clergy as a testimony to their piety before the Lord during the procession to the altar. Though once a private prayer of preparation for the priest, the *Confiteor* has now become a general confession that invokes the support of the communion of saints and, specifically, of the congregation gathered for the Eucharist. The *Confiteor* became part of the Mass in 1570 (Council of Trent). Though the prayer is not a substitute for the sacrament of reconciliation, its recitation is considered an appropriate preparation for Eucharistic celebration.[28]

The *Confiteor* begins with the words, "I confess to Almighty God." When we confess our sins at the beginning of Mass, we do something that has biblical antecedents. In the Old Testament, people sometimes confessed their sins in a formal public ceremony of repentance (Neh 9:2). At other times, an individual would spontaneously confess his sins (Ps 32:5; 38:18). The Wisdom Writings of the Old Testament encouraged the confession of one's sins (Prov 28:13; Sir 4:26).

The practice of confessing one's sins continues in the New Testament. In the stories about John the Baptist, we read about the crowds following the Baptist and confessing their sins in his baptism of repentance (Matt 3:6; Mark 1:5). In 1 John 1:8–9, we read, "If we say that we have no sin, we deceive ourselves, and the truth is not in us. If we confess our sins, he who is faithful and just will forgive us our sins and cleanse us from all unrighteousness." James exhorts Christians to "confess your sins to one another, and pray for one another, that you may be healed" (Jas 5:16). The season of Lent may be a particularly appropriate time to select the Penitential Rite.

We confess our sins not only to "almighty God" but also to our "brothers and sisters." "This makes the social dimension of our failures clear. It consists not only in the fact that we, through our misdeeds, have done injustice to our fellow human beings and have violated love but also in the fact that we have injured the Body of Christ and destroyed what others are working to build up."[29]

When we recite the *Confiteor* we are challenged to examine four areas of our lives in which we may have sinned:[30] "in my thoughts and in my words, in what I have done and in what I have failed to do." First, "in my thoughts." According to Wisdom 1:3, "Perverse thoughts separate men from God." According to Wisdom 1:5, "A holy and disciplined spirit will flee from deceit, and will rise and depart from foolish thoughts, and will be ashamed at the approach of unrighteousness." St. Paul exhorts the Philippians to guard their thoughts, keeping them focused on what is good: "Brethren, whatever is true, whatever is honorable, whatever is just, whatever is pure, whatever is lovely, whatever is gracious, if there is any excellence, if there is anything worthy of praise, think about these things" (Phil 4:8). Jesus, in the Sermon on the Mount, gives several warnings about ways in which we can fall into sin in our thoughts. According to Matthew 5:22, "Everyone who is angry with his brother shall be liable to judgment." Without ever physically touching a woman, we can fall into the sin of adultery of the heart through our lustful thoughts (Matt 5:27–28).

Second, we have "in my words." According to Psalm 52:2, "You are plotting destruction. Your tongue is like a sharp razor, you worker of treachery." Psalm 140:3 says, "They make their tongue sharp as a serpent's, and under their lips is the poison of vipers." According to Proverbs 18:21, "Death and life are in the power of the tongue, and those who love it will eat its fruits." According to James 3:6, "The tongue is a fire. The tongue is an unrighteous world among our members, staining the whole body, setting on fire the cycle of nature, and set on fire by hell." In other passages in the Bible, many ways of speech can be used to harm others. For example, gossip (2 Cor 12:20; 1 Tim 5:13; Rom 1:29), slander (Rom 1:30; 1 Tim 3:11), insult (Matt 5:22), lying (Col 3:9), and boasting (1 Cor 5:6; Jas 4:16). All these sins are to be confessed in the *Confiteor*.

Third, "in what I have done." Here we are talking about those actions that directly hurt other people or our relationship with God. In this connection, one might make mention of the Ten Commandments as the basis for examining one's conscience here.

Fourth, "in what I have failed to do." Here we are dealing with the good things that we failed to do, what we may call "sins of omission." As James says, "Whoever knows what is right to do and fails to do it, for him it is sin" (Jas 4:17).

Finally, we should draw attention to two points about the new translation of the *Confiteor*. First, whereas the old one says, "I have sinned," the new one says, "I have greatly sinned." This is a more accurate translation of the Latin[31] and echoes David's repentant words to God after his adultery with Bathsheba: "I have sinned greatly in that I have done this thing" (1 Chr 21:8). Second, whereas the old translation says, "Through my fault," the new one says, "Through my fault, through my fault, through my most grievous fault." These words are said while we strike our breasts as a sign of repentance.

The priest then gives the absolution in the following words: "May almighty God have mercy on us, forgive us our sins, and bring us to everlasting life." This prayer of absolution should not be underestimated. "They are certainly not words of sacramental absolution for sins that require confession, but there can hardly be any doubt of their theological and sacramental significance for repentant sinners."[32] The Sign of the Cross should not be made at this point either by the priest or by the assembly. We should note that in the Tridentine Missal, the *Confiteor* ended with two declaratory formulae: "May almighty God have mercy on you...," followed by "May the almighty and merciful Lord grant us pardon, absolution, and remission of all our sins." It was this *second* formula that had the character of a quasi-absolution that was accompanied by a Sign of the Cross. In the present Roman Missal, however, this second formula has been left out and the Sign of the Cross has *not* been transferred to the other formula.

The second form of the Penitential Rite is a two-fold exchange between the priest and the congregation that acknowledges the social nature of sin and asks for the Lord's mercy. The priest says, "Have mercy on us, Lord" and the people answer, "For we have sinned against you." The priest says further, "Show us, O Lord, your mercy," and the people answer, "And grant us your salvation." The absolution by the priest (as above) then follows.

The third form is arranged around a three-fold litany of praise to the Lord that the priest or deacon invokes and to which the assembly responds after each entry. It takes the following form:

> *The priest:*
>   You were sent to heal the contrite of heart:
>   Lord, have mercy.   *Or:*   Kyrie, eleison.
> *The people reply:*
>   Lord, have mercy.   *Or:*   Kyrie, eleison.
> *The priest:*
>   You came to call sinners:
>   Christ, have mercy.   *Or:*   Christe, eleison.
> *The people reply:*
>   Christ, have mercy.   *Or:*   Christe, eleison.
> *The priest:*
>   You are seated at the right hand of the Father to
>   intercede for us:
>   Lord, have mercy.   *Or:*   Kyrie, eleison.
> *The people reply:*
>   Lord, have mercy on us.   *Or:*   Kyrie, eleison.
> *The absolution by the priest follows.*

Other forms of this Penitential Rite may be composed. This is suggested by the new Order of Mass, which says at the beginning of the third alternative of the Penitential Rite, "The following or other invocations may be spoken by the priest or another minister, but the priest always gives the final blessing." The litany of praise may be freely improvised, but this must be done in line with certain principles. First, these invocations are addressed to Christ as Lord, and not to the Father, Son, and Holy Spirit. We should bear in mind that in the earliest texts, *Kyrie* (= Lord) was associated with the hymn in Philippians 2, where it is proclaimed, "Jesus Christ is Lord to the glory of God the Father." It is always Christ who is to be addressed, and not the Father or the Spirit (or Mary, or one of the saints). Second, it is not proper to let the litany of praise focus on human sinfulness. It is not meant to be a kind of examination of conscience. Rather, the focus should be on Christ, the channel of God's love and mercy. Because the invocations focus on Christ, they should not include the word *we*. It is thus improper to have an invocation that runs like this: "Lord Jesus, for the times we have not seen you present in our neighbors." In this last invocation, the focus is on us, rather than on God's mercy shown in Jesus. These invocations should never be turned into an examination of conscience. Third, the invocations should be brief, direct, and adapted to the season of the year, the day's feast, or the images and metaphors of the day's Scripture readings.

THE RITE OF BLESSING AND SPRINKLING OF WATER

On Sundays, the usual Penitential Act may be replaced by the blessing and sprinkling of water as a reminder of baptism. The Sundays of the Easter Season and Pentecost are the most appropriate time for this rite (*GIRM* 51). It serves as a link with the renewal of baptismal vows and sprinkling with water that takes place during the Easter Vigil. It is particularly fitting for the worshipping community, a priestly people by virtue of their baptism, to start the celebration of Mass on Sunday with this sprinkling, especially as each Sunday is a particular celebration of the Easter mystery. In contrast, during the season of Lent, as the Church prepares with its catechumens for baptism, it is better to use a standard Penitential Rite. For the rest of the year, the sprinkling of water may be frequently celebrated to stress that Sunday is always the "little Easter," the day of baptism and new life. Because baptism is entry into the Church, the rite is also appropriate at Masses that celebrate a local church's anniversary of dedication or a patronal feast.

In order to relate the sprinkling rite to baptism even more (if the church architecture allows it), it is a good idea to begin Mass by blessing the water at the baptismal font itself. It is full of significance, as it reminds us of our baptism and asks for a renewal of baptismal grace and a cleansing of our sins. If the greeting and blessing take place at the door, the priest may sprinkle the people during the entrance procession. During the sprinkling, the ministers could make their way from the font to their seats. If it is not possible to bless the water at the baptismal font, it can be blessed in the sanctuary, at the presidential chair. It is not good liturgically to bless the water to be used for the sprinkling in the sacristy, or at the rectory, and then sprinkle the people as the priest enters the church. The only exception to this is on Easter Sunday when the water to be used for the sprinkling would have been blessed the night before during the Easter Vigil.

When the congregation is large, it is not good for the presider alone to do the sprinkling, as the Opening Rite becomes disproportionately long. In such situations, it will be better to have water in several containers. After the presider blesses the water, he and others sprinkle different sections of the church. A generous amount of water should be used during the Rite of Sprinkling so that the symbolism of the cleansing waters of baptism is made very clear. The song that is sung during the sprinkling of the blessed water should have "an explicitly baptismal character."[33]

If the Rite of Blessing and Sprinkling of Water is used, the *Kyrie* ("Lord, have mercy") is not said. After the sprinkling, the priest says the following prayer: "May almighty God cleanse us of our sins, and through the Eucharist we celebrate make us worthy to sit at his table in his heavenly kingdom." This is followed by the Gloria when it is prescribed.

LORD HAVE MERCY (*KYRIE ELEISON*)

If the *Kyrie* has not been included in the Penitential Rite, it is now sung or recited, normally responsorially. The *Kyrie*[34] is an ancient chant by which the congregation acclaims the Lord. Already in the fourth century, it was the response of Greek Christians to petitions recited in the liturgy.[35] The *Kyrie* was adopted by the Roman Church from the Eastern liturgies, where it formed the response to various litanies of intercession. Toward the end of the fifth century, Pope Gelasius I introduced the Greek litany *Kyrie Eleison* into the Roman Rite, which replaced the solemn prayers of Intercession. That text was further revised and simplified by Pope Gregory the Great in the sixth century, resulting in a shortened form of the *Kyrie* litany.[36]

The *Kyrie* is by its nature a chant in which the faithful acclaim and implore the Lord's mercy. For this reason, all should have a part in it. It should not be sung by the choir or cantor alone. Normally, it is sung by all, alternating with the cantor or choir.

With the first word (*Kyrie*), we pay homage to Christ, whom Paul frequently describes as *Kyrios*, in the sense of the divine ruler. The phrase was used in heathen antiquity to pay homage to the gods or to a ruler who was revered as a god. In view of the fact that Christians in the early Church were often required to burn incense as an offering to the emperor as the *kyrios*, it can be more easily understood that this acclamation became a conscious acknowledgment that Christ is the true *Kyrios* (Lord).

The second word, *eleison*, is a cry for divine mercy. As the blind, the lame, the lepers, and sinners once called on the Lord Jesus to have mercy on them and Jesus responded by showing himself to be a helpful Lord, so we today, with our various physical and spiritual needs, trustfully call on Christ the Lord and ask him to be merciful. The *Kyrie Eleison* is really a shortened form of the cry of the two blind men: "Lord, have mercy on us, O Son of David" (Matt 20:31).

GLORIA

Next, we have the *Gloria* ("Glory to God in the Highest").

Glory to God in the highest,
and on earth peace to people of good will.
We praise you,
we bless you,
we adore you,
we glorify you,

we give you thanks for your great glory,
Lord God, heavenly King,
O God, almighty Father.

Lord Jesus Christ, Only Begotten Son,
Lord God, Lamb of God, Son of the Father,
you take away the sins of the world,
    have mercy on us;
you take away the sins of the world,
    receive our prayer;
you are seated at the right hand of the Father,
    have mercy on us.

For you alone are the Holy One,
you alone are the Lord,
you alone are the Most High,
Jesus Christ,
with the Holy Spirit,
in the glory of God the Father.
Amen.

Known as the greater doxology at Mass, the *Gloria* is the opening refrain of the Latin version of the hymn "Glory to God in the Highest." It is sung or recited after the Penitential Rite by the congregation, the choir, or both. The *Gloria* is regarded by scholars as one of those nonbiblical "psalms" that can be traced back to the primitive Church and that were composed on the model of the New Testament hymns. The date and authorship are unknown, though it was used in morning prayers as far back as the fourth century. An early version of the *Gloria* appeared in the *Apostolic Constitutions*, and it became a standard element in Eastern matins.[37] Even though it is very ancient, it did not become a common part of Sunday Eucharist in the West at which a priest presided until the eight century. It was introduced into the Roman Rite for Christmas at the beginning of the sixth century by Pope Symmachus (d. 514), then into Masses for Sundays and the feasts of martyrs if a bishop was presiding, and finally into these Masses no matter who the celebrant was. The *General Instruction* states,

"The text of this hymn may not be replaced by any other text" (*GIRM* 53).

The *Gloria* is by nature a festive hymn and is normally sung entirely, or in part, by the people. It should be sung by the whole congregation, or else by them in alternation with the choir. It may also be recited. The *Gloria* is still an occasional element in the Mass, used on Sundays outside of Advent and Lent, and on solemnities and feasts. It is particularly appropriate during the seasons of Christmas and Easter.

This song of praise is "saturated with words from Sacred Scripture."[38] The opening line comes from the words sung by the angels over the fields of Bethlehem, announcing to the shepherds the good news of Christ's birth: "Glory to God in the highest, and on earth peace among men with whom he is pleased" (Luke 2:14). In what follows, God is praised, blessed, adored, and glorified. In many passages in the Bible, too many to list here, God is praised. In other passages, human beings are said to bless God. This has to be taken in the sense of "praising" God. In other passages, God is adored or worshipped by human beings and he is also glorified. God is also given thanks because of his "great glory."

God the Father in the Gloria

The *Gloria* goes on to address God as "almighty Father" and "heavenly king." God is often referred to as "God Almighty" (Gen 17:1; Exod 6:3), or "Lord Almighty" (2 Cor 6:18), or just simply "the Almighty" (Pss 68:14; 91:1). In the Book of Revelation, the angels and saints in heaven praise God frequently as the "Lord God Almighty" (Rev 4:8; 11:17; 15:3; 19:6). In speaking of God as "almighty" and "heavenly king" in this song, we give him praise for his omnipotent reign over heaven and earth. However, God is also referred to as "Father." As a Father, he seeks what is good for his children.

Christ in the Gloria

After speaking of God the Father, the *Gloria* goes on to speak of the Son. Jesus is referred to as "Only Begotten Son" and "Son of the Father." There are a number of New Testament passages that point to Jesus' divine Sonship (e.g., John 5:17–18; 10:30–38; 2 Cor 1:19; Col 1:13; Heb 1:1–2).

Jesus is referred to as Lord (*kyrios*). This is significant since the Septuagint translates *Yahweh* by the Greek term *kyrios* (see LXX Gen 2:4, 8; 3:1; 6:3; Exod 5:1; 6:1; 7:5; 15:26; 20:2, 5; etc.). Indeed, the term *Lord* is used to mean "God" in many parts of the Bible (see, e.g., Matt 1:20; 3:3; 22:37; Mark 13:20; Luke 1:6; 2:9; 3:4; 4:18–19; 19:38; John 1:23; 12:13, 38; Acts 2:34; 3:22; 4:26; 7:49; Rom 4:8; 9:28–29; 1 Cor 14:21; Heb 12:5; Jas 5:4, 21; 1 Pet 1:25; 3:12; Rev 1:8; 19:6).

The term *kyrios* or *Lord*, as we have seen, was a title for God. However, in the ancient Roman world, *kyrios* was the title given to the emperor. Thus, while calling Jesus "Lord" associated him with God (1 Cor 8:6; Phil 2:11), it went against the accepted practice in the empire. The New Testament proclaims that Jesus is Lord, not Caesar.

When the earliest Christians made the statement "Jesus is Lord" (see Rom 10:9; 1 Cor 12:3; Phil 2:11) in view of his resurrection, this implied that he had entered into the life of God and, therefore, shared in the power and authority of the Lord God, creator of heaven and earth. He was in virtue of his resurrection both "Messiah and Lord," who had been exalted "to God's right hand" (Acts 2:33–36). He is, as the Book of Revelation says, "King of kings and Lord of lords" (Rev 19:16), that is, supreme over all other earthly and cosmic powers (see Phil 2:10–11).

The full title, "Lord Jesus Christ," is found here in the *Gloria* as well as in the Niceno-Constantinopolitan Creed. It is one of the most frequently used designations for Jesus (see, e.g., Rom 13:14; 16:20; 1 Cor 1:2, 7; 2 Cor 1:13; 13:13; Gal 1:3; 6:14; Eph 1:2; 5:20; Phil 1:2; Col 1:3; 1 Thess 1:1; 5:9; 2 Thess 1:12; 2:1; Phlm 3, 25; Jas 1:1; 2:1; 1 Pet 1:3; 2 Pet 1:8; Jude 4). In saying these words, Christians affirm that Jesus is our Lord. This means that we recognize him as Lord of all and acknowledge his authority over our own hearts. Indeed, by calling him Lord we imply that the worship and obedience we pay to the risen Jesus is the worship and obedience we pay to God.

The *Gloria* goes on to speak of Jesus as God's "only-begotten Son." In the Gospel and Epistles of John, Jesus is called the "Son of God,"[39] while Christians are called "children of God"[40] who are "born of God." This distinction underscores the unique relationship of Jesus to the Father, which is further underlined by the Gospel's designation of Jesus as "the only Son" or "the unique Son"[41] (John 1:14, 18; 3:16; 1 John 4:9).

The Greek word (*monogenēs*) translated as "only" or "unique" was translated by the King James Version as "only begotten," which is used here in the *Gloria*. This translation was due to St. Jerome's translation of the Greek term with the Latin *unigenitus*—"only begotten"—which the King James Version then echoed. St. Jerome was responding to the Arian assertion that Jesus was "made" not "begotten."[42] In addressing him with this title, we "use the rich theological language of St. John and join him in praising Jesus as the divine Son, the eternal Word who was made flesh and dwelt among us."[43]

In speaking of Christ as "the Lamb of God," the *Gloria* alludes to Christ's redemptive mission. It recalls the theme of the Lamb's triumph over sin and the devil in the Book of Revelation (Rev 5:6–14; 12:11; 17:14) and the worship of the Lamb by the angels and the saints in heaven (Rev 5:8, 12–13; 7:9–10; 14:1–3). By addressing Jesus as the Lamb of God in the *Gloria*, we partake in the heavenly worship of the Lamb as revealed in the Book of Revelation.

The *Gloria* goes further to address Jesus as "Lamb of God" who takes away "the sins of the world." These words echo the words of John the Baptist in John's Gospel when he saw Jesus passing by (John 1:29). They reveal Jesus as the new Passover lamb who offers his life on the cross for the sins of humankind. Just as the lamb was sacrificed on the first Passover night in Egypt to bring deliverance to the Israelites, so Jesus is the new Passover lamb who by his death on the cross saves humankind from sin.

The *Gloria* goes on to speak of Christ being seated at the right hand of the Father. In the New Testament, there are a number of ways to describe Jesus' new and more powerful form of existence after his resurrection. One very common way of doing this is to speak of him as sharing royal power with the Father. The royal enthronement in Psalm 110:1 plays an important role here, even if it is not quoted in full (as in Acts 2:25; Heb 1:13): "The Lord said to my Lord, 'Sit at my right hand, until I make your enemies a footstool for your feet.'" Therefore, the phrase "on the right hand" points to such a sharing in power (see, e.g., Matt 27:29; Mark 10:37; Rev 2:1), as does the reference to Jesus "sitting at the right hand" (see Matt 26:46; Mark 14:62; 16:19; Luke 22:69; Acts 2:33; 5:31; 7:55–56; Rom 8:34; Eph 1:20; Col 3:1; Heb 1:3; 8:1; 19:12; 12:2; 1 Pet 3:22; Rev 5:1, 7).

The concluding words of the *Gloria* run as follows: "For you alone are the Holy One, you alone are the Lord, you alone are the Most High, Jesus Christ, with the Holy Spirit, in the glory of God the Father." In the Old Testament, God is often referred to as "the Holy One of Israel" (cf. Ps 71:22; Prov 9:10; Isa 1:4; Hos 11:9–11). This title of God as "holy" is used of Jesus in the New Testament. Jesus applies this title to himself in Revelation 3:7, and an angel gives it to him in Revelation 16:5. In John 6:69, Peter refers to Jesus as "the Holy One of God." Even the demons recognize Jesus as "the Holy One" (Mark 1:24; Luke 4:34).

As we have seen above, the title *kyrios*, or Lord, was an imperial title. Thus, anyone in the ancient Roman world who said that Jesus alone is the Lord would have been seen as an enemy of the Roman Empire. Many early Christians, in fact, died for this belief, refusing to worship the emperor or the Roman gods.

The *Gloria* concludes with mention of the Holy Spirit, the third Person of the Trinity. Jesus is praised "with the Holy Spirit, in the glory of God the Father." A number of passages in the New Testament speak of the Holy Spirit primarily as the *power* at work in human beings. In Paul, the Holy Spirit is a power (Rom 15:13, 19; 1 Cor 12:4; 1 Thess 1:5–6; 2 Tim 1:7) that dwells in Christians (Rom 8:9, 11; 1 Cor 3:16, 19; 2 Tim 1:14) and gives them life (Rom 8:11; 3:25; Gal 3:25) as a first-fruits (Rom 8:23) or seal (Eph 1:13) or pledge (2 Cor 1:22) of a future glory (2 Cor 4:16—5:5).

Other Opening Rites

When other rites are combined with the Mass, the Introductory Rites are modified. The rule is that there is no need to have two Introductory Rites; it is not proper to duplicate ritual elements.[44] On particular occasions, another opening rite may be used. These rites are used on certain special feasts, when the liturgy of the hours is combined with the Mass, or when special rites are celebrated during the Mass, for example, baptism, the Rite of Acceptance into the Order of Catechumens, marriage, or funeral rites. In the English language Order of Christian Funerals, the Funeral Mass normally begins with the reception of the coffin at the door of the church. The usual Penitential Rite is omitted and the Sign of the Cross and greeting should both be done at the door of the church, preceding the sprinkling of water and clothing of the coffin. When the procession reaches the sanctuary, the celebrant welcomes those present on behalf of the family of the deceased, after which he says the Opening Prayer or the Collect.

Sometimes, for example, on Passion (Palm) Sunday or on the Feast of Presentation of the Lord, when an entrance procession forms part of the rite itself, the Opening Rite follows the form given for the occasion. On Ash Wednesday, the Penitential Rite is omitted.

THE COLLECT

With the words "Let us pray," the presider introduces the Collect, inviting the assembly to prayer. Silence is to be observed after the invitation. The purpose of this silence is twofold: it is to make the members of the assembly aware of God's presence, and to offer them the opportunity to call their intentions to mind.[45]

The Collect concludes the act of gathering, formally opens the celebration, and serves as a transition to the Liturgy of the Word. The term *Collect* owes its origin to what is known as stational liturgy that took place in stational churches. Stational or station churches were churches in Rome designated to be the special location for worship on a particular day. This practice dates back to the early centuries of the Church. The pope (or his legate) would celebrate solemn Mass in one after another of the four greater and the three minor basilicas during the fourth and fifth centuries. The seven churches are St. John Lateran, St. Peter, St. Paul Outside the Walls, St. Mary Major, the Holy Cross in Jerusalem, St. Lawrence, and the Twelve Apostles. Other churches were added to the list as needed for various liturgical occasions, bringing the total number of churches to forty-five.

The term *Collect* as used in the Mass originates from the Roman Stational Liturgy, which was intended to conclude the entrance procession and its chant. In the Roman Liturgy celebrated at that time, the processional assembly was called the *Collecta*, that is, a gathering of the faithful.[46] The Collect gathers into one the silent sentiments of the community and gives them collective expression, often in the form of a petition that the community might realize the fruits of the celebration. It is deliberately brief so that all individual worshippers may include their individual prayers in it and know that they are included.

The Collect, the first of the presidential prayers, has four elements. First is the priest's invitation to pray. This is followed by a brief silence—"brief," yet long enough to help the community to be conscious of being in the presence of God and to formulate their own prayer. Then follows the body of the prayer, which expresses "the character of the celebration." This comes out more clearly in Collects of feasts and proper seasons than Ordinary Time, as many of the latter have a rather generic content. The content of these prayers consists of an address to God, followed by a relative clause that focuses on the theme of the celebration and by a petition. The ancient Roman custom was to direct this prayer to the Father through the Mediator Jesus Christ in the Holy Spirit. Only since the tenth century have there been Collects directly addressed to Christ. These were written under the influence of the Gaulish liturgy.

All the Collects have a Trinitarian conclusion, such as, "Grant this through our Lord Jesus Christ who lives and reigns in the unity of the Holy Spirit, one God, for ever and ever." The form of this conclusion depends on whether the petition is addressed to the Father or the Son. The *General Instruction* prefers the first (more ancient) form: "In accordance with the ancient tradition of the Church, the collect prayer is usually addressed to God the Father, through Christ, in the Holy Spirit, and is concluded with a trinitarian, that is to say the longer ending" (*GIRM* 54).[47] After the body of prayer comes the people's "Amen," which unites them to the prayer and enables them to make it their own.

Like all the presidential prayers, the Collect is said with raised and extended hands. This is called the "stance of the *orantes*" that we spoke of in chapter four, where we discussed liturgical postures and actions. The congregation responds to the opening prayer by saying "Amen."

It is not good liturgical practice to change the prayer endings so that the liturgical assembly cannot respond with their "Amen." Sometimes some priests say "forever" or "forever more" instead of "forever and ever," or "through Christ our Lord and brother" instead of "through Christ our Lord." These modifications may seem insignificant, yet "in terms of ritual action, of stimulus and response, of expectations, and of repetitions, such minor changes can throw an assembly off-balance and leave them hanging in mid-air. If the assembly does not know when to say its proper response because the priest presiding has changed the cues, in effect the leader of prayer has deprived the assembly of its rightful part in the liturgical action!"[48]

CHAPTER SIX

The Liturgy of the Word

AS HAS BEEN SAID ABOVE, THE MASS IS MADE UP OF THE Liturgy of the Word and the Liturgy of the Eucharist, which are so closely connected as to form one act of worship. The liturgical assembly listens to the Word of God, reflects on it in silence, assimilates it, and applies it to their lives. Moved by it, they profess their faith and intercede for the needs of the Church and the world.

The following are the elements of the Liturgy of the Word:

1. The Readings
2. The Responsorial Psalm
3. The Gospel Acclamation
4. The Gospel Reading
5. The Homily
6. The Profession of Faith
7. The Prayer of the Faithful

1. The Readings

The origins of the Liturgy of the Word are probably to be found in the biblical tradition. Jesus took part in the "liturgy of the word" in the synagogue (Luke 4:16–21), as did Paul (Acts 13:13–43). The proclamation of the Word formed part of Old Testament worship, for example, the ceremony for the establishment of the covenant (Exod 24:3–11) and ceremonies for the renewal of the covenant (Josh 24:1–28; Neh 8:1–8; 9:3–38). The first Christians were familiar with the synagogue liturgy, but the influence of the synagogue celebration of the Word on the development of the Christian Liturgy of the Word is not easy to determine.[1]

For the early Christians, the first liturgical book was the Bible. The readings began at the point at which the previous liturgy had left off, and they continued until the presider gave the signal to stop. The practice of reading from the Scriptures, both the Old and the New Testaments, was universal throughout the Church, though the number of readings varied from place to place. However, the normal practice was to choose one reading from the Old Testament, one from the New Testament non-Gospel material (epistles, Acts, and Revelation) and one from the Gospels. It became obligatory in the whole Church that the final and climactic reading be taken from one of the Gospels. These other New Testament readings in turn came after "the law of Moses and the prophets and the psalms" (cf. Luke 24:44).

In our liturgy today, there are normally three readings on Sundays and solemnities. For feasts, on the other hand, two readings are assigned. If, however, according to the norms a feast is raised to the rank of a solemnity, a third reading is added, taken from the Common (*GIRM* 357). When there is more than one reading, it is preferable to assign the readings to different readers. This means that parishes will need to assign the first two readings to two different readers, while the Gospel is read by either the deacon or the priest.[2]

It is liturgically not proper for the Word of God to be proclaimed from worship aids or typewritten pages. It is better for the Word of God to be read from a lectionary or the *Book of the Gospels*. In the *Introduction to the Lectionary* we read,

> Because of the dignity of the word of God, the books of readings used in the celebration are not to be replaced by other pastoral aids, for example, by leaflets printed for the preparation of the readings by the faithful or for their personal meditation. (no. 37)

In some places, it is customary for readers to go to the presider to receive a blessing before doing the first or second reading. However, this is not necessary. We should note that when readers and extraordinary ministers of Holy Communion are formally instituted in their ministry, they receive a solemn blessing. This blessing prepares them for their ministry at every liturgy in which they carry out their duties. It is, therefore, unnecessary for them to receive extra blessings.

Regarding the blessing given to a deacon by the presider, we should note that this blessing (or the prayer said by the priest in the absence of a deacon) is part of the ritual words and gestures that point to the Gospel as the climax of the Liturgy of the Word. It should be observed that, apart from the reader of the Gospel receiving a special blessing, other ritual elements are included, such as candles, a special book (the *Book of the Gospels*), incense, a preparatory acclamation, and the posture of standing. These are not prescribed for the first and second readings. As the blessing of the deacon forms only one part of a number of ritual elements, it does not usually draw attention to itself, especially if it is done unobtrusively, while the congregation sings the Alleluia.

It should be observed, in contrast, that the non-gospel readings are proclaimed in a more restrained manner. The assembly sits, there are no introductory acclamations, incense and candles are not used. In conclusion, "The blessing of readers is a practice that has the potential to distract the assembly from its primary focus, which is the proclaimed word. It would be better if it were not introduced into contemporary liturgical practice."[3]

During the Liturgy of the Word, it is better for the reader to hold the lectionary and the *Book of the Gospels* at the ambo so that the congregation may see them, rather than leaving them half-hidden on the ambo. When a book of Scripture is being used in the proclamation of God's Word, it should be visible as the sacrament of God's presence.

The non-gospel readings should not be read by the priest if others who can read them are available. The ministry of reading Scripture in church is a function that differs from the office of leadership exercised by the deacon and the priest. Therefore, even if there are many deacons and priests during the celebration of Mass, the reading of Scripture (except for the Gospel) should be done by nonordained lectors.

It is the custom in some places that each reading is introduced by a short commentary. The *General Instruction* does not prescribe this and it is unnecessary. It implies that the congregation is not capable of understanding what is going to be read. Any commentary on the readings should form part of the priest's homily. In this connection, Keplers says that it is the purpose of the homily "to break open God's Word and unearth the kernel of wisdom emerging from the scriptural texts which the Church offers us for that day."[4]

FIRST READING

The first reading is taken from the Old Testament, except during the Easter season, when it is taken from the Acts of the Apostles. It usually has some correspondence to the Gospel. By taking readings from the Old Testament, the Church wants to make it clear that the Old Testament is also divine revelation and that its purpose ultimately is to serve the saving events of Christ's life. After the first and the second readings, the lector says "The Word of the Lord." This expression is an acclamation, a statement of faith that elicits the assembly's response, "Thanks be to God." Thanksgiving is a common feature of worship in the Old Testament: see, for example, 1 Chronicles 16:4; Psalms 42:4 and 95:2. It is also found in the New Testament in Colossians 2:7 and 4:2. The specific words "Thanks be to God" were used by Paul to thank the Lord for delivering him from sin and death (Rom 7:25; 1 Cor 15:57; 2 Cor 2:14).

SECOND READING

The principle for selecting the second reading is that there should be some correspondence in theme to the mystery of the feast being celebrated. On Sundays of Ordinary Time, however, the principle of semicontinuous reading is used. These readings are chosen from the letters of Paul and James. The letters of Peter and John are read during the Christmas and Easter seasons.

2. The Responsorial Psalm

The Responsorial Psalm comes after the first reading. The Responsorial Psalm was most likely introduced into the Roman liturgy by Pope Celestine I (422–32).[5] Its text is usually linked to the readings of the day. It is the assembly's response to the Word that has been proclaimed, and it should be sung whenever possible. This is in view of the fact that the psalms, the songs and hymns of Israel, were usually sung. The cantor may sing each verse of the psalm and the people sing the response. Alternatively, the whole psalm may be sung by the congregation. If recited, the reader should read the psalm as poetry, with appropriate expression. Even when the Responsorial Psalm cannot be sung, it is possible to enrich its reading with instrumental music. Readers should not introduce their reading with expressions such as "Responsorial Psalm" or "The response to the psalm is…"

Since the Responsorial Psalm forms part of the Word of God, it is proper that the person singing or reading it does so from the ambo, the same place where the other readings are proclaimed. If the reader cannot sing the Responsorial Psalm and it has to be sung by someone else (e.g., the choirmaster), that person may do so from another place and not from the ambo (cf. *GIRM* 60). If a particular Responsorial Psalm cannot be sung, it can be replaced with another psalm that can be sung.

3. The Gospel Acclamation/Alleluia

After the second reading comes the Alleluia, or depending on the season, the acclamation before the Gospel. *Alleluia* (Halleluiah) is a joyful liturgical expression of praise that is found in the Books of Psalms, Tobit, and Revelation. Its liturgical use dates from the early Church and is now used throughout the year except during Lent. *Alleluia* (Halleluiah) is a Greek transliteration from a Hebrew word meaning, "praise the Lord." In the Old Testament, it is found frequently in the Psalter (e.g., Psalms 104—6, 111—13, 115—17, 135, 146—50). The plural imperative form of the verb indicates that the term was a directive to the worshiping congregation in the temple and was meant to evoke a response. In time, it became an independent exclamation of joy, so that the Greek-speaking Jews simply transliterated it instead of translating it. In all Christian liturgical rites, the Alleluia is addressed to the risen Lord, corresponding to Revelation 19:1–7. Since it is such an Easter cry of homage, it is given a special place in the Easter season.

The Gospel acclamation/Alleluia expresses the people's greeting of the Lord and their faith in his presence as he addresses them in the gospel reading. It is an acclamation to Christ, who will be present in the Gospel. Except during Lent, it consists of the Alleluia with its corresponding verse. The Alleluia or Gospel acclamation looks forward to the gospel reading. It is not a response to the previous reading, from which it is separated by a distinct pause.

In accordance with the character of the Alleluia, it must be sung; it is less effective when merely recited. According to the *General Instruction*, "The *Alleluia* or the Verse before the Gospel, if not sung, may be omitted" (*GIRM* 63c). However, as DeGrocco notes in connection with the Gospel acclamation/Alleluia, "Interestingly, there is no prohibition against reciting this, although many parishes prefer to omit it when it is not sung, citing a certain fittingness that it is better to omit a text that is meant to be sung rather than reading it."[6]

The Alleluia should not be sung alone by the cantor who intones it or by the choir, but by the whole congregation. The Gospel acclamation has traditionally accompanied the Gospel procession, in which the *Book of the Gospels* is carried to the ambo accompanied by lights and incense. During the singing of the Alleluia or the Gospel acclamation, all stand: this posture expresses the congregation's reverence for, and their readiness to receive, the One who is coming.

If incense is used at the reading of the Gospel, it is prepared after the second reading and before the Gospel procession. During the Lenten season in preparation for Easter, the acclamation before the Gospel consists of a greeting of welcome to Christ (for example, "Glory and praise to you, Lord Jesus Christ!") and a verse.

THE SEQUENCE

In addition to the two chants between the readings, another song has found a place before the Gospel since the early Middle Ages. It is called the "sequence," a name derived from the Latin *sequentia*, meaning "continuation." This song developed as people began to add texts to the joyful melodies at the end of the Alleluia verses. There were many of these sequences, but the Missal of Pius V, published in 1570, limited the number to four. The post-Vatican II liturgy makes sequences obligatory at Easter (*Victimae Paschali Laudes*) and Pentecost (*Veni Sancte Spiritus*), and optional for Corpus Christi (*Lauda Sion Salvatorem*) and Our Lady of Sorrows (September 15, *Stabat Mater*). The sequence is sung before the Alleluia because the Alleluia is the immediate preparation for the Gospel.

4. The Gospel Reading

The English word *Gospel* is derived from the Old English *godspel* ("good tidings"), which is a rendering of the Greek *euangelion* ("good news"). The word *Gospel* is used to refer to a selection from one of the four Gospels that is read in the Mass. The proclamation of the gospel reading is never omitted, even at Masses with children, at which a shortened Liturgy of the Word is permitted. Because the proclamation of the Gospel is the high point of the Liturgy of the Word, it is distinguished from the other readings by special marks of honor. Its proclamation is reserved to a deacon or, in his absence, a priest.

The deacon who is to proclaim the gospel reading prepares himself by bowing before the priest celebrant and asking for a blessing saying, "Your blessing, Father." The celebrant says,

> May the Lord be in your heart and on your lips,
> that you may proclaim his Gospel worthily and well,
> in the name of the Father, and of the Son, ✠ and of the
>   Holy Spirit. (*RM*, Order of Mass 14)

If the main celebrant is a bishop and there is no deacon, the Gospel is read by a priest who asks for and receives the blessing in the same manner as would a deacon (*GIRM* 212). However, in a concelebration in which the presider is not a bishop, the concelebrant who proclaims the Gospel in the absence of a deacon neither requests nor receives the blessing of the presider (*GIRM* 212). The *General Instruction* prescribes that such a priest should bow toward the altar while reciting the following prayer: "Cleanse my heart and my lips, almighty God, that I may worthily proclaim your holy Gospel" (*GIRM* 132; *RM* 14). In spite of the prescription of the *General Instruction* that the priest should bow toward the altar while reciting the prayer, one sometimes sees priests bowing toward the tabernacle instead, as if it were "more reverent" to bow toward the reserved Sacrament. During the liturgy, the altar is the primary architectural symbol of Christ (*GIRM* 298), and must be reverenced as such.

According to the *General Instruction*, "When the *Alleluia* is begun, all rise, except for a Bishop, who puts incense into the thurible without saying anything and blesses the Deacon or, in the absence of a Deacon, the concelebrant who is to proclaim the Gospel" (*GIRM* 212). Similarly, the *Ceremonial of Bishops* says that only the bishop may put incense into the thurible while seated.[7] For the proclamation of the Gospel, it is required that "those present turn towards the ambo as a sign of special reverence for the Gospel of Christ" (*GIRM* 133).

The presiding priest should not read the Gospel if another priest or deacon is present. According to the *General Instruction*,

> The function of proclaiming the readings is by tradition not presidential but ministerial. Therefore the readings are to be read by a reader, but the Gospel by the Deacon or, in his absence, by another Priest. If, however, a Deacon or another Priest is not present, the Priest Celebrant himself should read the Gospel. (*GIRM* 59)

Some presiding priests suggest that since they will give the homily, they should also read the Gospel. However, it should be noted that giving a homily is a presidential function, whereas reading the Gospel to the congregation is a ministerial function. These two actions should not be confused. The presider should never proclaim the Gospel if another priest or deacon is present.[8]

For the proclamation of the Gospel, the *Book of the Gospels* is reverently taken from the altar and carried in procession to the ambo. The deacon or priest carries the *Book of the Gospels* "slightly elevated" (*GIRM* 133). The book is intended to be carried in procession and there is, therefore, the need for it to be highlighted. However, as DeGrocco notes, "Priests (and Deacons) should resist the urge to show the book to the assembly in a way

that mimics a blessing or other exaggerated or spontaneous gestures."[9] It is placed on the ambo and carefully opened. If incense is
used, the book is incensed with three swings of the thurible, to the
center, the left, and the right.[10]

The deacon (or priest) greets the people with "The Lord be
with you," and while announcing the Gospel passage, he makes
the Sign of the Cross first on the book, then on his forehead, lips,
and breast. The faithful likewise sign themselves in this way and
then respond, "Praise to you, Lord Jesus Christ" (*GIRM* 175).
The custom of signing on the forehead, lips, and breast before the
reading of the Gospel as well as signing the book comes from the
eleventh century and remains as a ritual gesture for the assembly.
This gesture is a reminder to the one who proclaims the good news
that he should revere its message in what he thinks (the mind), in
what he says (the lips), and in his heart (the breast). According to
the *Ceremonial of Bishops*, after the deacon (or priest) has traced
the cross on his forehead, lips and heart, "the bishop signs himself
in the same way...and all present do the same."[11] The congregation is thereby encouraged to do the same.

The meaning of at least part of this gesture is taken from the
blessing that the priest gives to the deacon ("May the Lord be in
your heart and on your lips, that you may proclaim his Gospel
worthily and well"), or that the priest says to himself if there is no
deacon ("Cleanse my heart and my lips, almighty God, that I may
worthily proclaim your holy Gospel") (*RM*, Order of Mass, 13).

Even if the gospel reading itself is not sung, it may be helpful
to sing the greeting and title of the gospel reading at the beginning and "The Gospel of the Lord" at the end, in order to allow
the people to sing their acclamation. On more solemn occasions,
it may be a good idea to repeat the sung Alleluia at the end of the
gospel reading.

The deacon or priest concelebrant who reads the Gospel concludes the reading by saying "The Gospel of the Lord." It is a
widespread practice for the deacon or priest who reads the Gospel
to lift up the *Book of the Gospels* (or a lectionary) while singing
or saying "The Gospel of the Lord," but this is not good liturgical
practice. As the DeGrocco notes, "The book itself is not the Gospel, but rather the Gospel is the living proclamation of the Spirit-
inspired words of the Evangelists and words of Christ that have

been announced to the assembly and that now rest in the minds, on the lips, and in the hearts of all present."[12] The deacon or priest may lift the book a little while kissing it, quietly saying, "Through the words of the Gospel..."

After the proclamation of the Gospel, when the deacon is assisting a bishop, he carries the book to him to be kissed, or else kisses it himself, saying quietly, "Through the words of the Gospel may our sins be wiped away" (RM, Order of Mass, 16). After the reading of the Gospel, a bishop may bless the assembly with the *Book of the Gospels* (GIRM 175). The practice of the bishop giving a blessing with the *Book of the Gospels* on certain solemn occasions is relatively new in the liturgy. The practice was introduced in the Roman Rite by Pope John Paul II during papal liturgies both in Rome and abroad, and is also found in some usages of the Byzantine Rite. For some time it was considered as a prerogative exclusive to the Holy Father, even though some bishops also began to impart this blessing, probably influenced by televised papal Masses.

The norm legitimizing the practice (GIRM 175) does not specify how this blessing is to be carried out. The general practice seems to be that, after proclaiming the Gospel, the priest or deacon brings the open book to the bishop to be kissed. The priest or deacon then closes the *Book of the Gospels* and gives it to the bishop who makes a simple Sign of the Cross with the book in a manner similar to that of Benediction with the monstrance. In other cases, the book is brought, already closed, to the bishop, who takes it, kisses it, and then imparts the blessing. The rubric does not indicate on what solemn occasions this blessing is imparted and apparently leaves the decision to the bishop himself.

The congregation sits for the readings but stands to hear the Gospel. This expresses their joy, reverence, and alertness. In this sense, their standing becomes a confession without words.

Laypeople are not permitted to read the Gospel. At Mass, the proclamation of the Gospel belongs first to the deacon, if he is assisting, then to the priest celebrant when there is no deacon present and when there are no concelebrants. A bishop celebrating Mass may not read the Gospel when there is a deacon or priest assisting him. A layperson may not read the Gospel at Mass, but laity may read other readings and lead the Responsorial Psalm. In addition, where necessary, lay readers may take part in the reading of the passion on Palm Sunday and Good Friday.

5. The Homily

The homily follows the reading of the Gospel. From the earliest days of the Church's liturgy, the Word of God was not read on its own. It was always followed by a homily, which explained the meaning of the biblical passages that had been read and drew out the application for people's lives. In the early Church, the bishop typically celebrated Sunday Mass and gave the homily. Yet the liturgical practice of explaining Scripture readings did not start with Christianity. It is rooted in ancient Jewish custom. In the Book of Ezra, for example, the book of the law was not merely read to the people. The Levites "helped the people to understand the law" (Neh 8:7). They read from God's law "and they gave the sense, so that the people understood the reading" (Neh 8:8). The Jewish synagogues followed a similar practice. Readings from Scripture were accompanied by explanations. Jesus himself practiced this custom. He expounded on a reading from Scripture in his hometown synagogue in Nazareth (see Luke 4:18–30).

According to the Second Vatican Council, the homily must have four characteristics. Homiletic preaching is biblical, liturgical, kerygmatic, and familiar.[13]

BIBLICAL

The homily must be biblical. It must be based on the readings. It was the practice in the synagogues that biblical passages that were read were explained (cf. Luke 4:16ff.; Acts 13:14ff.). It was necessary to interpret and apply the biblical message to the contemporary situation. Jesus' homily on the Book of Isaiah in the synagogue of Nazareth signals the prophetic nature of the scriptural exposition: "Today this scripture is fulfilled in your hearing" (Luke 4:21).

The Second Vatican Council insisted, "All the preaching of the Church must be nourished and regulated by Sacred Scripture" (*Dei Verbum* 21). Preaching was to "draw its content mainly from scriptural and liturgical sources" (*Sacrosanctum Concilium* 35) and the homily was described as flowing "from the sacred text" (*Sacrosanctum Concilium* 52).

LITURGICAL

The homily must also be liturgical. It must have the character of the ancient homilies that invited the worshipping assembly to the mysteries of Christ celebrated at the Eucharist. The Second Vatican Council called for a renewed understanding of the relation between the Liturgy of the Word and the Eucharist.

KERYGMATIC

The homily must also be kerygmatic. The word most frequently used for preaching in the New Testament is *keryssein,* "to proclaim." The preacher is like the herald (*keryx*) who returns from the battle to proclaim the happy message (*kerygma*) of victory to a people waiting in anticipation. The metaphor of the herald suggests that preaching is beyond the words of a mere human messenger. These are the saving words of God that are spoken through the herald. It is not the preacher but Christ the Lord who is preaching (2 Cor 4:5). This type of preaching does not depend upon the persuasive words of rhetoric but upon the demonstration of spirit and power (1 Cor 2:4). Kerygmatic preaching obliges the listeners to make a response. Such preaching is found in the apostolic preaching of Acts (e.g., 2:14–40; 3:12–26; 10:28–43). The Second Vatican Council spoke of the need for the homily to be permeated by a kerygmatic character. It stressed "the proclamation of God's wonderful works in the history of salvation, the mystery of Christ, ever made present and active in us, especially in the celebration of the liturgy" (*Sacrosanctum Concilium* 35).

FAMILIAR

The word *homily* comes from the Greek *homou* (together) and *homilos* (a crowd). The word refers to a familiar conversation with a group of people or a pastor conversing with a flock in words and images that they recognize. The crowd is not some random mob of strangers but a gathering of friends, people familiar to the preacher. It is not a conversation in which the speaker tries to impose his views or to persuade the listeners. It is rather talking to people heart to heart in a liturgical context in the light of God's Word that has been read.

The word *homily* is used to describe the conversation that the two disciples engaged in as they were on their way to Emmaus "talking [*homiloun*] as they went about all these things that had happened" (Luke 24:14). The story of Emmaus reflects the pattern of early Christian worship. Before the risen Lord proclaims the good news, he listens and enters into the two disciples' story of distress and lost hope. His interpretation of the things that went on in Jerusalem "these days" is different from their own. Jesus, the preacher, throws light on their story and makes their hearts burn. According to *The Decree on the Ministry and Life of Priests* (no. 4), if today's preaching is to be effective, it must explain the Word of God "not…in a general and abstract way, but rather by applying the lasting truth of the Gospel to the particular circumstances of life."

The homily is important for nourishing the Christian life:

> The purpose of the homily is to draw out the message of the good news for us here and now. The homily follows upon the gospel as its extension, its application. It is not meant to be a repetition or summary of what we have already heard. It is intended to help us penetrate and experience more fully what we have already heard and to lead us to celebrate the Eucharist wholeheartedly.[14]

According to Edward Foley,

> The homily is not so much about clarifying ideas as it is about inviting the faithful and even inquirers into a deeper relationship with God through Christ; thus, it is rightly understood as an act of first evangelization and re-evangelization.[15]

If it is to fulfill its purpose, the homily must be the fruit of meditation, carefully prepared, and in length, style, and content, adapted to the needs and capacities of all present. Pope Francis speaks in a similar vein when he says in *Evangelii Gaudium* (no. 145), "Preparation for preaching is so important a task that a prolonged time of study, prayer, reflection and pastoral creativity should be devoted to it."

In the Catholic Church, a distinction is made between *homily* and *sermon*. The latter is the type of preaching that is not necessarily linked to the biblical readings and can be heard in nonliturgical contexts. The homily, on the other hand, explains the mysteries of the Christian faith and its guiding principles. This is often done from the readings of the day as well as from the other texts and rites of the liturgy. The homily, as a living exposition of the Word of God, helps the faithful to assimilate it and apply it to their lives.

Dennis C. Smolarski explains the difference between a sermon and a homily:

> A sermon is a holy speech, a sacred oration—but, of its nature, it need not be connected to Scripture. A homily should start with the context of the celebration, particularly the feast being celebrated, or, if there is no feast, the experience of the Scripture just proclaimed. It should be a holy reflection on the Scripture, "breaking the bread" of God's written word for the assembly so that those present can be nourished by it (cf. *GIRM* 65). It should offer practical applications to the contemporary experience, and a challenge to the way lives are lived in the contemporary culture. It is not an academic lecture containing absolute truth as perceived by the homilist.[16]

On Sundays and holy days, a homily must be given at all Masses celebrated with a congregation; it should not be omitted without a serious reason. A homily is strongly recommended on the weekdays of Advent, Christmas, Lent, and Easter, and on other occasions when people come together in large numbers. Indeed, a homily is recommended for almost all Masses with a congregation.

During Mass, the presider usually gives the homily. A deacon or, at a concelebrated Mass, one of the concelebrants may be asked to give the homily (see canon 767 §1). The preaching of the homily is part of the gift and mission of holy orders reserved to the sacred minister, priest, or deacon. Nonordained faithful are not allowed to give it, even if these are "pastoral assistants" or catechists.

This exclusion is not based on the preaching ability of sacred ministers or their theological preparation, but on the function that is reserved to them in virtue of having received the sacrament of holy orders. For the same reason, the diocesan bishop cannot validly dispense from the canonical norm, since this is not merely a disciplinary law but one that touches upon the closely connected functions of teaching and sanctifying. For the same reason, the practice, on some occasions, of entrusting the preaching of the homily to seminarians or theology students who are not clerics is not permitted. Indeed, delivering the homily should not be regarded as training for some future ministry.[17]

It should also be noted that on June 20, 1987, the Commission for the Authentic Interpretation of the Code of Canon Law (since 1988, the Pontifical Council for the Interpretation of Legislative Texts) reaffirmed canon 767 §1 and stated that the local diocesan bishop does not have the power to dispense from this law. The *Instruction on Certain Questions regarding the Collaboration of the Non-Ordained Faithful in the Sacred Ministry of Priests* (jointly published by eight Vatican departments in 1997) applies the same canon in the section, "Practical Provisions," article 3.[18]

In this connection, Jeremy Driscoll observes that the homily given by an ordained minister is intended to be a sign or "guarantee" that the preaching is passing on "the Church's apostolic faith and not merely the private thoughts and experiences of an individual."[19] It is the particular responsibility of bishops as successors of the apostles to teach the apostolic faith. Since priests and deacons, by virtue of their ordination, share in this particular responsibility, they also may proclaim the Gospel and deliver the homily at Mass.

The homily given during a funeral should not be turned into a tribute. While lessons can be drawn from the life of the deceased, the homily should not be turned into a eulogy. As the *General Instruction* says, "At Funeral Masses there should usually be a short Homily, but to the exclusion of a funeral eulogy of any kind" (*GIRM* 382). DeGrocco's comment on this is very apt:

> A Homily focuses on the Paschal Mystery of Christ's
> Death and Resurrection and our participation in it; a

eulogy simply focuses on the deceased. A Homily brings out Christ's saving deeds; a eulogy focuses on the accomplishments of the deceased. A Homily breaks open the Scripture readings and is connected to them; a eulogy is simply a series of talking points with no relation to the Word of God....A Homily is preached to the living; a eulogy is about the deceased.[20]

The one who gives the homily during Mass should be a participant in the whole celebration, and thus experience the proclamation of the Word on which the preaching is based and the consummation of the celebration in Eucharistic Communion. It is not liturgically proper for a priest or deacon who is not taking part in a Mass to appear just at the time of the homily, to deliver it and then disappear.

Regarding the location from which the homily can be given, the *General Instruction* says, "The Priest, standing at the chair or at the ambo itself or, if appropriate, in another worthy place, gives the Homily" (*GIRM* 136). From this, it is clear that the priest *stands* in one of three locations to give the homily: at the chair, or at the ambo, or at another suitable place. However, only a bishop can *sit* and give the homily. According to the *Ceremonial of Bishops*, the bishop "gives the homily seated in the chair (cathedra), unless he prefers some other place in order to be easily seen and heard by all."[21] The idea of the bishop sitting and giving the homily has biblical support in Matthew 23:2–3, when Jesus says that the scribes and Pharisees derive their teaching authority from sitting on the seat of Moses: "The scribes and the Pharisees sit on Moses' seat; therefore, do whatever they teach you and follow it; but do not do as they do, for they do not practice what they teach." In addition to this, there are references to Jesus sitting down and teaching the crowds (cf. Matt 5:1ff., 26:55; Luke 5:3; John 8:2).

In particular circumstances, such as in an unrenovated church or at a celebration with children, the homilist may need to get closer to the congregation in order to communicate effectively.

The homily should not begin and end with the Sign of the Cross. The practice of making the Sign of the Cross before and after the homily is a remnant from times past when the homily was considered an interruption in the liturgy and, therefore, needed pious parentheses.[22] This was the case in medieval times, when the homily became a speech independent of the liturgy and thus of the sacred text read or sung in the liturgy.[23] The practice is no longer recommended, since the homily is part of the liturgy itself. In the early 1970s, a question about this practice, along with whether it is appropriate to use a greeting to the assembly to begin the homily, was posed to the Congregation for Divine Worship. The following was the answer given:

> Generally speaking it is inadvisable to continue such customs because they have their origin in preaching outside Mass. The homily is part of the liturgy; the people have already blessed themselves and received the greeting at the beginning of Mass. It is better, then, not to have a repetition before or after the homily.[24]

It is recommended that a period of silence be observed after the homily so that the people may take the Word of God to heart and prepare a response to it in prayer (*GIRM* 66).

6. The Profession of Faith

After the homily and the silence that follows, the Niceno-Constantinopolitan Creed is either sung or recited. The recitation of the Creed after the Gospel and the homily expresses the assembly's verbal response to the story of salvation proclaimed in the Scriptures and celebrated most fully at the Eucharistic table. Before they celebrate the mystery of faith in the Eucharist, believers call to mind the rule of faith in a formula approved by the Church. The recitation of the Creed during the Mass is an act of praise and testimony by which Christians confess before God and one another what God has done and is doing in and through Jesus Christ by the power of the Holy Spirit. The repetition of the Creed every week during Sunday Mass narrates the saving events that are the basis of Christian faith: God's activity in creation, redemption in Jesus Christ, and presence in and through the Spirit who enlivens, enlightens, guides, and heals the human and Christian communities.

The Niceno-Constantinopolitan Creed is composed of the Creed of Nicaea (AD 325), which was revised at the Council of Constantinople (381). The Creed of Nicaea was originally the theological confession resulting from the first Council of Nicaea, convened by the emperor Constantine to resolve Church divisions related to Arianism.[25] This Creed was probably based on earlier creeds from Jerusalem and Antioch, and was drafted to counter the Arian teaching that the Son was the highest creation of God and thus differed in essence from the Father. The Creed upholds the unity of God, insists that Christ was "begotten from the Father before all time," and declares that Christ is "of the same essence (*homoousios*) as the Father." Thus, the Son is God in every respect.

The Niceno-Constantinopolitan Creed is actually an enlargement of the teaching of the Creed of 325, most likely ratified by the Council of Constantinople (381). Further expanding on this, the Chalcedonian Definition was prepared by more than five hundred Greek bishops at the Council of Chalcedon in 451, in response to the erroneous teachings regarding the person of Christ proposed by Apollinarius, Nestorius, and Eutyches. The Definition states that Jesus Christ is perfectly God and perfectly man, that he is consubstantial with God as to his divinity, and with humankind as to his humanity. Moreover, humanity and deity are joined in the God-man "without confusion, without change, without division, without separation."[26]

The Niceno-Constantinopolitan Creed also upheld the divinity of the Holy Spirit and his procession from the Father. In the West, the phrase "who proceeds from the Father" was later altered to read, "from the Father and the Son." This so-called *Filioque* clause affirms the double procession of the Spirit, following the teaching of Hilary, Ambrose, Jerome, and Augustine, and appears in the Athanasian Creed, but it was rejected by the Eastern Church. It became the major doctrinal issue in the schism between East and West that came to a head in 1054. Chalcedon represents the definitive statement, albeit in Greek ontological language, of how Jesus Christ was God and man at the same time. This creed is of great ecumenical importance, for it is still accepted by Catholics, Orthodox, and the great majority of Protestant churches.

The Creed is a summary statement of the faith used in the early Church as a rule or standard for Christian belief. Originally, catechumens were required to profess the faith of the Church during the rite of baptism. To make sure that they had the correct faith, candidates for baptism were required to give their assent to a short formula of Christian belief. In answer to three questions about belief in the Father, Son, and Spirit, the candidate would respond, "I believe" (*credo*). In the course of time, under the influence of the Church's catechetical ministry, there was a move from interrogatory to declaratory creeds. Declaratory creeds appeared in the third century as part of the catechetical instruction given before baptism.

The Creed appeared in the celebration of the Mass later, during the confused struggles against Arianism. In May 325, the Council of Nicaea declared Arius a heretic after he refused to sign the formula of faith stating that Christ was of the same divine nature as God.

The Creed appeared in the East in the first quarter of the sixth century. It appeared in the West at the time when the Visigoths rejected Arianism. The Council of Toledo (589) decided to imitate Eastern usage and put the Creed just before the Our Father. It did not become part of the Roman liturgy until early in the eleventh century.[27]

The present practice of standing and reciting the Niceno-Constantinopolitan Creed after the Gospel and homily has its roots in local custom in Antioch in the fifth century, and gradually spread through East and West. The origin and nature of the Creed indicate that it is more naturally recited than sung. If sung, it should be in a way that involves the whole assembly.

According to the present Roman Rite, the Creed must be sung or recited at Masses on Sundays and solemnities. Since the (simpler) Apostles' Creed originated in the liturgy of baptism of the Western Church, it may be used in Masses with children. The celebrant is not allowed to omit the Profession of Faith at Sunday Mass or on the solemnities when it is not optional. The Creed *may* also be said or sung on other appropriate occasions.

There are some official alternatives to the Nicene Creed that may be used during Mass. (1) Episcopal conferences may allow the use of the Apostles' Creed as an option at Sunday Mass. It may be good for catechetical reasons to use this creed, since it ensures that the faithful, especially children, learn the ancient baptismal creed. However, from a liturgical perspective, its use is a departure from the classical liturgical tradition of saying or singing the great conciliar Creed of the Councils of Nicaea and Constantinople. (2) At all Masses on Easter Sunday, the Creed may be replaced by the Renewal of Baptismal Promises. Then the faithful are sprinkled with blessed Easter water. This gives everyone a chance to celebrate the sacramental meaning of the Paschal Mystery, even if they did not take part in the Easter Vigil. (3) At the Easter Vigil and the Ritual Masses for baptism and confirmation, the Creed is omitted because the Profession of Faith has been made in the baptismal promises.

THE MEANING AND BIBLICAL BACKGROUND OF THE CREED

We will now examine the Creed in detail, looking at its meaning and its biblical background.[28]

God as One

I believe in one God,
the Father almighty,
maker of heaven and earth,
of all things visible and invisible.

The Creed begins with the words "I believe." In English, this is a departure from the previous translation, which had "we believe." This new translation brings the English-speaking world into conformity with the rest of the Western world by using the singular *I* for its opening. After the Second Vatican Council, English was the only major Western language that translated the singular "I believe" in the Latin (*credo*) with the plural "we believe." The singular *I*, however, gives the Creed a more personal touch and challenges each individual to make the faith his or her own. As the *Catechism of the Catholic Church* explains, "I believe" expresses "the faith of the Church professed personally by each believer" (CCC 167).

The Creed begins with an affirmation of belief in one God. Belief in one God calls to mind the ancient confession of Israel, "Hear, O Israel: The LORD is our God, the LORD alone" (Deut 6:4).

Yahweh, as God was sometimes called in the Old Testament, was first regarded as the chief tribal god of the Jews (Exod 3:14–15). Thus, Yahweh is sometimes presented as the first among many gods (see, e.g., Pss 29:1; 82:1–6; 86:8–10; 89:5–8; 91:11). The idea of Yahweh being the "first" among the gods ultimately led to the belief that Yahweh alone was God, the one God of all the earth and of all peoples.

This conviction is clearly found in the Book of Isaiah, where the gods of the nations are simply regarded as idols, the works of human hands. They do not really exist, except in the imagination of their worshippers. They cannot save but can only enslave their worshippers (see Isa 40:12–31; 42:5–9; 45:12–21; see also Pss 96:4–5, 135:5–18). As Yahweh says, "I am the first and I am the last; besides me there is no god" (Isa 44:6). The faith of the Jews thus remained essentially monotheistic. The same monotheistic view of God is found in the New Testament, but with a particular emphasis on the sovereignty of this one God over all peoples.

God as Father

In the Creed, God is called "Father." The Jews did not often use the title "father" for Yahweh. When Yahweh was called father, it was as father of the people of Israel. Yahweh's "fatherhood" is revealed especially in his creating a people and nurturing it. In Psalm 68:5, God is called the "father of orphans and protector of widows." In Hosea, Yahweh says,

> When Israel was a child, I loved him,
>   and out of Egypt I called my son.
>
> ...It was I who taught Ephraim to walk,
>   I took them up in my arms;
>   but they did not know that I healed them.
> I led them with cords of human kindness,
>   with bands of love.
> I was to them like those
>   who lift infants to their cheeks.
>   I bent down to them and fed them. (Hos 11:1–4)

The New Testament refers to God many times as "father." He is a father in relation to human beings and he is the Father of Jesus Christ. Christians know God to be their Father because Jesus calls him Father, reveals himself as the Son of God, and through the Holy Spirit, makes it possible for us also to become sons and daughters of God by adoption.

In Matthew's Gospel, Jesus tells his disciples that God is their "father in heaven" (5:16, 45, 48; 6:1, 14, 32; 7:11, 21) or simply "your father" (6:4, 6, 8, 15, 18, 26; 10:20, 29), and he asks them to pray to "our father who art in heaven" (6:9). But Jesus also speaks of God as his own Father in a direct and intimate manner. He speaks of "my father who is in heaven" (see Matt 10:32, 33; 12:50; 16:17) and "my father" (Matt 20:23; 25:34, 41). In John's Gospel, Jesus also speaks of God as his Father, referring to "my father" (2:16; 5:17, 43) or simply "the father" in relation to "the son" (3:35; 4:23; 5:19).

God as All-Powerful (Almighty)

The expression "all-powerful" is found in only a few places in the New Testament (see 2 Cor 6:18; Rev 1:8; 4:8; 11:17), but the *idea* of God's omnipotence is found in many places. In his prayer in the garden of Gethsemane on the eve of his death, Jesus prayed: "Abba, Father, for you all things are possible; remove this cup from me; yet, not what I want, but what you want" (Mark 14:36). Similarly, the angel Gabriel told Mary that she could conceive even as a virgin because "nothing will be impossible with God" (Luke 1:37). On the question of rich people entering the kingdom of God, Jesus stated, "What is impossible for mortals is possible for God" (Luke 18:27). In Romans, Paul talks about the power of God that can be known from the nature of creation (Rom 1:20).

God as Maker

The Creed goes on to speak of God as the "maker of heaven and earth, of all things visible and invisible." The expression "heaven and earth" clearly contains an allusion to Genesis 1:1. The translation of this part of the Creed is different from the old one, which read, "maker of all that is seen and unseen." The new translation more correctly echoes the language of Paul who spoke of the creation of all things "in heaven and on earth...visible and invisible" (Col 1:16). To the words "heaven and earth" are added the expression "all things visible and invisible." The expression "heaven and earth" could be understood in a way that did not include everything that existed. The phrase "all things visible and invisible," therefore, makes it clear that God is responsible for absolutely everything that exists, not only things unseen but also all material things.

> I believe in one Lord Jesus Christ,
> the Only Begotten Son of God,
> born of the Father before all ages.

The Creed goes on to describe Jesus as being "Only Begotten." We discussed the meaning of this in our discussion of the *Gloria*. The Creed says further that this only-begotten Son was "born of the Father before all ages." We need to take note of two things here. First, here "being born" should not be taken in a physical sense. The Creed is not referring to the birth of Jesus as a human being. Rather, the birth spoken of here takes place within the life of God. As creatures living in space and time, we can speak of things eternal only by making use of temporal categories, and so we must use the phrase "before all the ages."[29] Second, when God the Father is spoken of as "begetting" Jesus Christ, this does not refer to him as making something; it refers to a sharing by the Father out of himself. This is made clear by the phrase "of the Father."[30]

> God from God, Light from Light,
> true God from true God,
> begotten, not made, consubstantial with the Father;
> through him all things were made.

The Creed speaks of the Son as "God from God" and "true God from true God." In the Old Testament and most of the New Testament, the title "God" is used of the Father. It is bold on the part of the Creed to apply the title to the Son in spite of the fact that the New Testament does not often use it of Jesus Christ.

It is possible that the title "God" is given to Jesus in a number of passages in the New Testament. These include the following passages: Romans 9:5; Titus 3:4; Hebrews 1:8; John 1:1, 18; and 20:28.[31] The description of Jesus as "true God from true God" may have been influenced by the language of the Fourth Gospel. In 1 John 5:20, Jesus, speaking of the Father, uses the expression "the true God." In his final prayer in the Gospel of John, Jesus again refers to the Father as "true God" (17:3). The adjective "true" distinguishes the authentic from the false or the apparent.

In using the expression "true God from true God," the formulators of the Creed intended to reject the teaching of Arius, who taught that in the Trinity, the Son of God is inferior to the Father, that the Son is a creature, and that there was a time when the Son was not. Arius claimed to have biblical support for his teaching. The passages that he cited included Proverbs 8:22, Acts 2:36, Romans 8:29, Colossians 1:15, Hebrews 3:2, and John 17:3, and the passages in the Gospels that speak of Jesus' ignorance, especially Mark 13:32. At first sight, many of these passages seem to indicate the subordination of Jesus to the Father. However, there are other New Testament passages that give the opposite impression. Arius failed to take these passages into account. He made much of the Old Testament passages that presented Wisdom as the first of God's creatures that assisted God in the creation of the world (see Prov 8:22–31; Sir 24:1–9).

The Creed further says that the Son is *consubstantial* with the Father. This term is not found in the Bible. In AD 325, the Council of Nicaea was convened to deal with a controversy in the Church regarding the relationship among the persons of the Trinity. Arius taught that Christ was more than human but not fully divine. The Council condemned the teaching of Arius, and the Greek term used by the Council to affirm that Christ was "of the same substance" as the Father was *homoousios*. This was adopted by the Council of Nicaea to state the orthodox faith against Arian denials of the divinity of Christ. In St. Athanasius's interpretation of the term, it means that all divine predicates made of the Father can also be made of the Son, except the name "Father." At the Council of Chalcedon, *homoousios* was also used to state that the one Christ was of the same substance as the Father in his divinity and of the same substance as we humans in his humanity.[32]

We should note that in the old translation of the Roman Missal in English, instead of "consubstantial with the Father," we had "one in being with the Father." The new translation is closer to the theological language used by the Council of Nicaea (AD 325), which stated that the Son was "of the same substance" (in Greek, *homoousios*) as the Father.

The Creed goes on to state that "through him all things were made." Arius had referred to the Son as a creature, "a thing made." According to the first line of the Creed, God the Father is "maker." The Creed now says that the one who is "begotten not made" is the one through whom God has made "all things." It follows that, if he is the one through whom all things are made, he is not one of the things made. According to John 1:3, the Son had a role to play in creation: "All things came into being through him, and without him not one thing came into being." The Creed, like John, stresses the Son's role in creation.

For Paul also, the Son had a role to play in creation. He speaks in 1 Corinthians 8:4–6 of "one Lord Jesus Christ, through whom are all things and through whom we exist." In Colossians 1:15–16, Paul says, "In him all things in heaven and on earth were created, things visible and invisible, whether thrones or dominions or rulers or powers—all things have been created through him and for him." Hebrews 1:2 speaks of the Son through whom God has spoken in the last of days and "through whom he also created the worlds."

The phrase "Light from Light" has biblical roots. Light was the first thing that God created by his word of command (Gen 1:3–5). In the psalms, light is often associated with God: "The Lord is my light" (Ps 26:1), and "in your light we shall see light" (Ps 35:9; see also Pss 42:3; 55:13; 77:14). Psalm 88:15 declares to be blessed those who walk "in the light of your countenance." In Isaiah 2:5, the house of Jacob is invited "to walk in the light of the LORD." Isaiah says further that the people who walked in darkness have seen a great light; "those who lived in a land of deep darkness—on them light has shined" (Isa 9:2). In the New Testament, light is also associated with the presence of the divine. Paul says that God "dwells in unapproachable light" (1 Tim 6:16). Peter speaks of God calling the chosen "out of darkness into his marvelous light" (1 Pet 2:9). James speaks of God as "the Father of lights with whom there is no variation or shadow due to change" (James 1:17).

For us men and for our salvation he came down from
   heaven,
and by the Holy Spirit was incarnate of the Virgin
   Mary,
and became man.

In the expression "for us men," the word *men* translates a
Greek word (*anthropos*) that means "humanity," "mankind,"
which is gender-inclusive. It does not use the Greek word for "a
man" (*aner*). Thus, "for us men" should be understood in an
inclusive sense to refer to all "human beings." In other words,
the Son of God became human, suffered and died as other human
beings do, for the sake of human beings.

The Creed further says of Christ, "He came down from
heaven....He ascended into heaven." The language of "coming
down" or "descending" and "ascending" should be understood
symbolically. In speaking in this manner, those who formulated
the Creed clearly echoed the language of the Fourth Gospel. In
John's Gospel, Jesus uses such language of himself. We find this,
for example, in the bread of life discourse, where he says, "For the
bread of God is that which comes down from heaven and gives
life to the world" (John 6:33). John 6:50 speaks of "the bread that
comes down from heaven, so that one may eat of it and not die."
John 6:58 says, "This is the bread that came down from heaven,
not like that which your ancestors ate, and they died. But the one
who eats this bread will live forever." Jesus makes it clear that the
image applies to himself: "I have come down from heaven, not to
do my own will, but the will of him who sent me" (6:38; see also
6:42). In this context, "heaven" refers to the place of "the one
who sent me," namely God. "The language of heaven and earth
therefore expresses not a change in place but a change in condition
from the divine realm to the human."[33] John makes it clear that
the Son alone is the one who comes from and goes back to God:
"No one has ascended into heaven except the one who descended
from heaven, the Son of Man" (John 3:13).

With the expression "he came down from heaven," the Creed
wants to say two things at the same time: first, that Jesus Christ
who became man is "from heaven," that is, of divine origin; and

second, that Jesus Christ has "come down out of heaven," that is, he is truly among us in our world.

The expression "and by the Holy Spirit was incarnate of the Virgin Mary, and became man," is undoubtedly an allusion to the annunciation narratives of Matthew and Luke. In Matthew, Mary is said to be pregnant before she had sexual relations with Joseph, which caused Joseph to seek to divorce her quietly (Matt 1:18–19). However, he was told by the angel Gabriel not to fear taking Mary as wife, "for the child conceived in her is from the Holy Spirit" (Matt 1:20). In Luke, Mary is spoken of as a "virgin" (Luke 1:27) to whom the angel announces that she will "conceive in your womb and bear a son, and you will name him Jesus" (1:31). When Mary says that she has no experience of sex ("I am a virgin," 1:34), the angel answers, "The Holy Spirit will come upon you, and the power of the Most High will overshadow you; therefore the child to be born will be holy; he will be called Son of God" (1:35).

The old translation speaks of Jesus' conception as follows: "By the power of the Holy Spirit he was born of the Virgin Mary, and became man." The new translation more correctly reflects the Latin text of the Creed, which uses the Latin word *incarnatus* ("became incarnate"). The use of *incarnate* refers to "the fact that the Son of God assumed a human nature in order to accomplish our salvation in it" (CCC 461). This translation makes it clear that the Son of God "was not just born of the Virgin Mary. The Eternal Son of God who is of the same substance as the Father actually took on human flesh."[34]

When the Creed speaks of Christ becoming man and of his birth, all bow, but on the feasts of Christmas and Annunciation all kneel (*GIRM* 98). "This is a gesture of reverence in response to the incomprehensible way in which God has condescended to begin the redemptive work of Christ. At this point we do just what the wise men from the East did when they saw the child and his mother: 'They knelt down and paid him homage' (Matt 2:11)."[35]

Death and Resurrection of Jesus

For our sake he was crucified under Pontius Pilate,
he suffered death and was buried,
and rose again on the third day

By using the phrase "for our sake," the Creed makes it clear that Jesus chose to be put to death to show solidarity with his fellow human beings. The phrase is very scriptural. In Paul, we find expressions like these: "Christ died for the ungodly" (Rom 5:6), "Christ died for us" (Rom 5:8), "Christ died for our sins" (1 Cor 15:3), "for our sake he made him to be sin" (2 Cor 5:21), "Christ loved us and gave himself up for us" (Eph 5:2), "Christ became a curse for us" (see Gal 3:13), and others (Rom 14:15; 15:3; 1 Cor 1:13; 8:11; 2 Cor 8:9; Gal 1:4; 1 Tim 2:6; Titus 2:14).

Other New Testament writers also see Jesus as one who suffered on behalf of humankind. Hebrews says that Christ died "in order to sanctify the people by his own blood" (Heb 13:12). 1 Peter declares that "Christ suffered, the righteous for the unrighteous" (see 1 Pet 3:18), and that "Christ also suffered for you" (2:21). We find a similar idea expressed in the Gospels. Mark 10:45 speaks of the Son of Man who came "to give his life as a ransom for many." In Luke's account of the Last Supper, Jesus tells his disciples, "This is my body, which is given for you," and "This cup that is poured out for you is the new covenant in my blood" (Luke 22:19–20). In John, Jesus speaks of himself as the Good Shepherd who "lays down his life for the sheep" (John 10:11).

Jesus gave himself for humankind through a death by crucifixion. That Jesus suffered this kind of death is attested to by both believers and nonbelievers. There is evidence for this in both the Gospels and in Acts (Matt 27:15–37; Mark 15:1–39; Luke 23:28–49; John 19:19–30; Acts 3:13–16; 4:27). There are references to the crucifixion also in the New Testament letters (1 Cor 1:18—2:8; 2 Cor 13:4; Gal 3:1; Phil 2:8; Col 1:20; 1 Tim 6:13; Heb 12:2; 1 Pet 2:24). Jesus' crucifixion is also attested to by ancient non-Christian sources, including Tacitus, Josephus, and Lucian of Samosata.

In 1 Corinthians, Paul gives a summary of the good news that he had received and had handed on to the Corinthian Christians. It begins, "…that Christ died for our sins in accordance with the scriptures, and that he was buried" (1 Cor 15:3–20).

The Creed speaks of Christ being "buried." In the Gospels, there are references to the burial with some variations (see Mark 15:42–47; Matt 27:55–66; Luke 23:50–55; John 19:38–42). The burial symbolizes Jesus' descent into the world of the dead, which in the Old Testament was called Sheol, or Hades in the Greek translation of the Old Testament. In Peter's speech at Pentecost, he quoted Psalm 16 with reference to Jesus' death: "You will not abandon my soul to Hades, or let your Holy One experience corruption" (Acts 2:27).

The statement that Jesus "rose again on the third day" agrees with what Paul says in 1 Corinthians 15:4: "He was raised on the third day in accordance with the scriptures." The Creed uses the active verb "he rose" instead of the passive used by Paul, "he was raised." This variation is often found in the New Testament, which uses both the passive, indicating an activity by God even when there is no explicit reference to God as subject (see Matt 16:21; Rom 4:24), and the active, sometimes with God as subject (see Acts 2:24; 1 Cor 15:15; 2 Cor 1:9) and sometimes with Jesus as subject (Mark 8:31; 1 Thess 4:4).

Christ is said to have risen from the dead "on the third day." The New Testament in some places also uses in this connection the expression "after three days" (Mark 8:31; 9:31; 10:34; Matt 27:63; Luke 24:21), but in other places, we have "on the third day" (1 Cor 15:4; Luke 9:22; 18:33; 24:7; Acts 10:40; Matt 16:21; 20:19). According to the Gospels, Jesus was crucified on the day before the Sabbath, that is, a Friday (see John 19:31; Luke 23:56; Mark 15:42; Matt 27:62), and his empty tomb was discovered on "the first day of the week," that is, on Sunday (Mark 16:1–2; Matt 28:1; John 20:1; Luke 24:1), so "on the third day" is accurate enough. The resurrection of Jesus from the dead means that he is no longer in the world of the dead; he is now with God in heaven. His resurrection, then, is not resuscitation, a return to earthly life. It is his entry as a human person into the eternal life of God.

> He ascended into heaven
> and is seated at the right hand of the Father.

The fact that Jesus ascended into heaven is found in the New Testament (Acts 1:9; Mark 16:19). In the Gospel of John, there are some references to Jesus "going" and "going back" and "ascending" to the Father (see John 13:1; 14:3, 12:28; 16:5, 10; 17:11, 13). When Jesus appears to Mary Magdalene in the garden after his resurrection, he tells her, "I am ascending to my Father and to your Father, to my God and your God" (John 20:17). The seating of Jesus at the right hand of the Father means that he occupies a position of authority in the new realm.

> He will come again in glory
> to judge the living and the dead
> and his kingdom will have no end.

In the Gospels, there are references to Jesus, the Son of Man, coming in glory at the end of time. For example, in Matthew 16:27 we read, "For the Son of Man is to come with his angels in the glory of his Father" (see also Matt 24:30; 25:31; Mark 8:38). On the question of the Son coming to judge the living and the dead, we note that in the Old Testament, God is presented as a judge of the world (Gen 18:25; Deut 32:36; Exod 5:21; LXX Ps 5:10; Sir 32:12; Isa 30:18; Jer 11:20; Ezek 7:8). In the New Testament, we come across the belief that Jesus shares God's role as judge. According to Romans 2:16, God will judge the secrets of humankind "on the day" and Paul adds that this will be done "through Jesus Christ."

The Creed goes on to say, "...and his kingdom will have no end." In the Gospels, there are many references to the "kingdom of God" or the "kingdom of heaven" (Matthew). The kingdom here is not to be taken in a geographical sense; it rather refers to God's reign or sovereignty over creation.

The Holy Spirit

> I believe in the Holy Spirit, the Lord, the giver of life,
> who proceeds from the Father and the Son,
> who with the Father and the Son is adored and
>   glorified,
> who has spoken through the prophets.

The Holy Spirit is said to proceed from the Father "and the Son" (Latin: *Filioque*). The phrase *Filioque* seems to have been added to the Nicene-Constantinopolitan Creed at the Third Council of Toledo in 589. Pope Leo III was not in favor of the addition of the *Filioque*, but he allowed it to remain. Although the Western Church accepted it as an article of faith by the end of the fourth century, the formula did not receive approval for general liturgical use before the early part of the eleventh century. It was only in 1014, and under pressure from St. Henry, that the Church of Rome accepted the Creed, which, however, never became a part of every Mass.

The phrase *Filioque* was strongly condemned by Photius, the patriarch of Constantinople in 867 and 879. Eastern Christians viewed this as a nonbiblical tampering with the Creed, a subordination of the Holy Spirit to the Son, and a denigration of the Father's unique identity in the Trinity. The *Filioque* thus became a key reason, among many other political and theological factors, for the eventual schism between Western and Eastern Christians in 1054. An attempt was made at the Council of Ferrara-Florence in 1439 to reconcile the two points of view, but it was not successful. The Eastern and Western churches have remained separate, and the doctrine enshrined in the term *Filioque* stands as one of the primary points of difference between them.

The Holy Spirit is said to be adored and glorified together "with the Father and the Son." God alone is worthy of being adored or worshipped. The statement that the Holy Spirit "is adored" means "is to be adored" or "deserves to be adored."

It should be observed that in the New Testament, use of the word *worship* is generally restricted to God (God the Father: see 1 Cor 14:25; Rev 22:9) and false gods (Rev 13:4, 8, 12, 15). The risen Christ is paid such homage (Matt 28:9; Luke 24:52; see also Matt 2:2, 8, 11). However, in the New Testament, nothing is said explicitly about the Spirit being worshipped. When the Creed says that the Spirit is worshipped, it may be making a deduction based on what Scripture says about the identity and work of the Spirit. This is a theological inference that may probably find support in the passage in John in which Jesus discusses true worship with the Samaritan woman: "But the hour is coming, and is now here, when the true worshipers will worship the Father in spirit and truth...and those who worship him must worship in spirit and truth" (John 4:23–24). Since the Holy Spirit is later identified in the Gospel as "the Spirit of Truth" (John 14:17), it was not difficult for the early Christians to attribute worship to the Holy Spirit.

The Holy Spirit is said to be "glorified." The closest the New Testament comes to connecting the Holy Spirit and glorification is the statement in John 16:14 that the Paraclete "will glorify me." In this connection, Johnson says,

> Thus, when it says "and glorified" the creed extrapolates beyond the explicit scriptural evidence for the nature and role of the Holy Spirit. It does so on the basis of believers' continuing experience of the Spirit, especially their growing recognition that the grace that comes to them in the gift of the Holy Spirit is in reality a share in the divine life, and therefore a participation in God's glory.[36]

The Church

> I believe in one, holy, catholic and apostolic Church
> I confess one Baptism for the forgiveness of sins
> and I look forward to the resurrection of the dead
> and the life of the world to come. Amen

The Creed speaks of the Church as being "one, holy, catholic and apostolic." The Church is one in the sense that its members live a life of real unity. The oneness of the Church means that to be fully itself, the Church must maintain harmony and union among its members. Overcoming prejudices and factions belongs to the essential task of the Church. It is supposed to be "a seed of unity" for the whole human community (*Lumen Gentium* 9) and cannot really fulfill this if not united within itself.

According to Luke, the early Christians in Jerusalem were united: "All who believed were together and had all things in common" (Acts 2:44), and "the whole group of those who believed were of one heart and soul, and no one claimed private ownership of any possessions, but everything they owned was held in common" (Acts 4:32).

The ideal of a united Church is expressed by Paul, when he urges the Christians at Ephesus to bear "with one another in love, making every effort to maintain the unity of the Spirit in the bond of peace. There is one body and one Spirit, just as you were called to the one hope of your calling, one Lord, one faith, one baptism, one God and Father of all, who is above all and through all and in all" (Eph 4:2–6). Paul, however, adds that within this unity, there is also diversity: "But each of us was given grace according to the measure of Christ's gift....The gifts he gave were that some would be apostles, some prophets, some evangelists, some pastors and teachers, to equip the saints for the work of ministry, for building up the body of Christ" (Eph 4:7, 11–12; see also 1 Cor 12:4–11).

The Church is also said to be "holy." Holiness is a necessary condition for the Church in its task of reconciling the human community to God. Holiness applies to the members of the Church as well as to its official activities. In the Old Testament, the people of Israel are challenged to be holy: "You shall be holy, for I am holy" (Lev 11:44–45). The ideal of holiness is also found in the New Testament. Paul tells the Thessalonians that God wills their sanctification or holiness (1 Thess 4:3, 7; cf. 1 Cor 1:2; 6:11; Eph 5:26; 1 Thess 3:13; 5:23). Indeed, the title "the saints" refers to ordinary members of the Church and not an elite class within the Church (Rom 1:7; 1 Cor 6:1–2; 14:33; 2 Cor 1:1; Eph 1:1; Phil 1:1; Col 1:4; 1 Thess 5:27; 1 Tim 5:10).

Even though believers "have been sanctified" through the gift of the Holy Spirit and baptism (1 Cor 1:2; 6:11; Eph 5:6), they are still "called to be holy." This tension is recognized by Paul, for whom being called to holiness is a process of personal and communal transformation (1 Cor 1:2; 2 Cor 7:1; 1 Thess 3:13; 4:3). The Church is the dwelling place of the Holy Spirit, and thus it can be regarded as a holy temple of God; however, it must also express that holiness in its behavior (1 Cor 6:19–20).

The Church is also said to be "catholic." The term *catholic* (Greek *katholikos*, "universal," from *katholou*, "in general") was first used in the letter of St. Ignatius of Antioch to the Smyrnaeans (about AD 110). The term was later used by Clement of Alexandria in his *Stromata* (*Miscellanies*). The word was accepted as a technical term by the beginning of the third century. The formal principle of the Catholic Church was expressed by the French theologian Vincent of Lérins as "that which has been believed everywhere, always, and by all. This is what is truly and properly catholic."

Catholicity, as applied to the Church, means the quality of being universal, complete, or all-embracing. As a mark of the Church, catholicity means nonelitism or being open to all.

It does not necessarily mean that all human beings must belong or that Christians must earnestly entice others away from their traditional religions or personal convictions. It means rather that the Church must make everyone welcome, excluding no categories (racial, linguistic, cultural, economic, etc.). Whether this leaves Church membership still a "small flock" among the world's large populations is not important as long as the Church is doing and being what it is called to do and be (*Lumen Gentium* 9).[37]

The word *Catholic* is not found in the Bible, though the idea is well rooted in the New Testament, which speaks of the Church as "the fullness of him [Christ] who fills all in all" (Eph 1:23). Because of its relationship to Christ, the Church has a mission to all nations and to all generations (Matt 28:19–20). The ideal of inclusiveness or all-embracing nature of the Church was demonstrated by Jesus in his call to the outcast and the marginalized and his offer of table fellowship to sinners. The early Church extended the ideal of inclusiveness by the decision of the Council of Jerusalem to include Gentiles without the condition that they be circumcised and observe the Mosaic Law.

The Pauline and Deutero-Pauline letters repeatedly speak of the capacity of Christianity to overcome the division between rich and poor, free and slave, male and female, Jew and Gentile, Greek and barbarian. This ideal is expressed by Paul, for example, in Galatians 3:28: "There is no longer Jew or Greek, there is no longer slave or free, there is no longer male and female; for all of you are one in Christ Jesus." If the Church is catholic, it must embrace cultural differences. In his Letter to the Ephesians, Paul argues that the Church is essentially a place where differences are reconciled. The "dividing wall" of hostility that separated Jew and Greek expressed the alienation of human beings from God. The reconciliation between God and humankind achieved through the death and resurrection of Jesus must be expressed by reconciliation between human beings:

> But now in Christ Jesus you who once were far off have been brought near by the blood of Christ. For he

is our peace; in his flesh he has made both groups into one and has broken down the dividing wall, that is, the hostility between us. He has abolished the law with its commandments and ordinances, that he might create in himself one new humanity in place of the two, thus making peace, and might reconcile both groups to God in one body through the cross, thus putting to death that hostility through it. (Eph 2:13–16)

Speaking of the catholicity of the Church, *Lumen Gentium* says,

This characteristic of universality which adorns the people of God is a gift from the Lord Himself. By reason of it, the Catholic Church strives constantly and with due effect to bring all humanity and all its possessions back to its source In Christ, with Him as its head and united in His Spirit. (no. 13)

In virtue of this catholicity, each individual part contributes through its special gifts to the good of the other parts and of the whole Church. Through the common sharing of gifts and through the common effort to attain fullness in unity, the whole and each of the parts receive increase (*Lumen Gentium* 13). According to Avery Dulles, the catholicity of the Church "is the diversified unity enabling it to reconcile in itself the contrasting values of diverse peoples and cultures, to elevate these through the gifts of grace, and thus to achieve an unexcelled plenitude through mutual enrichment....The diverse gifts of the Spirit contribute to the multisplendored unity of the body of Christ."[38]

The last mark of the ideal Church is that it must be "apostolic." Apostolicity refers to continuity with the mission and ministry of the apostles. In the early centuries, the Church sought this continuity principally in the teaching and the carrying on of the authentic life and worship. We must point out that after the sixteenth century reformations, Catholics use the term *apostolicity* mostly in reference to the validity of holy orders and the succession of bishops by accepted standards of consecration.

I confess one Baptism for the forgiveness of sins

Baptism is the universal rite of initiation, performed with water, in the name of the Trinity (Father, Son, and Holy Spirit). The Catholic Church does not consider baptisms valid if they were performed without using the trinitarian formula. Baptism is the sacrament of regeneration and initiation into the Church that was begun by Jesus, who accepted baptism from John the Baptist and also ordered the apostles to baptize in the name of the Father, the Son, and the Holy Spirit (Matt 28:19).

It is clear from the New Testament that there is a connection between baptism and the forgiveness of sins. According to Mark 1:4, John the Baptist proclaimed "a baptism of repentance for the forgiveness of sins." We are told further in the same context that "people from the whole Judean countryside and all the people of Jerusalem were going out to him, and were baptized by him in the river Jordan, confessing their sins" (see also Luke 1:77; 3:3). In his preaching, Jesus himself spoke of the forgiveness of sins (Matt 9:2, 5; 12:21; 26:28; Mark 2:5–10; Luke 5:20–24; 7:47–49; John 1:29; 8:1–11), and commissioned the disciples to continue proclaiming the forgiveness of sins (Luke 24:47; John 20:23).

The Acts of the Apostles tells us that baptism was a means by which sins were forgiven. At Pentecost, Peter exhorts the crowd, "Repent, and be baptized every one of you in the name of Jesus Christ so that your sins may be forgiven; and you will receive the gift of the Holy Spirit" (Acts 2:38).

The Creed states that this baptism is "one." This finds support in what Paul says in Ephesians, "There is one body and one Spirit, just as you were called to the one hope of your calling, one Lord, one faith, one baptism, one God and Father of all, who is above all and through all and in all" (Eph 4:4–5).

and I look forward to the resurrection of the dead

For its last statement, the Creed uses words other than *believe* or *confess*, they are *look forward to*. The Greek word used here means "expect" and the translation "look forward to" captures the active sense of anticipation in the original. The doctrine of the resurrection of the dead is something biblical. In the Old Testament, this belief is found in a number of passages, the clearest of which is Daniel 12:2, "Many of those who sleep in the dust of the earth shall awake, some to everlasting life, and some to shame and everlasting contempt." The New Testament is replete with references to the resurrection of believers, the most extensive treatment being found in 1 Corinthians 15:35–58. The two phrases "resurrection of the dead" and "life of the world to come" are closely linked in origin and meaning.

Amen

The Creed ends with the ancient Hebrew word *Amen*. *Amen* usually concludes a prayer, often a prayer said by someone else, and means "may it be in the manner you have spoken." It declares our agreement and confirmation. Those reciting the Creed say "Amen" to their own profession.

7. The Prayer of the Faithful

After the Creed comes "the Universal Prayer, that is, the Prayer of the Faithful or Bidding Prayers."[39] In the 2010 translation of the *General Instruction*, The International Commission on English in the Liturgy (ICEL) attaches "Bidding Prayer" to the "Prayer of the Faithful," giving the impression that the two are synonymous (*Order of Mass* 20). However, this is not the case. The prayer of the faithful "brings to mind its character as the common prayer of the baptized (the faithful) or the priestly people, while bidding prayer refers to the manner in which the prayer is performed."[40] The Latin text speaks of *oratio universalis*, literally, "universal prayer" (*GIRM* 69). Another translation of the Latin text is "general intercessions."[41] However, the term *general intercessions* is "a dynamic interpretation of the *oratio universalis*, which in liturgical practice consists of intercessions of a general character and intention. 'Universal Prayer' does not explicitly say this."[42]

The Prayer of the Faithful is one of the most ancient parts of the Mass, already mentioned by Justin Martyr in AD 155. Justin wrote to the Roman Emperor explaining what Christians did when they met to celebrate the Eucharist. In this letter, he gives an outline of the prayers and rituals used by Christians. He mentions the intercessory prayers offered after the readings from Scripture and the homily: "Then we all rise together and offer prayers for ourselves...and for all others, wherever they may be, so that we may be found righteous by our life and actions, and faithful to the commandments, so as to obtain eternal salvation."[43]

According to Hippolytus of Rome, this prayer was a prerogative of the faithful. The newly baptized could take part in it only after they had left the baptistery. Catechumens were required to leave the Eucharistic celebration before this prayer began. It is for this reason that the Universal Prayer is also known as "the Prayer of the Faithful." The expression "Prayer of the Faithful" was used to refer to these prayers said by those already baptized in the absence of the catechumens, who were not yet among "the faithful" and were therefore not present for these prayers.

The practice of intercessory prayer goes back even further in Christian history. When Peter was imprisoned by Herod, the Christians in Jerusalem "prayed fervently for him," and that night an angel came to release him from his chains (Acts 12:1–7). In his Letter to Timothy, Paul advised him and other Christians to intercede for all people:

> First of all, then, I urge that supplications, prayers, intercessions, and thanksgivings be made for everyone, for kings and all who are in high positions, so that we may lead a quiet and peaceable life in all godliness and dignity. This is right and is acceptable in the sight of God our Savior, who desires everyone to be saved and to come to the knowledge of the truth. (1 Tim 2:1–4)

The Church continues this same practice in the celebration of the Eucharist when, after hearing the Word of God, it exercises its priestly function by interceding for all humanity. The Church prays not only for its own needs but also for those of the world, for civil authorities, for those oppressed by any burden, and for the local community, particularly those who are sick or who have died.

Such prayers said for others are especially effective when they are said by the Christian community because Christ is then united with those praying, according to Matthew 18:19–20, "Again, truly I tell you, if two of you agree on earth about anything you ask, it will be done for you by my Father in heaven. For where two or three are gathered in my name, I am there among them."

As a rule, the Prayer of the Faithful moves from the broad and universal to the particular and the local. It should follow this order: (1) for the needs of the Church; (2) for public authorities and the salvation of the world; (3) for those who are in any kind of difficulty; (4) for the local community. It should be noted that "the needs of the Church" is much broader than the hierarchy and the expression "public authorities" encompasses more than elected officials. Although four topics are mentioned, it does not necessarily mean that one cannot exceed that number. In particular celebrations, such as confirmation, marriage, or funerals, and so on, the intercessions may refer more specifically to the occasion (*GIRM* 46). In such cases, more intentions may be offered for those who are present.

According to paragraph 71 of the *General Instruction*, the Prayer of the Faithful should follow this pattern: The presider (and not a concelebrant or other minister) introduces the Prayer of the Faithful from the presidential chair by inviting the faithful to pray for the needs of the Church and the world. The deacon, cantor, or another minister announces the "intentions," which are formulated so that he or she is addressing the assembly. Typically, the deacon presented the intentions because he was the one who knew the particular needs of the community (who needed food, charity, who was sick, who had died, etc.).

The intentions should be short and clear enough for the faithful to understand and to give the response without difficulty. It could take the following form: "Let us pray for all sick people, especially those in our parish. For this we pray to the Lord." Each "intention" usually concludes with the same words (e.g., "For this we pray to the Lord") so that the assembly knows when to offer their common response (e.g., "Lord, hear our prayer"). This common response is the prayer.

As much as possible, the presiding priest should *not* offer the intentions unless there is no one who can do it. It should be noted that the intentions are invitations addressed to the assembly inviting them to pray for specific topics of concern. Both the priest's introduction and the intentions to be prayed for are addressed to the assembly, not to God. The petitions should not be addressed directly to God the Father or to Jesus. In this connection, we should note that in some parishes, these rules are not observed, especially when these prayers are said spontaneously. Some people say prayers that are addressed to God or to Jesus. Some go like this: "O God our Father, we thank you for all that you have done for us. We ask you to bring healing to all those who are sick." However, in these prayers, God should not be addressed directly. These intentions are invitations or biddings *to the faithful*, who then pray for the proposed intention silently and in a common petition. A petition for healing, for example, should run like this: "Let us pray for the sick that God in his goodness will bring healing to them." The petitions are prayed from the ambo or another suitable place.

By tradition, the Prayer of the Faithful is in the style of a litany, and litanies are intended to be sung, and should be sung whenever possible. Where this is not possible, a deacon or some other minister can recite the intentions and a cantor can sing the concluding invitation and response. In such a case, the text of the concluding invitation could be adapted to suit the text of the response. For example, the cantor might sing the response, "Lord, in your mercy," and the assembly would conclude, "Hear our prayer." In this case, the entire phrase, "Lord, in your mercy, hear our prayer," would be regarded as a single response to the intention, sung in two parts: the first half by the cantor and the second half by the entire congregation. Where the responses are generally not sung, it will be enough for the congregation to respond as "Lord, in your mercy, hear our prayer."

On the question of who writes the Prayer of the Faithful, the Introduction to the *Lectionary* states, "The deacon, another minister, or some of the faithful may propose intentions that are short and phrased with a measure of flexibility" (no. 30). Apart from the written intentions read by the deacon or someone else, members of the congregation can be asked to offer their own spontaneous intentions. However, they should be trained not to turn intentions into long prayers addressed to God. Priests should let such people know that such intercessions are simply invitations to the worshipping community to pray for specific needs.

When should the Prayer of the Faithful be included in the Mass? The *General Instruction* says, "It is desirable that there usually be such a form of prayer in Masses celebrated with the people" (*GIRM* 69). In practice, the Prayer of the Faithful is a normal part of the Mass on all Sundays and solemnities. It is appropriate on major feasts and memorials. But it is not obligatory to have these prayers at every weekday Mass. For reasons of time—for example, when workers attend Mass early in the morning on their way to work—this Universal Prayer may be omitted. However, the priest could include a short form of it in each weekday Mass.

After the last intention and response, the presider (and not a concelebrant or other minister) concludes the Prayer of the Faithful by extending his hands and offering a simple prayer with the short ending, for example, "Almighty God, our Father, you know all our needs. Accept these prayers we confidently make, through Christ our Lord." Those who do the intercessions should return to their places only after the concluding prayer has ended. This ensures that the distraction of people moving during the prayer is avoided.

In some parts of the world, including England and Wales as well as some parts of Ghana, it is customary to include a prayer to Mary (usually the "Hail Mary") or a reference to "joining our prayer with hers." However, "a Marian invocation, direct or indirect, is, strictly speaking, inappropriate in the General Intercessions, which like all the prayers of the Mass, are addressed to the Father through the Son."[44] This view was endorsed by Cardinal Francis Arinze, former Prefect for the Congregation of Divine Worship and Discipline of the Sacraments, in a private conversation that the author had with him on this subject during the Synod of Bishops in Rome in October 2008. He said that a prayer to Mary during Mass is inappropriate, pointing out that it is never done during any of the papal Masses. However, he added that a prayer or a hymn to Mary (such as the *Salve Regina* or *Regina Caeli*) is permitted after the blessing at the end of Mass and that this is sometimes done in papal Masses.

CHAPTER SEVEN

The Liturgy of the Eucharist and the Concluding Rites

Preparation of the Altar

AFTER THE PRAYER OF THE FAITHFUL, THERE COMES THE Liturgy of the Eucharist. At this point in the Mass, the altar is prepared. Until now, apart from its veneration by the priest at the beginning, the altar has not been the center of attention. It remains almost bare and unused during the Liturgy of the Word. Lighting may be directed toward the altar at this time. A corporal is laid out and all the vessels needed for the celebration are placed on it. In addition to the corporal, purificators and the Roman Missal are brought to the altar at this time. These tasks are carried out by a deacon, acolyte, or other members of the assembly. The United States bishops offer the useful comment that these items should be brought reverently but without ceremony from a side table.[1] The chalice may be left at the credence table if the deacon chooses to prepare the chalice there (*GIRM* 178).

The Offering of Bread and Wine

When Jesus ate the Last Supper with his disciples, he took bread and wine, gave thanks to God over them, broke the bread, and gave the bread and cup as his body and blood to his disciples. As early as the second century, these actions of Jesus were to some extent given solemn form: the paten (with the bread) and cup (with the wine) were carried to the altar after the Liturgy of the Word. A little later, Hippolytus tells us that this service was the work of a deacon.[2] In time, a new element was introduced to this originally simple rite: the faithful brought to the church the foods they had on their own tables at home.

This custom is explicitly attested to in the West. St. Cyprian, for example, rebukes a matron who dared to come to the Eucharistic celebration with empty hands: "You are rich and well-to-do; yet you celebrate the 'Lord's Supper' even though you…come to it without an offering and receive a part of the offering brought by a poor person. Consider the widow in the gospel…"[3] According to St. Augustine, his mother did not allow a day to pass without bringing her offering to the altar.[4] In Africa and at Rome, there was a procession of offerers at the beginning of the Eucharistic liturgy, parallel to the Communion procession. The offerers came to the bishop and his ministers and gave them the gifts while a psalm was sung. In Gaul, however, the faithful put the bread and wine in the sacristy before the beginning of Mass. These gifts were then brought to the altar in solemn procession by the deacons and other ministers at the beginning of the Eucharistic liturgy proper. By contributing the bread and wine, Christians made it clear that they wanted to share in the fruits of the Eucharist.

In practice, however, the Church carefully distinguished between the bread and wine intended for consecration and all other food and drink. The Council of Carthage in 397 laid down this rule: "In the celebration of the Mass nothing is to be offered except what is in accord with the tradition that originates in the Lord himself, namely, bread and wine mixed with water."[5] But this same Council allowed first fruits (only those of wheat and the vine were allowed) and of milk and honey to be brought for a Christian initiation: "Although these are offered on the altar, they receive a separate blessing, in order to show that they are clearly distinct from the sacrament of the Lord's body and blood."[6] Apart from bread and wine, then, everything else, even if contributed at Mass, had to be set aside away from the altar; this was a way of stressing the different status of these other gifts. It must be added that the gifts of bread and wine are the common offering of the entire worshipping community, since these are the symbols that will be prayed over and transformed.

Preparation of the Gifts

After the Universal Prayer, all sit (including the presiding priest) and the collection is taken. This is an important part of the Mass and therefore it is not liturgically proper to prepare the bread and wine at the altar while the collection is being taken. The collection forms part of the gathering of offerings for the celebration. Some of those offerings are bread and wine, money and gifts. All of these things are offerings brought by the community to be presented to the priest. It is not proper to accept some offerings and prepare them at the altar while the other offerings are still being collected.

At the beginning of the Liturgy of the Eucharist, the gifts that will become the Body and Blood of Jesus are brought to the altar. This taking of the bread and wine is a preparation of the gifts. It is not in itself the sacrifice or offering, but a preparation for the Eucharistic Prayer. The faithful are encouraged to bring forward, and even to provide, the elements through which Christ's offering will be made present, together with money and other gifts for the sustenance of Christ's body, especially the poor and the needy.

Presentation of the Gifts

After the collection has been taken, there is the procession with the bread, wine, money, and other gifts (especially on Sundays and special occasions). These gifts are first designated "for the poor" and then "for the Church" (*GIRM* 73). It is important that some of these gifts are actually given to the poor. According to the *General Instruction*, "It is a praiseworthy practice for the bread and wine to be presented by the faithful" (*GIRM* 73).

It is liturgically incorrect to include things such as the chalice, the purificators, the Missal, the water, and so on, in the procession during the Presentation of the Gifts. These items are not offerings and they should not be carried in procession but should rather be brought reverently from the credence table.

The elements of bread and wine are brought in the procession in vessels that can be seen by all the assembly. Ideally, the bread and wine should each be contained in single vessels, so that the priest and people may be seen to be sharing the same food and drink in the sacrament of unity.

Where should the presiding priest receive these gifts? According to the *General Instruction*, the gifts are to be received "at an appropriate place by the Priest or Deacon" (*GIRM* 73). In many places, it is customary for the priest to receive the gifts at the edge of the sanctuary where Communion is normally distributed. However, it has been argued that receiving the gifts at this point "subtly reinforces the notion that the laity should not enter the 'sanctuary.'"[7] Depending on the architecture and the availability of space in the sanctuary, it should be possible for priests to receive the gifts at the chair. For example, at papal Masses, the Holy Father remains seated at his chair during this part of the liturgy to receive the gifts.

In places where many gifts are usually brought in the procession, it may be better for the priest to receive the bread and wine first. These can be placed on the credence table until the priest is ready to receive them at the altar. The money is taken and placed in a safe place away from the altar. This may be near the credence table or even in a safe place in the sacristy. Offertory gifts brought along with the bread and wine, money or other gifts for the poor, should not be placed on the altar but put in some other suitable place (*GIRM* 73 and 140). As the *General Instruction* says, "Even money or other gifts for the poor or for the Church, brought by the faithful or collected in the church, are acceptable; given their purpose, they are to be put in a suitable place away from the Eucharistic table" (*GIRM* 73).

In some places, especially where the congregation is small, the priest at this point invites the members of the congregation to stand with him around the altar during the Eucharistic Prayer. However, this is liturgically incorrect as, during the Liturgy of the Eucharist, "only the presiding celebrant remains at the altar. The assembly of the faithful take their place in the Church outside the *presbyterium*, which is reserved for the celebrant or concelebrants and the altar ministers."[8]

Placing of the Gifts on the Altar

The priest accepts the vessel containing the bread from the deacon or an altar server. He quietly says the appropriate prayer as he holds the vessel *slightly* above the altar. He allows the vessel containing the bread to touch the altar only after the prayer. In the meantime, at the credence table, the deacon (or concelebrant) pours the wine and water into the chalice (as he says the pre-scribed prayer) and holds it (and any other flagon or carafe) for the presiding priest until needed. Again, it is only after the appro-priate prayer has been said that the chalice touches the altar. It is not required to make a sign of the cross to bless the water as was required in the Tridentine Mass.

When there is no deacon, the priest prepares the chalice him-self. In this case, it should not be put on the corporal but on the right side of the altar and prepared there. Then, the priest takes it, holds it slightly raised above the altar, says the blessing, and puts it on the corporal. Ideally, once the bread and the wine have been put on the corporal, they should not be moved or even touched until the institution narrative.

The gifts should not be on the altar before the Presentation of the Gifts. In some parishes, the author has seen the chalice, ciborium, wine, water, and everything else needed placed on the altar *before* the beginning of Mass! This is not proper since they should touch the altar only *after* the prayers are said. In addition, they should not be put on the altar by the servers, deacon, or people since it is the formal duty of the presiding priest to "place" the bread and wine upon the altar (*GIRM* 75, 141, 142) after he accepts them from the people or deacon. As Smolarski says,

> A careful reading of the rubrics of the sacramentary and of the text of the *GIRM* indicates that there is no justification for the all-too-common practice of a priest receiving the bread and wine, placing them on the altar, lifting each high in the air while saying the prayer and then placing them on the altar a second time. Placing the Eucharistic elements on the altar is an action that should be done once and only once![9]

It is important to stress the strong symbol of one bread and one cup during the Mass. Ideally, there should not be more than one chalice and one ciborium on the altar at this point in the Mass. If a large quantity of bread will be needed for Communion, then a ciborium big enough to contain all the hosts should be used. As for the wine, the symbolism of one cup may be difficult to retain when there are many communicants. Some liturgists have proposed the use of one or more large decanters, carafes, or flagons in addition to the chalice. They propose that extra chalices and ciboria can be brought at Communion time. Consecrated hosts will be put in the ciboria and the consecrated wine will be poured into the chalices from the flagons.

However, it should be pointed out that *Redemptionis Sacramentum* is not in favor of using flagons or decanters during Mass. It says, "If one chalice is not sufficient for Communion to be distributed under both kinds to the Priest concelebrants or Christ's faithful, there is no reason why the Priest celebrant should not use several chalices....It is praiseworthy, by reason of the sign value, to use a main chalice of larger dimensions, together with smaller chalices" (no. 105). According to paragraph 106, "The pouring of the Blood of Christ after the consecration from one vessel to another is completely to be avoided, lest anything should happen that would be to the detriment of so great a mystery. Never to be used for containing the Blood of the Lord are flagons, bowls, or other vessels that are not fully in accord with the established norms."

In this connection, we should mention the recommendation of the *General Instruction* that "it is most desirable" that the faithful also receive Communion from what is consecrated at that Mass.[10] In this regard, we should mention the exception made on Holy Thursday, when extra hosts are consecrated for distribution at the Good Friday commemoration of the Passion.

This means that ordinarily, at the Preparation of the Gifts, the priest should ensure that there are enough hosts to be used at Communion during Mass. Indeed, no Vatican document on liturgy issued since the Second Vatican Council states that consecrated hosts in the tabernacle can be used during the Communion rite. Indeed, they state that it is allowed to take Communion from the tabernacle to give to those unable to attend Mass because of illness, and that it is necessary to reserve the sacrament for the sick and the dying. Whenever these documents speak of consecrated hosts in the tabernacle, they do not say that they should be used during Mass.

In fact, the opposite is mandated. In 1742, Pope Benedict XIV stated that the Church should end the practice of reserving Communion in the tabernacle to be used during the liturgy. He added that the faithful should be encouraged to receive Communion from the elements consecrated at that Mass. This exhortation was quoted by Pope Pius XII in his encyclical *Mediator Dei* in 1947, and subsequently was repeated in 1963 by the Second Vatican Council's *Constitution on the Liturgy*, the Roman Instruction *Eucharistum Mysterium* in 1967, the 1969 *General Instruction*, the 2002 *General Instruction*, and in various other decrees and liturgical documents since the Council.

Even though the norm is that Communion should be received from the bread and wine consecrated at a particular Mass, it does not mean that a priest may never use consecrated hosts reserved in the tabernacle during Mass. In emergencies, hosts can be taken from the tabernacle and used during Communion, but this must be the exception rather than the rule. Indeed, when priests plan the liturgy carefully, they should be able to avoid such situations. They should be able to estimate (perhaps by carefully counting for several weeks) how many people normally receive Communion at a given Mass and plan accordingly. The Communion in the tabernacle should be used primarily for the sick. Thus, generally, there should *not* be more than one ciborium in the tabernacle, and preferably no more than about fifty hosts in it. Since Mass is celebrated daily in most churches, the hosts taken to the sick can be from those consecrated the same day. The exception to this is the Commemoration of the Last Supper on Holy Thursday, when extra hosts are consecrated to be distributed on Good Friday.

At the Preparation of the Gifts, the paten is slightly raised but not "elevated" during the prayer "Blessed are you, Lord God of all creation...." The bread remains on the paten as a sign that it is being set aside and thus *offered* to God, so that it may become the Body of Christ.

Prayers over the bread and wine *may* be said aloud when there is no singing. Modeled on Jewish table prayers, they are sometimes called *berakoth* (singular *berakah*), the Hebrew word for "blessings." The first one over the bread reads,

> Blessed are you, Lord God of all creation,
> for through your goodness we have received
> the bread we offer you:
> fruit of the earth and work of human hands,
> it will become for us the bread of life.

This is modeled on the blessing over the bread in the Jewish meal, which reads,

> Blessed be thou, JHWH, our God, King of the universe,
> who bringest forth bread from the earth.

The prayer over the wine in the Mass reads,

> Blessed are you, Lord God of all creation,
> for through your goodness we have received
> the wine we offer you:
> fruit of the vine and work of human hands,
> it will become our spiritual drink.

This is modeled on the Jewish blessing over the wine, which reads,

> Blessed be thou, JHWH, our God, King of the universe,
> who givest us this fruit of the vine.

These prayers "acknowledge that the bread and wine derive from the bountiful munificence of the Creator and are being offered to him, not in their natural state—grain and grapes—but made into bread and wine by the work of human hands."[11]

Before the priest raises the chalice during the prayer of preparation, he pours a little water into the wine. This action has biblical roots, first, in the classical world's custom of not drinking wine unless mixed with water. Jesus probably followed this custom at the Last Supper. Beyond this, Christian tradition has seen various symbols in this action:[12]

1. Some see in this a reference to the blood and water that flowed from Christ's pierced side (John 19:34). This event was seen as symbolizing the birth of the Church and of the sacraments.

2. For some people, wine and water were symbols of the divine and human natures in Christ. The mixing of water and wine at this point is derived from a Christmas liturgy commemorating the incarnation when the divine (wine) and the human (water) came to be united. The prayer at the mixing of water and wine speaks of the wonderful exchange between Christ's divinity and our humanity: "By the mystery of this water and wine may we come to share in the divinity of Christ who humbled himself to share in our humanity."

3. Another symbol is found in the ancient Ethiopian liturgy, which contains the following statement in the eighth-century "Anaphoras in Honor of Mary": "As the water and wine in the chalice cannot be separated from each other, so never permit us to be separated from you and your Son, the Lamb of Salvation."

Some priests raise both the paten and chalice at the same time and offer the bread and wine together in a single action, adapting the words, "Blessed are you...." They may do this to save time or to simplify the Preparation of the Gifts, but it is not allowed. The two prayers that accompany the actions of offering the bread and the wine are similar but distinct. The priest is not obliged to say these prayers aloud. Indeed, the first option is to say them quietly, whether or not there is music or singing accompanying these actions. The advantage of this option is the elimination of repetitiveness that some priests may want to avoid when they say "Blessed are you, Lord God of all creation..." only once.

Incensation of the Gifts and the Altar

After the bread and wine have been elevated, the presider incenses the gifts and the altar. How should the gifts be incensed? According to the *General Instruction*, "The Priest incenses the offerings with three swings of the thurible or by making the Sign of the Cross over the offerings with the thurible before going on to incense the cross and the altar" (*GIRM* 277). In spite of the stipulation of the *General Instruction*, even today some celebrants continue to use the elaborate triple crosswise and triple circular incensations during the Preparation of the Gifts. This way of incensing was prescribed by the 1570 Missal. However, we must bear the following statement in mind:

> It must never be forgotten that the Missal of Pope Paul VI has, since 1970, supplanted the one called improperly "the Missal of St. Pius V," and completely so, in both texts and rubrics. When the rubrics of the Missal of Paul VI say nothing or say little on particulars in some places, it is not to be inferred that the former rite should be observed. *Therefore, the multiple and complex gestures for incensation as prescribed in the former Missal...are not to be resumed.*[13]

During the celebration of a funeral Mass, the celebrant, after incensing the gifts and the altar, also incenses the coffin or casket. This is done before the altar server incenses the congregation. After the priest has incensed the gifts and the altar, he is incensed by the deacon or another minister. Then, if there are concelebrating priests, they are also incensed.

The Washing of the Hands

After the incensation, the celebrant washes his hands. This practice recalls rites for the priests of the Old Testament. When priests and Levites were consecrated, they had to undergo ritual washings before they could carry out their duties in the sanctuary (Exod 29:4; Num 8:7). The priests were required to wash their hands (and feet) in a bronze basin of water before they could enter the tabernacle or approach the altar of incense (Exod 30:17–21). According to Psalm 24, this ritual was of great importance to the people as they prepared to enter the Temple:

> Who shall ascend the hill of the Lord?
>   And who shall stand in his holy place?
> Those who have clean hands and pure hearts....
>   (Ps 24:3–4)

We should note that clean hands are associated with a pure heart. In the psalm, ritual handwashing was a symbol of the internal cleansing of heart that was required before a person could draw near to God's presence in the sanctuary.

The Jewish Passover ritual also provides a historical background for this rite. Before the father of the family broke the blessed bread and distributed it to the gathered family and friends, he washed his hands as a sign of purification. Therefore, there is a spiritual, ritual background to what became a custom in the Roman Rite. We should also bear in mind that the earliest descriptions of the Presentation of the Gifts at Mass included all kinds of foodstuffs apart from the bread and wine. These foods, such as wine, cheese, oil, and fresh fruits and vegetables were brought forward during the Mass so that they could later be given to the poor. This was normally done by deacons. It was necessary for the priest to wash his hands before touching the Eucharistic gifts at the altar and at Communion. It may also have been necessary for him to wash his hands after he incensed the Eucharistic gifts.

Because these practices died out (or were rarely engaged in) and because of the sacred character of the Eucharist, the ritual of washing hands acquired greater symbolic, spiritual value. It came to symbolize interior purification and integrity of heart. Some scholars contend that the spiritual meaning became attached to handwashing in parts of Europe and eventually became the practice in Rome. In any event, it is still part of the Mass and in the revised *Missal*, when he washes his hands the priest says inaudibly one verse adapted from Psalm 51:

> Wash me, O Lord, from my iniquity
> and cleanse me from my sin. (*RM* 28)

The washing of hands is not optional, and is done even if there has been an earlier washing of hands, for example, when the bishop has already cleansed the chrism from his hands at a confirmation Mass or when the celebrant has washed his hands after imposing blessed ashes on Ash Wednesday.

In the washing of hands, it is not proper for the priest to dip only his fingers in a bowl of water or to allow only a few drops of water to trickle over his thumbs. It is preferable for the priest to use a large jug and basin, not a small water cruet and a dish. The bishop's ewer and basin can serve as an example.

According to the *General Instruction*, the washing of hands by the priest must take place at the side of the altar (*GIRM* 76). The center of the altar is reserved for the offering of the Eucharistic sacrifice.

Prayer over the Offerings

The Prayer over the Offerings closes the liturgical unit of the Preparation of the Gifts. This prayer is introduced by "Pray, brethren…" According to *GIRM* 146, the people then rise and make their response to the priest's invitation to pray. This is in line with the stipulation of *GIRM* 43, namely that "The faithful should stand…from the invitation, *Orate Fratres* (*Pray, brethren*)." In the view of Martin Connell and Sharon McMillan, "Pastorally this could suggest that the people are standing even before the priest offers the invitation, so that this text is a true invitation to pray rather than cue to stand."[14]

Since the "Pray, brethren…" is now viewed as a lengthened "Let us pray,"[15] the presider should not say "Amen" after the assembly's response, "May the Lord accept…." According to the current missal, it is the assembly that responds with "Amen" after the prayer over the offerings.

The new translation of the "Pray, brethren" runs as follows: "Pray, brethren, that my sacrifice and yours may be acceptable to God, the almighty Father." This differs from the previous translation, which had "our sacrifice." This translation was criticized for seeming to blur the distinction between the ministerial priesthood and that of the baptized. The new translation, "my sacrifice and yours," has been criticized for giving the impression that there are two sacrifices. However, according to Chupungco, we should not interpret "my sacrifice and yours" as two separate sacrifices.[16] He points out that the Latin does not say "my sacrifice and your sacrifice." Rather, the Latin word translated as *and* ("my sacrifice *and* yours") should be understood as "my sacrifice, which is also yours."[17] In this interpretation, there is only one sacrifice, although there are different ministers and functions within the sacrificial act. Chupungco concludes, "The thinking that seeks to distinguish one sacrifice from another based on the difference between an ordained priesthood and the priestly assembly is not supported by the Latin text."[18]

After the principal celebrant has said the prayer over the offerings, the concelebrants approach the altar and stand around it. They should do this in such a way that they do not obstruct the carrying out of the rites and so that whatever the priest does may be seen clearly by the faithful. They should not be in the deacon's way when he needs to go to the altar to perform his ministry (*GIRM* 215).

After concluding the prayer over the gifts, the priest should make a distinct pause to make clear that the Preparation of the Gifts (the "taking") is complete and that the Eucharistic Prayer (the "giving thanks") is now about to begin.

The Eucharistic Prayer

The Eucharistic Prayer, which begins with the Preface and ends with the doxology just before the Lord's Prayer, has its roots in Jewish table prayers. At the beginning of a Jewish meal, the father of the family or the one presiding over the meal would take bread and pronounce a blessing (*barakah*) that praised God, saying, "Blessed are you Lord, our God, king of the universe, who has brought forth bread from heaven." The bread would then be broken and distributed to the participants, who would start to eat the various courses of the meal. If it was a Passover meal, there would be a reading of the *haggadah*, which retold the story of the Jews' deliverance from Egypt and explained its significance to those present. Toward the end of the meal, the presider recited a second and longer blessing over a cup of wine. This blessing contained three elements: (1) praise of God for creation; (2) thanksgiving for his redemptive work in the past; and (3) supplication for the future, that God's saving works would continue in their lives and be brought to their climax in the sending of the Messiah who would restore the Davidic kingdom. The early Eucharistic Prayers seem to have followed this general pattern. They included the recitation of a blessing over bread and wine. This recitation retold the saving event of Jesus' death and resurrection and the three-fold structure of offering praise to God for creation, thanksgiving for his saving deeds, and supplication. Our modern Eucharistic Prayers contain these ancient Jewish elements.

HISTORICAL OVERVIEW

The Roman Canon or Eucharistic Prayer I

From the beginning, the Church did not have just one text of the Eucharistic Prayer; rather, various forms developed. The oldest of the traditional Eucharistic Prayers used in the Latin Rite is the Roman Canon. The Roman Canon (or Eucharistic Prayer I in the current Roman Missal) is one of the most esteemed prayers in the Church's liturgical history. Its remote origins are uncertain. It is indeed possible that some parts of it were originally in Greek. Important elements of the text, as we know it, come from the fourth century when the Roman Church first formally adopted Latin as its liturgical language.[19] The earliest available evidence for it comes from the lectures of St. Ambrose of Milan in which he instructed candidates for the sacraments of initiation (*De Sacramentis* 5:21). Apart from St. Ambrose, the prayer may have been known to the late-fourth-century writer known as Ambrosiaster. He refers in his writings to a phrase found in the Roman Canon, namely "your high priest Melchizedek." In the late sixth century, Pope Gregory the Great stated that the prayer was written during the pontificate of Pope Damasus (366–84).

The "Roman Canon," with some changes, continued to be used in the whole Church until the Second Vatican Council. Although the *Constitution on the Sacred Liturgy* of the Second Vatican Council had not spoken of the reform of the Eucharistic Prayer, members of Study Group 10 of the *Consilium* (the group responsible for implementing the Council's reform) met to discuss the possibility of revising the Roman Canon. They attempted to reform the Roman Canon with its many intercessions and its weak elements of praise and thanks, but it became obvious such a revision was impossible. The *Consilium* ultimately concluded that no attempt should be made to alter such a venerable text, and that in view of the use of multiple anaphoras (Eucharistic Prayers) in the Eastern churches, the Roman Church might adopt several new, additional Eucharistic Prayers. Pope Paul VI accepted this suggestion, saying, "The present anaphora is to be left unchanged; two or three anaphoras for use at particular specific times are to be composed or looked for."[20]

Thus, the Roman Canon appeared in the 1970 edition of the Roman Missal virtually unchanged. However, two changes were made to the institution narrative. First, the words, "which will be given up for you," were added to the words over the bread in order to make the institution formula identical in all the Eucharistic Prayers. Second, the words "the mystery of faith" were removed from the words over the cup and were instead inserted after the narrative to introduce the memorial acclamation.

Other Eucharistic Prayers

Apart from the Roman Canon, members of Study Group 10 of the *Consilium* discussed creating new Eucharistic Prayers by going back to the sources. On May 23, 1968, the *Consilium* announced that Pope Paul VI had approved three new Eucharistic Prayers together with eight new prefaces for the Roman Rite. On November 1, 1974, the Congregation for Worship presented, on an experimental basis, two prayers for Masses of reconciliation and three prayers for Masses with children. Meanwhile, the corpus of prefaces in the Roman Missal had increased to more than eighty. Thus, the Roman Church enriched its Eucharistic Prayers by adopting the practice of the Eastern churches of having many Eucharistic Prayers rather than a single one and by adding considerably to its own practice of having variable prefaces for the Roman Canon and for Eucharistic Prayers II and III.

The creation of the new Roman Eucharistic Prayers was greatly influenced by the anaphoras found in the liturgies of the Eastern churches. In the Byzantine Rite since the sixth century, the Eucharistic Prayer has simply been called the "anaphora."

Eucharistic Prayer II

One of the new Eucharistic Prayers approved by Pope Paul VI on May 23, 1968, this prayer contains much ancient material. It was intended to be a modern adaptation of the Eucharistic

Prayer found in the *Apostolic Tradition*, an early "church order," rediscovered and published in the early twentieth century.

To this original prayer was added a *Sanctus*, with its introduction; a bridge from the *Sanctus* to the remainder of the prayer; a consecratory epiclesis before the institution narrative; the reformulation of the institution narrative; the memorial acclamation; and the intercessions. At the same time, some of the original wording of the *Apostolic Tradition* was also changed.

Eucharistic Prayer III

This is a new creation based on a proposal of the Italian liturgical scholar Dom Cipriano Vagaggini. It is distinguished primarily by the way it arranges the individual structural elements in an organic and clear manner. In so doing, it does not merely rely on the Roman Canon but also incorporates ideas and texts from the liturgy and theological tradition. It incorporates a text from the Mozarabic liturgy: "Father, you are holy indeed...to the glory of your name," and one or two phrases from the Eastern and Gallican liturgies, such as, "On the night he was betrayed." It has no preface of its own.

Eucharistic Prayer IV

Eucharistic Prayer IV is based on the Alexandrian Anaphora of St. Basil. It contains a preface that is never changed and, beginning at this point, extends the thanksgiving in praise of God's acts of salvation through the *Sanctus* to the paschal mystery of Christ and the sending of the Holy Spirit. It then moves on through the epiclesis of the Holy Spirit to the account of the institution of the sacrament. This comprehensive praise of the history of salvation is like a confession that praises the whole Christian faith. The use of this Eucharistic Prayer in a Mass in which the Creed is recited would result in undesirable duplication.

THEOLOGY OF THE EUCHARISTIC PRAYER[21]

The Eucharistic Prayer is the Great Thanksgiving that the worshipping community says over the bread and the cup during the celebration of Mass and has the following features. First, it is a prayer of thanksgiving, expressed especially in the Preface, which gives thanks to God for the whole work of salvation. Especially in Jesus Christ, God has brought salvation to humankind. The prayer also gives thanks to God for some particular aspect of the work of salvation. It is in this part that the nature of the day, feast, or liturgical time is specified. The worshipping community acknowledges what God has done for it in praise and thanksgiving.

Second, the Eucharistic Prayer is a prayer of remembrance. In it, the Church celebrates the memorial of Christ, recalling especially his passion, resurrection, and ascension. Theologically, this means that what Christ achieved in the past by his death, resurrection, and ascension continues to be efficacious in the present. Thus, when the worshipping community, in obedience to Jesus' command to celebrate the supper in his memory, recalls his death, resurrection, ascension, and coming again, the effects of the past acts are made present in the worshipping community.

Third, the Eucharistic Prayer is a prayer of offering. In it, the assembly recalls the once-for-all offering of Jesus Christ and joins to it an offering of praise and thanksgiving over the bread and the wine. These are gifts from God's creation, yet in this act, they become for the assembly the Body and Blood of Jesus Christ, whose own words at the Last Supper are recalled in the prayer.

Fourth, the Eucharistic Prayer is a prayer of supplication, in particular that the Holy Spirit might come upon the gifts and upon those who will share in them.

Fifth, as the prayer recalls the reconciliation willed by God and won by Jesus Christ, the Eucharistic Prayer has an underlying theme of reconciliation because the assembly is the gathering of those who have been baptized "for the forgiveness of sins." This reconciliation reaches its highest expression in Holy Communion, to which the table prayer is intimately bound. The assembly's sharing of the bread and the cup, the signs of Jesus Christ's Body broken and his Blood poured out for the forgiveness of sins, demonstrates that the Church is a community of reconciliation because it has accepted the reconciliation won for it in Jesus Christ.

Finally, the whole prayer is intended to function as a prayer of sanctification or consecration. By it the priestly people finds itself renewed in its baptismal commitment, and the gifts of bread and wine become for the assembly the Body and Blood of Jesus

Christ, whose consumption unites the communicants more deeply in the Body of Christ, the Church. This consecration is intensely manifested in the recitation of the Lord's words and in the petition that God may send the Holy Spirit upon the gifts and upon those who receive them.

CHOOSING A EUCHARISTIC PRAYER

Even though the Eucharistic Prayer is the most important of all the prayers that have to be said by the priest (*GIRM* 30), very often it does not receive the attention it requires during the preparation of the liturgy. It is not good to use the same Eucharistic Prayer very often. Priests should try to vary them, depending on the type of celebration being held.

As far as Eucharistic Prayer I is concerned, it may be better not to use it on a typical Sunday in view of its length and peculiar literary structure. It includes rather long intercessions but almost no element of praise or thanksgiving. On the other hand, it includes special insertions for major feasts—so it may be good to use it on such feasts or on the feast of some saint mentioned in its intercessions.

Eucharistic Prayer II is, overall, too short for Sunday celebrations, but might be suitable if sung. Eucharistic Prayer III seems to be appropriate in terms of length and content, and might be appropriate on Sundays, but if it is used too often, it ceases to be effective. Eucharistic Prayer IV contains a very good proclamation of salvation history, which provides an excellent context for praise and thanksgiving. However, if it is used, it must be used with its own preface. For this reason, it cannot be used on solemnities that have their own prefaces.

Selecting the appropriate Eucharistic Prayer is only one element in making this part of the Mass lively. Other important elements are singing and posture. Ideally, the *Sanctus*, the memorial acclamation, and the *Amen* should be sung on Sundays and solemnities. Indeed, the whole Eucharistic Prayer could be sung.

PARTS OF THE EUCHARISTIC PRAYER

According to the *General Instruction*, the main elements of the Eucharistic Prayers are the following: thanksgiving (as especially expressed in the Preface); the acclamation of the *Sanctus*; the epi-clesis, or invocation of the Holy Spirit; the institution narrative and consecration; anamnesis (remembering); offering; interces-sions; and concluding doxology (*GIRM 55*). We shall look at the four Eucharistic Prayers commonly used in our liturgy in the light of these main elements. The elements of thanksgiving (including the Preface), the acclamation of the *Sanctus*, the institution narra-tive and consecration, and the concluding doxology are practically the same in all four Eucharistic Prayers. I will examine these in the commentary on Eucharistic Prayer I but will not revisit them in the other three Eucharistic prayers.

Eucharistic Prayer I

Opening Dialogue and Preface

The Eucharistic Prayer begins with an opening dialogue that serves to unite presider and assembly in offering its Great Thanks-giving with their hearts lifted up. Thus, at the outset, the prayer is seen as the assembly's prayer and not simply that of the presider, who proclaims it in the assembly's name. This prayer is called the Preface. The word *preface* used in this context does not mean a prelude to the Eucharistic Prayer. Rather, it is the first part of it. "Preface" here refers to a proclamation, a speaking out before God and the worshipping assembly, and not a foreword or pre-lude. The priest, before God and the assembly, "glorifies God the Father and gives thanks to him for the whole work of salvation or for some particular aspect of it, according to the varying day, festivity, or time of year" (*GIRM* 79a). The Preface thus expresses the main theme of the Eucharistic Prayer, that is, the giving of thanks. The purpose of the dialogue in the Preface is to unite the presider and the congregation to offer its Great Thanksgiving with their hearts lifted up.

It is important for concelebrants to take their places near the altar before the Preface begins. This means that they should go after the Prayer over the Offerings, not after the *Sanctus* as is often done. As DeGrocco says, "Concelebrating Priests participate as Priests in the entire Eucharistic Prayer, and therefore, should be at the altar for the entire Prayer, which begins with the Introductory Dialogue of the Preface."[22] According to the *General Instruction*, the presiding priest should keep his hands extended in the *orans* position for the entire Introductory Dialogue and the Preface; he should not join his hands until he concludes the Preface and as all begin to sing or say the Holy, Holy, Holy (*GIRM* 148).

This three-part dialogue begins with the words, "The Lord be with you," to which the congregation responds, "And with your spirit." In the people's response, the Pauline form is adopted, "with your spirit," patterned on 2 Corinthians 13:13 and Philippians 4:13. The formula "evokes the possession of the Spirit, the particular Christian gift that is necessary to Christian action and here, in particular, to the liturgical action."[23] At this point in the Mass, both the priest and the people need the Lord to be with them as they prepare to enter into the mystery of the Mass.

Next, the priest says, "Lift up your hearts" (Latin: *sursum corda*). In this invitation, the adverb in Latin (*sursum*) suggests an upward movement. This prayer calls to mind the exhortation in the Book of Lamentations: "Let us lift up our hearts as well as our hands to God in heaven" (Lam 3:41). The prayer also calls to mind Paul's words to the Colossians, "So if you have been raised with Christ, seek the things that are above, where Christ is, seated at the right hand of God. *Set your minds on things that are above*, not on things that are on earth" (Col 3:1–2). Finally, the priest says, "Let us give thanks to the Lord our God." The Bible is replete with the theme of thanksgiving. For example, in Psalm 136:1–3, we have, "O give thanks to the LORD for he is good…" (see also Ps 107:8, 15, 21, 31). Similarly, Paul says that Christians should be "abounding in thanksgiving" (Col 2:7), "giving thanks in all we do" (see Col 3:17) and "in all circumstances" (1 Thess 5:18), especially in worship (cf. 1 Cor 14:16–19; Eph 5:19–20; Col 3:16).

In response to what the priest says about giving thanks to God, the congregation says, "It is right and just." The word *right*[24] here recalls 2 Thessalonians 1:3, "We must always give thanks to God for you, brothers and sisters, as is right." The word *right* here signifies that "in the order of the grace given in Jesus Christ it is meet-proper-fitting to give thanks, for through him faith and charity abound."[25]

The people's response also says that it is "just"[26] to give thanks to God. *Just* in the Old Testament refers to the quality of acts done according to the Law. We find this, for example, in Deuteronomy

1:16, "Judge *rightly* between one person and another, whether citizen or resident alien." It has been suggested that *right* and *just* are synonymous.[27] "Right" (*aequum*) is a quality that belongs to judgment (e.g., Lev 24:22) and to the treatment of others: thus "right and just" translates Paul's admonition in Colossians to masters to treat their slaves "justly and fairly," realizing that they too have a Master in heaven (Col 4:1). The variable prefaces that follow normally begin by reaffirming these words of the assembly's response, then adding a second pair "our duty and our salvation."[28]

After the assembly has responded to the presider's invitation to give thanks, the Preface states the motives for giving thanks. In the case of Eucharistic Prayers I, II, and III, which have variable prefaces, some aspect of the mystery of faith is generally singled out. Its content is determined by the liturgical season, feast day, or particular ritual celebration. Eucharistic Prayer IV focuses mainly on God and on what he has accomplished for humankind in creation and redemption. In the children's Eucharistic Prayers, the children may be asked for their motives for thanksgiving before the dialogue begins.

The Eucharistic Prayer is always expressed in the first person plural. The whole worshipping community celebrates the Eucharist, even if the priest speaks in the name of all. It is the responsibility of the priest to proclaim the prayer with and for the people.

THE *SANCTUS*

It has become traditional in the Eucharistic Prayer to link the praise of God by the assembly to that of the heavenly liturgy so that with one voice all creation praises God. At the end of the Preface, we have the *Sanctus*, the great song of God's glory, which the congregation sings. It consists of two parts, each of which is closely linked to a passage of the Bible. The first part comes from the calling of the Prophet Isaiah. In a vision, he sees the Lord on his throne, surrounded by seraphim with six wings, who call to another: "Holy, holy, holy is the LORD of hosts; the whole earth is full of his glory" (Isa 6:3). Similar to this passage from Isaiah is one from Revelation 4, where John speaks of strange animal-like creatures gathered before God's throne. We read, "Day and night without ceasing they sing, 'Holy, holy, holy, the Lord God the Almighty, who was and is and is to come'" (Rev 4:8).

The second part of the *Sanctus* is derived from the shouts of praise spoken by the crowds of people during Jesus' triumphant entry into Jerusalem (Mark 11:1–11; Matt 21:1–11; John 12:12–17). Matthew reports the greeting of the crowd as "Hosanna to the Son of David! Blessed is the one who comes in the name of the Lord! Hosanna in the highest heaven" (Matt 21:9). In the West, Caesarius of Arles mentions the addition of the *Benedictus* in the first half of the sixth century (*Serm.* 72.2).

The acclamation of the *Sanctus* is thus based on Scripture. Its first part glorifies God, whose glory fills heaven and earth. The Hebrew word *Hosanna* in the second section originally meant "Pray, save (us)." However, it soon became an acclamation that glorified and praised God. That is how it is used in our text. Taken together with the phrase "in the highest" (*in excelsis*), it calls to mind the angels' song *Gloria in excelsis Deo* ("Glory to God in the highest"). This acclamation of praise also applies to the Son of God "who comes in the name of the Lord." His coming becomes a saving presence in the celebration of the Eucharist.

In this song, God is addressed as "Lord God of hosts."[29] Here *hosts* translates the Hebrew word *Sabaoth* and means an army of angels, evoking God's power over the universe and against evil. To the praise of God there is added a blessing of the one who comes (Christ) "in the name of the Lord," in the name of the *Kyrios*, and who is one with the Father in his lordship.

The *Sanctus* reminds us that when we gather to celebrate the Eucharist, "we do it in union with the liturgy of praise and offering to God that goes on eternally and perfectly before God's throne in heaven."[30] The meaning of the *Sanctus*, which the whole congregation sings, can be identified as "a way to join them with the heavenly liturgy where choirs of angels sing the divine praises."[31]

After the *Sanctus*, the Eucharistic Prayer continues with these words:

> To you, therefore, most merciful Father,
> we make humble prayer and petition
> through Jesus Christ, your Son, our Lord:

that you accept and bless these gifts, these offerings,
these holy and unblemished sacrifices...

God is addressed as "most merciful Father." The "most merciful"[32]
was an imperial title that was often found in many inscriptions[33]
and was borrowed by Christians. Here it refers to the attitude of
God, the supreme Lord, toward the weakness and lowliness of his
subjects.

Next in the Eucharistic Prayer, the worshippers "make hum-
ble prayer and petition" through Christ, that God may "accept
and bless these gifts, these offerings, these holy and unblemished
sacrifices." The idea of approval or acceptance of sacrifice is well
attested in Scripture, starting with the sacrifice of Abel: "Abel for
his part brought of the firstlings of his flock, their fat portions.
And the LORD had regard for Abel and his offering, but for Cain
and his offering he had no regard" (Gen 4:4–5). God is asked to
accept the gifts. No offering is of itself worthy of acceptance by
God. We ask God to bless our offering and make it worthy of
himself. In this connection, Mazza says,

> When offerers pray for acceptance, they are acknowl-
> edging that their outward worship is not magical and
> does not have power to produce its effect automatically.
> A prayer for acceptance is a solemn proclamation that
> God is supremely free and remains transcendent even
> in regard to a cult which he himself has prescribed and
> which the offerers carry out exactly as ordered.[34]

The gifts to be offered are referred to in three different ways: "these
gifts, these offerings, these holy and unblemished sacrifices." This
threefold way of referring to the gifts is a Latin rhetorical device to
add emphasis and has been interpreted in different ways. According
to Josef A. Jungmann,[35] we have a gradation in the way the three
terms designate the material offerings: the gifts themselves (*dona*)
presented as a public service (*munera*) to be offered in tribute to
God (*sacrificia*). In the view of Mazza,[36] they are offerings for the
dead (*dona*), for the living (*munera*) and offerings to be used in the
sacrifice (*sacrificia*).

The prayer for God to accept our offering is followed by an intercession for the Church:

> which we offer you firstly
> for your holy catholic Church.
> Be pleased to grant her peace,
> to guard, unite and govern her
> throughout the whole world,
> together with your servant N. our Pope
> and N. our Bishop,
> and all those who, holding to the truth,
> hand on the catholic and apostolic faith.

God is asked to "accept and bless these gifts, these offerings, these holy and unblemished sacrifices which we offer you first of all for your holy catholic Church." When the Church is called "catholic" here, it should not be understood in the modern sense of Roman or in the etymological sense of "universal." From the third century on, the word *catholic* in this context was not taken to mean "universal" but referred only to the Great Church and what concerned it, as opposed to the sects. Therefore, the term was used to refer to the Church, which was orthodox in contrast to the sects.[37] The celebrant prays in this part of the Canon that God may give his Church peace, guard it, unite it, and govern it. The four verbs used here point to all of God's blessings, including the blessings of the messianic age.

The Eucharistic Prayer next prays for "N. our Pope and N. our Bishop." In the early centuries of the Church, the title "pope" was synonymous with "bishop"; it was only in the sixth century that the title was reserved by Christians for the Bishop of Rome. Therefore, in its earliest form, when the Canon prayed for "our pope," it was praying simply for the bishop in each local church. After the word *pope* came to be used exclusively of the Bishop of Rome, it was found necessary to alter the text of the Canon to cater for the necessary commemoration of the local bishop. At this stage, the words "together with N. our bishop" were added to "our Pope."[38]

If the one celebrating the Mass is a bishop, in the prayers, after the words "N., our Pope," he adds, "and me, your unworthy servant." If, however, the bishop is celebrating Mass outside his own diocese, after the words "N., our Pope," he adds, "me, your unworthy servant, and my brother N., the Bishop of this Church of N" (*GIRM* 149). It is important to note this, since it marks a departure from previous practice where the bishop, in celebrating Mass outside his diocese, would simply say, "N., our Pope and N., our bishop."

In connection with the practice of praying for the pope and the local bishop during the Mass, the *Catechism of the Catholic Church* says,

> Since he has the ministry of Peter in the Church, the *Pope* is associated with every celebration of the Eucharist, wherein he is named as the sign and servant of the unity of the universal Church....The bishop's name is mentioned to signify his presidency over the particular Church, in the midst of his presbyterium and with the assistance of *deacons*. (CCC 1369)

Apart from praying for the pope and the local bishop, the congregation prays for "all those who, holding to the truth, hand on the catholic and apostolic faith." At first sight, this seems to refer to all the faithful who hold on to the orthodox faith and protect it. However, scholars have made a comparative study of texts in parallel liturgies and have concluded that those being prayed for are the bishops who form a single body with the pope, the Bishop of Rome. Therefore, here intercession is being made for the entire episcopal body. "The prayer thus asks that the Father would grant peace and the fullness of his blessings to the entire Church and therewith to the pope of Rome and the episcopal college that forms one body with him."[39] In a similar vein, Gilbert Ostdiek says, "Historically, this phrase refers to the college of bishops, who share with the pope the role of *cultores fidei*."[40]

The Commemoration of the Living

> Remember, Lord, your servants N. and N.
> and all gathered here,
> whose faith and devotion are known to you.

For them,
we offer you this sacrifice of praise
or they offer it for themselves
and all who are dear to them:
for the redemption of their souls,
in hope of health and well-being,
and paying their homage to you,
the eternal God, living and true.

Those for whom the prayer is said are believers "whose faith and devotion" are known to God. They are spoken of as servants (Latin: *famuli*), a title which ultimately refers to a "family" to which a person belongs, not as son or daughter nor, on the other hand as a slave, but as a faithful servant who is loved by the master.

For these servants and "all who are dear to them we offer you this sacrifice of praise or they offer it for themselves and all who are dear to them." Those who offer this "sacrifice of praise" are primarily those whose names are mentioned so that the congregation will know who they are. This part of the Canon is not a general "commemoration of the living" but a specific "commemoration of the offerers." The commemoration also includes all those around the altar, that is, all the participants in the liturgy. "For them and all who are dear to them we offer you this sacrifice of praise or they offer it for themselves and all who are dear to them." This means that either the offerers are themselves present, or they are absent, in which case the celebrant offers the sacrifice of praise on their behalf.[41]

The offering is made in the first place "for the redemption of their souls." This may refer to deliverance from the penalties due for sin or even of deliverance from sin itself through penance for sins committed daily. The offering is made in the second place "in hope of health and well-being." While "health"[42] has a primarily spiritual connotation, "well-being"[43] includes both spiritual and material welfare.

In communion with those whose memory we venerate,
especially the glorious ever-Virgin Mary,
Mother of our God and Lord, Jesus Christ,
✠ and blessed Joseph, her Spouse,

your blessed Apostles and Martyrs,
Peter and Paul, Andrew,...
and all your Saints;
we ask that through their merits and prayers,
in all things we may be defended
by your protecting help.
[Through Christ our Lord. Amen.]

At this point, the Church prays that the fruits of the sacrifice of the Mass may be experienced throughout the Church and the world. For this reason, the prayer introduces the theme of the communion of saints into the celebration. The Eucharist celebrates not only communion with God but also the communion of the faithful among themselves. It therefore becomes necessary to mention and commemorate the faithful who already experience the glory of the Father and, among them, especially those who were the founders of the local church or gave special witness to its faith.

Eucharistic Prayer I contains two different lists: the first includes twenty-six saints altogether: Mary, Joseph, twelve apostles, and twelve martyrs. Among the twelve apostles mentioned, we find not Matthias (who replaced Judas) but Paul who called himself an apostle (1 Cor 1:1). Paul was martyred in Rome and his tomb remains there. St. Joseph's name was not present in the first Eucharistic Prayer until recently. It was inserted by edict of Pope John XXIII on December 8, 1962, the closing day of the first session of the Second Vatican Council, which the pope had entrusted to the patronage of St. Joseph.

We should note that the Vatican's Congregation for Divine Worship and the Discipline of the Sacraments has issued new texts that include the name of St. Joseph, husband of the Virgin Mary, in the other Eucharistic Prayers as well. The decree *Paternas Vices* (*Fatherly Care*) was promulgated on May 1, 2013, the Feast of St. Joseph the Worker, by the authority of Pope Francis, and made public on June 18, 2013. The new decree extends the inclusion of St. Joseph to Eucharistic Prayers II, III, and IV. Thus, in all these Eucharistic prayers, after the mention of "the Blessed Virgin Mary, Mother of God," we now have, "with blessed Joseph, her Spouse."

In the list of the twelve martyrs, we find five popes, one bishop, and two other clerics (Lawrence, a deacon, and Chrysogonus who, according to an uncertain legend, was part of the clergy of Rome). After these come four laymen, the two soldiers John and Paul and the two physicians Cosmas and Damian. All suffered martyrdom in Rome except Cyprian, who was the bishop of Carthage in North Africa, and was a friend of Cornelius.

The second list comes toward the end of the Eucharistic Prayer and here the Church prays for the dead and then those celebrating the Eucharist, asking for "some share and fellowship with your holy Apostles and Martyrs." The list that follows includes fifteen saints, all martyrs: John the Baptist, then seven men and seven women.

In both lists, the saints mentioned are, apart from the outstanding figures of the apostolic Church, the heroes and martyrs of the local church of Rome who do not necessarily enjoy universal significance or particular devotion elsewhere in the Church. Their names may be omitted from Eucharistic Prayer I. Praying in communion with Mary, Joseph, and the other saints of God, the assembly now intercedes for the living and the dead in union with the Lord, who forever lives to make intercession (cf. Heb 7:25).

THE INSTITUTION NARRATIVE AND CONSECRATION

After the *Sanctus/Benedictus*, the Eucharistic Prayer traditionally develops, however briefly, some image from it such as the holiness of God or the idea of fullness. In many contemporary prayers, this leads into a remembrance of the role of God and Jesus Christ in the history of salvation. In Eucharistic Prayers II and III, it serves principally as a transition to the first epiclesis upon the gifts of bread and wine that they might become the Body and Blood of Christ.

Forming an essential part of most Eucharistic Prayers is the institution narrative, which recalls what Jesus did at the Last Supper.[44] The New Testament contains four versions of this event: Matthew 26:26–28; Mark 14:22–24; Luke 22:19–20; and 1 Corinthians 11:23–26. It should be observed that the text used in the Roman liturgy does not literally correspond to the biblical accounts. Pope Paul VI was especially concerned that the words of institution should be the same in all Eucharistic Prayers:

TAKE THIS, ALL OF YOU, AND EAT OF IT,
FOR THIS IS MY BODY,
WHICH WILL BE GIVEN UP FOR YOU...

TAKE THIS, ALL OF YOU, AND DRINK FROM IT,
FOR THIS IS THE CHALICE OF MY BLOOD,
THE BLOOD OF THE NEW AND ETERNAL
    COVENANT,
WHICH WILL BE POURED OUT FOR YOU AND
    FOR MANY
FOR THE FORGIVENESS OF SINS.

DO THIS IN MEMORY OF ME.

In each of the four Eucharistic Prayers, the institution narrative is introduced by an allusion to Christ's passion, placing the story of the meal quite clearly into the passion narrative, as is the case in the Gospels. The introduction in the Roman Canon is the simplest, locating the narrative in time, "the day before he suffered." In the second and third Eucharistic Prayers, the institution narrative is introduced by reference to the night in which Jesus was betrayed. It should be observed that the words spoken over the bread, "which will be given up for you," are not found in any of the biblical accounts. They have been added to make them parallel the words over the cup ("which will be poured out for you and for many...").

The reference to "which will be given up"[45] is influenced by the biblical accounts of the Last Supper where the verb "give up" refers to the act of betrayal by the disciple Judas: "At the time he was betrayed" (Eucharistic Prayer II), "For on the night he was betrayed" (Eucharistic Prayer III), and "he gave himself up to death" (Eucharistic Prayer IV). By connotation, however, with the clear sense of Jesus' own willingness to give himself over, the verb "give up" recalls the Father's will in handing over his Son more explicitly than in Eucharistic Prayer I. The Latin word translated "which will be given up" is often used in the New Testament with reference to the Father's handing over of the Son and the Son's handing over of himself. The expression thus enhances the idea that the Church is calling to mind Jesus' voluntary sacrificial death.

We note that there are two changes in wording over the bread in the new Missal: "Take this, all of you and eat of it, for this is my body." In the previous translation it was: "Take this, all of you, and eat it." The prepositional phrase "of it"[46] after "eat" is not found in any of the institution narratives. However, the discourse on the bread of life (John 6:48–51) uses it: "This is the bread that comes down from heaven, so that one may eat *of it* and not die. I am the living bread that came down from heaven. Whoever eats *of this* bread will live forever" (John 6:49, my italics). "Eat of it" expresses the sharing of the bread among "all of you" and parallels the words over the cup, "drink from it."

In the new translation, the word *chalice* is used instead of *cup*. The use of *chalice* here may sound weird, even outmoded, to some people, as it may call to mind images of medieval chalices that were adorned with jewels. It should be noted that the Greek and Latin of all the institution narratives (Matt 26:27; Mark 14:23; Luke 22:20; 1 Cor 11:25) have *poterion* and *calix* respectively. In classical Latin, *calix* meant "cup, goblet, drinking vessel."[47] It should be borne in mind that as far as the biblical narrative is concerned, every modern English version of Scripture uses *cup* where the Vulgate has *calix*. This is the case in the Synoptic accounts of the Last Supper, at the agony in the garden, and in 1 Corinthians 11:25. *Cup* is the ordinary English translation for the term as it appears throughout Scripture.[48] We should note that *cup* is retained in the new translation in the second acclamation following the institution narrative.

Next, there is reference to "the blood of the new and eternal covenant." The word *covenant* translates a word[49] that is used in Latin versions of the Letter to the Hebrews, where the contrast is made between the two covenants and the two kinds of priesthood of these covenants.

Another change is found in the translation "which will be poured out for you and for many," where previously we had "for you and for all (men)." On October 17, 2006, the Congregation for Divine Worship and Discipline of the Sacraments in Rome sent a letter[50] to the presidents of the conferences of bishops regarding the translation of the Latin phrase that had been translated "for all," namely, *pro multis*. It directed them to correct the current translation "for all," because the Latin text says "for many." It affirmed that the phrase "for many" is the exact translation, while "for all" is not a translation but a catechetical explanation of the words Jesus pronounced over the cup.

Concelebrants are required to pronounce the words of consecration. According to the *General Instruction* (218),

> The parts pronounced by all the concelebrants together and especially the words of Consecration, which all are obliged to say, are to be recited in such a manner that the concelebrants speak them in a low voice and that the principal celebrant's voice is heard clearly. In this way the words can be more easily understood by the people.

The stipulation that concelebrants should speak in a very low voice is intended to ensure that their voices do not override that of the principal celebrant, especially if there are many concelebrants.

THE ELEVATION

After the priest has finished saying the words over the bread, he shows the consecrated bread to the people, and after that he does the same with the cup. The elevation of the elements at the consecration is a practice introduced in the thirteenth century that received the approval of the bishop of Paris around the year 1208. At that time, the faithful did not receive Communion frequently. In order to make up for this, they had a great desire to see the sacrament of the Body of Christ. They regarded the elevation as important, for it enabled them to see the sacrament. There was a tendency on the part of some celebrants to perform the elevation in such a way that the congregation might see it more easily. To check this practice, the bishop of Paris issued a decree shortly after 1200: "When priests take the host in their hands as they begin the *Qui pridie*, they are not immediately to elevate it very high so that the congregation can see it. Rather, they are to hold it in front of their breast until they have said the words 'This is my body' and only raise it higher so that all can see it."[51]

The Franciscans were not allowed to elevate the host. This

may have been because it was regarded as a novel French custom. However, it spread very quickly throughout Europe. The elevation of the chalice came later. In England, there is the story of a devout worshipper who cried out to the priest who did not raise the host high enough for him to see it: "Heave it higher, Sir John, heave it higher!" The gesture of elevation should be reverent, but not prolonged, as it might affect the unity and continuity of the Eucharistic Prayer.

The elevation immediately after the Consecration is a solemn *showing* of the consecrated host to the people (*GIRM* 150). Thus, it is not proper to leave the host on the paten at this elevation, for then the people cannot see it. It is also not correct to raise the paten beneath the host, as is sometimes done by some priests. Moreover, it is very important for the priest to take time over these elevations and to ensure that they are done reverently.

According to the *General Instruction*, after the elevation of the host and the chalice, "the Priest genuflects" (*GIRM* 43). The priest's reverential genuflection after the consecration became customary only around 1500. The priest must not replace the genuflection with a bow or some other gesture. After each elevation, the celebrant's genuflection is his affirmation before the community that Christ is now present on the altar under the appearances of bread and wine.

It may not always be possible for a priest to genuflect during consecration. A priest suffering from some physical disability or an ailment, such as arthritis, might find genuflecting very difficult or painful. Instead of genuflecting, he might bow reverently. Canon 930 §1 gives permission to priests who are unable to stand to celebrate Mass seated.

After the elevations, concelebrants bow deeply as the celebrant genuflects. If, for some reason, people have to stand during the consecration, it will be good for them to bow when the celebrant genuflects. Sometimes some celebrants genuflect only once, after the elevation of the chalice. This is not correct. They should genuflect after each elevation.

The deacon should kneel at the consecration. Unfortunately, in some places, deacons remain standing at the consecration. According to the *General Instruction*, "During the Eucharistic Prayer, the Deacon stands near the Priest, but slightly behind him, so that when necessary, he may assist the Priest with the chalice or the Missal. From the epiclesis until the Priest shows the chalice, the Deacon usually remains kneeling..." (*GIRM* 179). According to the *Ceremonial of Bishops*, no. 155, the deacon(s) ministering at the altar must kneel during the consecration. The reason is simple: deacons are not concelebrants. They should kneel at the epiclesis and stand after the elevation of the chalice, that is, after the celebrant genuflects, just before the acclamation. Before he kneels, the deacon removes the pall, if used, and uncovers any ciboria on the altar. However, if there is a good reason why the deacon cannot kneel (for example, physical limitation), then he can stand.

There is no binding rule that a bell should be rung before the institution narrative and during both of the elevations. However, the *General Instruction* explicitly permits it (*GIRM* 150).

One practice that has developed in some places is an organ accompaniment during the recitation of the Eucharistic Prayer. This practice is not acceptable. In responding to the question relating to this practice, the document *Official Interpretations of the General Instruction in the Notices of The Sacred Congregation for Divine Worship and the Discipline of the Sacraments* [1969–1981] quotes the *General Instruction*: "The nature of the 'presidential' parts requires that they be spoken in a loud and clear voice and that everyone listen to them attentively. Therefore, while the Priest is pronouncing them, there should be no other prayers or singing, and the organ or other musical instruments should be silent (*GIRM* 32)."[52]

The response to the query goes on to say:

> This is a clear rule, leaving no room for doubt, since it is a reminder of wrong practices that have greatly impeded and diminished the people's participation in this central part of the Mass. Further, it is obvious that the organ's so-called background music often puts into the background what should be foremost and dominant. A "background" accompaniment of the priest's homily would be out of the question: but in the Eucharistic prayer the word of the presider...reaches the peak of its meaning.

THE MEMORIAL ACCLAMATION

After the elevation of the chalice, the presider says or sings, "The mystery of faith" to which the people respond by saying or singing one of three acclamations. The acclamation is addressed to Christ. In the first two acclamations, the commemoration is given a clear eschatological horizon, while the third is a petition addressed to the Savior. The first acclamation reads as follows: "We proclaim your Death, O Lord, and profess your Resurrection until you come again." This acclamation is based on the anaphora of St. James and is reminiscent of 1 Corinthians 11:26 ("For as often as you eat this bread and drink the cup, you proclaim the Lord's death until he comes"). The second acclamation runs as follows: "When we eat this Bread and drink this Cup, we proclaim your Death, O Lord, until you come again." This acclamation is based more directly on 1 Corinthians 11:26. The third runs as follows: "Save us, Savior of the world, for by your Cross and Resurrection you have set us free."[53]

The memorial acclamation of the people in the Eucharistic Prayer confesses the Church's belief in the central mystery of our faith, the paschal mystery of Christ's death, resurrection, and presence among his people. Each of the three memorial acclamations provided may be used with any of the Eucharistic Prayers. Inserting an acclamation draws upon the practice of the Eastern liturgies to allow for the assembly's intervention in the course of the anaphora (Eucharistic Prayer).

The memorial acclamation is for the people, and so the priest should not join in singing or saying the acclamation. As DeGrocco says in this connection, "Here is another place where the dialogic nature of the Mass should be respected as the Priest and the people each have their distinct parts, not to be confused."[54]

The deacon is not allowed to make this proclamation, as is sometimes done in some churches. These words are strictly meant to be said by the celebrant of the Mass. Pope Paul VI made this clear in the Apostolic Constitution *Missale Romanum*, when he stated that the words *mysterium fidei* ("the mystery of faith") had been moved from the formula of consecrating the wine and were now to be said by the *priest* as an introduction to the acclamation made by the faithful. The rubrics for all the Eucharistic Prayers in the *Order of Mass* clearly indicate that the celebrant sings or says the *mysterium fidei.*

ANAMNESIS

The anamnesis or memorial prayer recapitulates what Jesus has accomplished for us. It is made as a response to the command of Jesus that the meal be celebrated in remembrance of him. The institution narratives of Luke (22:19) and Paul (1 Cor 11:24ff.) repeat Christ's instructions that this meal of his Body and Blood was to be held in the future. The words of institution, which are the same in all the Eucharistic Prayers, repeat this command: "Do this in memory of me." The congregation's acclamations have already remembered with praise and thanks the paschal mystery and Christ's coming again. This happens once again in the following prayer, the name of which is the Greek term *anamnesis.* This Greek word is difficult to translate into English. It has been translated by *memorial, commemoration, remembrance.* All these suggest a recollection of the past, whereas *anamnesis* means making present an object or person from the past.

Sometimes the word *reactualization* has been used to bring out the force of *anamnesis.* In Semitic thought, memorial is a "recalling to God" of a past person or promise. In this section of the Eucharistic Prayer, therefore, we pray that the benefits accruing from Christ's sacrifice, which took place in the past, may be made present to the faithful here and now. This formal remembering before God of the sacrificial life and death of Christ is linked with the offering of the bread and wine, through which the benefits of Christ's sacrifice will be received in Holy Communion. By faithfully taking part in this conceptually detailed remembering (memorial), we encounter repeatedly the presence of the saving love of the triune God. Since the Roman prayers at this point have already petitioned the descent of the Spirit upon the gifts earlier in the prayer, they limit themselves here to a petition for unity among the worshippers who will participate in the gifts.

THE EPICLESIS

We saw earlier that in the ancient Jewish table prayers, the blessing over the cup included a supplication that God should send the Messiah to Israel and restore the Davidic kingdom. Quite naturally, the early Christians included in the Eucharistic Prayer a similar supplication. In the liturgy today, we ask the Father to send the Spirit upon the gifts we offer and upon the Church. This is what is referred to as *epiclesis*. We must point out that both aspects are not always present in each Eucharistic Prayer. Both are found in the Eucharistic Prayers of the Roman Rite today, though they are divided up and placed separately within the prayers.

In these prayers, we find the first epiclesis after the *Sanctus* and before the institution narrative. At this point, the priest extends his hands over the gifts of bread and wine on the altar and prays that the Father will send the Holy Spirit upon them to change them into the Body and Blood of Christ. This is referred to as *consecratory epiclesis*. The second epiclesis comes later, after the anamnesis. Here the presider prays to the Father to send the Holy Spirit upon the Church to strengthen its communion, or oneness. This is called the *epiclesis for unity*.[55]

Already in the *Apostolic Tradition*, the Holy Spirit was invoked on the bread and wine in a petition asking for the unity of those who partook in the celebration. The third-century anaphora of Addai and Mari asks the Holy Spirit to "bless and sanctify" the offering, "that it may be to us for the remission of debts, forgiveness of sins, and the great hope of resurrection from the dead, and new life in the kingdom of heaven, with all who have been pleasing in your sight." In the Syro-Byzantine anaphoras, the epiclesis developed to the point of asking that the Holy Spirit would "make" the bread and wine the Body and Blood of Christ, "changing them by your Holy Spirit" (anaphora of St. John Chrysostom).

The Second Vatican Council saw the need for the role of the Holy Spirit to be more clearly recognized and celebrated in the life of the Church. This was done in the liturgy of the reformed Eucharistic rites, which place the Holy Spirit at the center of the Eucharistic action. The epiclesis is described as being effected through the power of the Holy Spirit, for it is especially by the Holy Spirit that the Church's prayer is efficacious (*GIRM* 79c).

On the importance of the consecratory epiclesis, Hudock says,

Just as the Spirit made Christ present on earth in his Incarnation and raised Christ from the dead into his glorious resurrection; just as the Spirit gave birth at Pentecost to the church, the body of Christ on earth; just as the Spirit compels and fuels the church's ongoing making-present of Christ through the works of evangelization, charity and justice—so we witness in the consecratory epiclesis that the Spirit makes Christ present for us, in a sacramental way, in the elements of bread and wine.[56]

The work of the Holy Spirit does not consist simply in making Christ present in the Eucharistic elements. From its inception, the Church has always seen the Eucharist as being about its unity and it has always seen the Holy Spirit as having a role to play in this. The *General Instruction* recognizes the power of the Holy Spirit in transforming the community when it speaks of the power of the Holy Spirit in enabling the act of receiving Communion "for the salvation of those who will partake of it" (*GIRM* 79c). This particular invocation in the Eucharistic Prayer is known as the "communion epiclesis" and is usually found after the anamnesis and offering in the Roman Rite prayers.[57] Even if the important elements of the consecratory epiclesis and the institution narrative are absent from a Eucharistic Prayer, there is always a prayer for the unity of the Church.

This prayer for the unity of the Church has a good biblical basis in Jesus' prayer for unity in John 17:11. We find the epiclesis for unity in the *Didache* ("Remember, Lord, your church...bring it together from the four winds")[58] and the *Apostolic Tradition* ("send your Holy Spirit upon the offering of your church...gathering her into one").[59] The need for the unity of the Church is also underlined by Paul in his letter to the Corinthian Christians, where he seeks to correct abuses in the celebration of the Eucharist.

In the view of some scholars, Eucharistic Prayer I or the Roman Canon does not have any invocation: it prays that God may accept the gifts and that the gifts may be taken to the heavenly altar. These two portions of the canon, found before and after the words of institution, have made some liturgists speak of a split-epiclesis, which is also found in the Alexandrian anaphoras. However, other scholars are of the view that it is possible to see an epiclesis in Eucharistic Prayer I in the prayer immediately before the institution narrative, even though there is no explicit mention of the Holy Spirit. The thrust of this prayer is that the participants in the Eucharist may receive its fruits. This petition employs the image of the two altars and the twofold movement associated with them: the offering of human beings ascends to God and then comes back in blessing upon those who have gathered for the Eucharistic celebration. This petition uses the daring imagery of the holy angel who will bring the gifts of the offering to the heavenly altar:

> In humble prayer we ask you, almighty God:
> command that these gifts be borne
> by the hands of your holy Angel
> to your altar on high
> in the sight of your divine majesty,
> so that all of us, who through this participation at the
>   altar
> receive the most holy Body and Blood of your Son,
> may be filled with every grace and heavenly blessing.

The angel mentioned here has a mediatorial role in worship. In the Old Testament, God is presented as surrounded by countless angels (cf. Dan 7). They, especially Michael, intercede with God. They convey prayers from all synagogues to God, and set them like crowns upon his head. Tobit 12:12 also bears witness to the mediatorial function of the angels in prayer. In the Book of Revelation, we read, "Another angel with a golden censer came and stood at the altar; he was given a great quantity of incense to offer with the prayers of all the saints on the golden altar that is before the throne. And the smoke of the incense, with the prayers of the saints, rose before God from the hand of the angel" (Rev 8:3–4). In this connection, Mazza remarks,

> We ought also to keep in mind that persons possessing
> a profound sense of the divine transcendence find it dif-
> ficult to think of direct contact with God; they prefer to
> have suitable mediators. The very concept of "angel"
> as mediator between God and human beings or even
> among human beings very nicely solves the problem.[60]

In this connection, we can safely say that angels bridge a spatial distance between God and humankind and bring their prayers to God. The angel mentioned in Eucharistic Prayer I fulfills such a function.

COMMEMORATION OF THE DEAD

> Remember also, Lord, your servants N. and N.,
> who have gone before us with the sign of faith
> and rest in the sleep of peace.
> Grant them, O Lord, we pray,
> and all who sleep in Christ,
> a place of refreshment, light and peace.

In this prayer, there are two commemorations. The first is of the dead, the second of the ministers of the present liturgy. The sign of faith with which the faithful have gone before us is baptism,[61] and the "sleep of peace" is the sleep of death, which does not interrupt the communion of the dead with the Church. They now "rest in Christ" and their state is one of "peace." We pray that God will give them "a place of refreshment, light and peace."

COMMEMORATION OF THE LIVING

> To us, also, your servants, who, though sinners,
> hope in your abundant mercies,
> graciously grant some share
> and fellowship with your holy Apostles and Martyrs:
> with John the Baptist, Stephen,
> Matthias, Barnabas,
>   (Ignatius, Alexander,
>   Marcellinus, Peter,
>   Felicity, Perpetua,
>   Agatha, Lucy,
>   Agnes, Cecilia, Anastasia)
> and all your Saints:
> admit us, we beseech you,
> into their company,
> not weighing our merits,
> but granting us your pardon,
> through Christ our Lord.

The second commemoration does not refer to the whole congregation as sinful. In this prayer, intercession is made for the leaders of the Christian community who because of their sins do not feel worthy to carry out their functions. A passage with a similar sentiment is the Anaphora of St. Mark: "Be mindful also, Lord, of us sinners, your unworthy servants, and, being a good and kindly God, wipe away our sins. Be mindful also, Lord, of me, a poor sinner and your unworthy servant."[62] The Roman Canon asks that the sinfulness of the ministers may not prevent their communion with the holy apostles and martyrs whose names are mentioned.

Eucharistic Prayer II

Eucharistic Prayer II begins with the words

You are indeed Holy, O Lord,
the fount of all holiness.

The words "indeed Holy" link this passage with the *Sanctus* and reassert the divine attribute. The text goes on to say that God is "the fountain of all holiness." God is the source of all holiness.

Eucharistic Prayer II has a two-fold epiclesis. The first one is found in the words

Make holy, therefore, these gifts, we pray,
by sending down your Spirit upon them like the
  dewfall,
so that they may become for us
the Body and Blood of our Lord, Jesus Christ.

In this Eucharistic Prayer, there is a movement from the holiness of God who is the source of all holiness to the sanctification of the gifts through the Holy Spirit.

The best-known case for the use of dew as a metaphor of divine action is that of Isaiah 45:8, "Let justice descend, you heavens, like dew from above, like gentle rain let the clouds drop it down" (NABRE). In Palestine, people greatly appreciate dew; it makes up for the rain that does not fall for half a year. Lack of dew is regarded as a disaster and a curse. Dew is an image for prosperity because it makes the soil fruitful. In Hosea 14:5, we read, "I will be like the dew to Israel; he shall blossom like the lily, he shall strike root like the forests of Lebanon." This means that God will be a source of grace on which all growth and development will depend. Deuteronomy 32:2 compares the effect of Moses' teaching in God's name to dew on the grass: "May my teaching drop like the rain, my speech condense like the dew; like gentle rain on grass, like showers on new growth." Dew here is an image of reawakening life. The use of dew in connection with the Holy Spirit in Eucharistic Prayer II "conjures up an image of the Spirit resting on the gifts as dew rests on the grass, as it is said that the Spirit comes upon or rests or remains on the Son."[63]

After the institution narrative and the acclamation, we have the words

> Therefore, as we celebrate
> the memorial of his Death and Resurrection,
> we offer you, Lord,
> the Bread of life and the Chalice of salvation,
> giving thanks that you have held us worthy
> to be in your presence and minister to you.

These words borrow from Eucharistic Prayer I the words "the Bread of life and the Chalice of salvation." The offering spoken of here is the memorial offering of the Church, the offering with thanksgiving of the bread and wine so that it is the sacrament of Christ's offering and of the Church's self-offering in and with him.

The question may be asked as to who makes the offering in the words "you have held us worthy to be in your presence and minister to you." In ecclesiastical Latin, the word translated as "to minister"[64] stands for any service offered for the worship of the Church. However, the text of the *Apostolic Tradition* would seem to point to the priestly service of the ordained. Nevertheless, "A proper grasp of the minister's service does not exclude the congregation in whose name the priest prays through the Son."[65]

Next, we have the words

> Humbly we pray
> that, partaking of the Body and Blood of Christ,
> we may be gathered into one by the Holy Spirit.

These are the words of the second epiclesis, which asks that all may be gathered or congregated as one in the sharing of the one bread and the one cup, thus highlighting a desire for communion and unity. These two themes—transformation of the gifts and the unity of the Church—reflect the vital role that the Holy Spirit plays in the Eucharist.

The intercessions, which are in three distinct sections, follow. First, there is the introductory prayer for the Church:

> Remember, Lord, your Church,
> spread throughout the world,
> and bring her to the fullness of charity,
> together with N. our Pope and N. our Bishop*
> and all the clergy.

This intercession commends to God the Church spread throughout the world, specifically mentioning the pope, the local bishop, and all the clergy. The use of the personal pronoun *her* for something like the Church is not usual in contemporary English, but in this context, it is meant to evoke images of the Church as our mother and the bride of Christ.[66]

The second section is the intercession for the dead:

> Remember also our brothers and sisters
> who have fallen asleep in the hope of the resurrection,
> and all who have died in your mercy:
> welcome them into the light of your face.

This remembrance of the dead includes both those who have died in the explicit hope of the resurrection and all those who have died in God's mercy. We ask that God will welcome them into the light. Here we have a strong anthropomorphic image of "the light of your [God's] face."

The third section is devoted to the living; the Church prays that they will have happiness at the end: "Have mercy on us all, we pray...." It is at this point that commemoration is made of Mary, the Virgin Mother of God, of the holy apostles, and all the saints "who have pleased you throughout the ages," an expression characteristic of the East. Finally, there is the remembrance and contemplation of the saints who are living in the vision of God and who contemplate the light of his face, that is, his "glory."

Eucharistic Prayer III

The first part of this prayer reads,

> You are indeed Holy, O Lord,
> and all you have created
> rightly gives you praise,
> for through your Son our Lord Jesus Christ,
> by the power and working of the Holy Spirit,
> you give life to all things and make them holy,
> and you never cease to gather a people to yourself,
> so that from the rising of the sun to its setting
> a pure sacrifice may be offered to your name.

The opening sentence speaks of the Lord as being "holy." The next few paragraphs contain four points. First, the work of God is described in trinitarian terms. The Son is the mediator, while the Spirit makes his work effective. Second, the Lord is said to "give life to all things and make them holy." Life and holiness are God's gifts mentioned here. The statement has a cosmic perspective. Third, there is an ecclesial dimension: "You never cease to gather a people to yourself." God gathers people to or around himself. He is in the midst of a people that he himself has gathered. Next, we have a passage that speaks of a pure sacrifice being offered to God "from the rising of the sun to its setting." This passage is taken from Malachi 1:11 and states that the worship of God will be universal.

In Eucharistic Prayer III, the two-fold epiclesis surrounds the institution narrative. The first one asks God to transform the bread and the wine into the Body and Blood of Christ by the power of the Holy Spirit:

> Therefore, O Lord, we humbly implore you:
> by the same Spirit graciously make holy
> these gifts we have brought to you for consecration,
> that they may become the Body and ✠ Blood
> of your Son our Lord Jesus Christ.

The Liturgy of the Eucharist and the Concluding Rites

While the priest is saying these words, he brings together his hands with the palms downward and extended over the elements to be consecrated. This action vividly portrays the life-giving power of the Spirit, who moved over the waters in the first days of creation and overshadowed Mary at the moment of the Incarnation. This is a laying on of hands and is the same sacramental gesture that is used in ordination, confirmation, the anointing of the sick, and the sacrament of reconciliation. In line with ancient tradition, if there are concelebrating priests, they stretch out *both* hands toward the elements (*GIRM* 59a). According to the *Ceremonial of Bishops* (no. 106), "The bishop and the concelebrants hold their hands outstretched over the offerings in Mass at the epiclesis before the consecration." If, however, a priest is holding a booklet containing the Eucharistic Prayers in one hand, then he can stretch out the other hand. The last words of the first epiclesis asking for the change of the elements are accompanied by two gestures of blessing: the priest joins his hands, extends them over the gifts, and blesses them by making the Sign of the Cross.

The second epiclesis prays that God may grant the Church a life of communion in Christ through the power of the Holy Spirit:

> Look, we pray, upon the oblation of your Church
> and, recognizing the sacrificial Victim by whose death
> you willed to reconcile us to yourself,
> grant that we, who are nourished
> by the Body and Blood of your Son
> and filled with his Holy Spirit,
> may become one body, one spirit in Christ.

The epiclesis in this prayer could be said to be only a quasi-epiclesis since it does not directly ask for the Holy Spirit but rather that the people, filled with the Holy Spirit, may be made one through the sacrament. The reference to the Spirit occurs within the intercessions for the Church.[67]

In Eucharistic Prayer III, the intercessions are in two parts. They begin with a commemoration of the Church in heaven:

> May he make of us
> an eternal offering to you,

so that we may obtain an inheritance with your elect,
especially with the most Blessed Virgin Mary, Mother
   of God,
with blessed Joseph, her Spouse,
with your blessed Apostles and glorious Martyrs...
and with all the Saints

For the dead, the church asks that they, as a perfect gift, may receive their inheritance "with the elect." The "elect" are usually the already blessed, but the term harkens back to baptism, the candidates for which are called the elect, and the Church itself is called a "chosen race," borrowing from 1 Peter 2:9. The prayer then turns to a commemoration of the entire Church, which is God's "pilgrim Church on earth."

The prayer for the Church and the world is introduced by reference to the victim of reconciliation. What is sought through this victim offered for our reconciliation is peace and charity in episcopal communion. In the tradition of the Roman Eucharistic Prayers, peace often means freedom from external interferences that would disrupt the life and worship of Christians. Thus, it is associated (as in the embolism to the Lord's Prayer) with freedom from "distress,"[68] that is, external incursions that would hinder the freedom of religion or religious practice.[69] In the interests of such peace among the peoples of this world, the Church needs to remain in a communion of faith and charity, promoted by communion with the pope and the episcopal order. It is for this reason that at this point mention is made here of the pope and the local bishop.

Eucharistic Prayer IV

Eucharistic Prayer IV draws heavily on the tradition of the Eastern Church (the Apostolic Constitutions of Antioch and the Byzantine Liturgy of St. Basil). It contains a preface that is never changed and, beginning at this point, extends the thanksgiving in praise of God's acts of salvation through the *Sanctus* to the paschal mystery of Christ and the sending of the Holy Spirit. It then moves on through the epiclesis of the Holy Spirit to the account of the institution of the sacrament.

In Eucharistic Prayer IV, the first epiclesis comes only after a long account of what God has done in salvation history and the mention of the Holy Spirit at Pentecost:

> Therefore, O Lord, we pray:
> may this same Holy Spirit
> graciously sanctify these offerings,
> that they may become
> the Body and Blood of our Lord Jesus Christ

The second epiclesis specifically addresses the unity of the Church and the transformation of the communicants into a living sacrifice. The play on words is Pauline, relating Communion from the one bread and the one cup to gathering those who partake into one body and one sacrifice in Christ.

The intercessions in Eucharistic Prayer IV are similar to those in Eucharistic Prayer I and II. However, Eucharistic Prayer IV differs from them in one way, namely the extension of the Church's concern beyond its own boundaries to include all the living who seek God with sincere hearts and all the dead who, in ways known to God alone, may have lived some form of faith. The prayer speaks of

> those gathered here before you,
> your entire people,
> and all who seek you with a sincere heart.

It continues: "Remember also those who have died in the peace of your Christ and all the dead, whose faith you alone have known."

The final petition is for all present and for all the Father's children, asking for them inheritance with the saints. This petition concludes in the same vein as that in which the prayer began, asking that these children may glorify God with all creatures in God's kingdom, through Christ whom he dispenses every good.

THE DOXOLOGY

In line with the Jewish way of praying found at the time of Jesus and his disciples, the Eucharistic Prayer concludes where it began, by ascribing praise and glory to God. This prayer is known as the *Doxology*, a short prayer of praise that is formulated to stress Jesus' role as mediator in the context of the Trinity. The Doxology sums up all the themes of the Eucharistic Prayer in a proclamation of God's name. Everything belongs to the Father. All honor and glory ascend to him in a Christ-centered movement that is expressed by means of three prepositions: "through, with, in." Our celebration has value and meaning because it is centered on Christ. The glory and honor go to him "in the unity of the Holy Spirit" for two reasons. The first is that the only acceptable worship is that in Spirit and in truth; the second is that the unity of God comes to us through that same Spirit.

The congregation ratifies the prayer by saying or singing *Amen*, often called the "Great Amen," as it comes after the Great Thanksgiving. Through Christ, with him, and in him, all is turned to the Father's glory by the action of the Holy Spirit. At the climax of the prayer, the consecrated elements are raised high.

During the recitation of the Doxology, the principal celebrant and the deacon hold up the consecrated bread and wine, each in its own vessel—the bread on the plate, the wine in the cup (*GIRM* 180). When there is a deacon—the traditional minister of the cup—he stands next to the priest and lifts up the cup during the Doxology. The priest takes the paten with the consecrated bread and lifts it up while singing or saying the Doxology. After the people have finished the *Amen*, the paten and chalice are placed again on the altar. If there is no deacon, a concelebrating priest may lift up the cup, but only one paten and one cup should be lifted during the Doxology. The author has seen instances where all the vessels containing the consecrated bread and wine are distributed among concelebrating priests! This is liturgically improper. The practice seems to arise from a sincere desire to "involve" all the concelebrants and "give them something to do." Only one chalice and one paten should be lifted up. Additional chalices and ciboria should remain on the altar even if there are many deacons or concelebrants at the celebration. If there is no deacon (or concelebrant), the priest holds both the paten and the chalice.

The elevation of the consecrated bread and wine during the Doxology is one of the oldest gestures of the Eucharistic Prayer in the Roman tradition. The elevation of the elements in the Mass today traces its origin to the seventh-century practice at papal Masses in Rome, in which a deacon would hold up the chalice and the pope would lift two loaves of bread. This gesture must be understood as an offering of the consecrated bread and wine to God rather than as a showing of these elements to the people. As the Eucharistic Prayer comes to an end, the presiding priest proclaims that "all glory and honor" is given "through...with... and in" Christ to our Almighty Father, and that this lifting up of "all glory and honor" through Christ to God is shown in gesture by the lifting up of the consecrated elements. At the Doxology of the Eucharistic Prayer, we make a solemn sign of *offering* the Body and Blood of Christ to the Father in the Holy Spirit, as the text proclaims: "Through Him, with Him, in Him..." For this reason, the consecrated host should be *on* the paten and *must not be shown to the people*, as at the consecration. Thus, it is not liturgically proper to hold the host vertically over the chalice, as some celebrants do. At this point, the Body and Blood of Christ should be raised significantly higher than is done at the preparation of the gifts.

The Doxology of the Eucharistic Prayer still forms part of the presidential prayer, and thus should be said by the presiding priest *alone*, although at concelebrations, the concelebrants *may* join him, but are not obliged to do so (cf. *GIRM* 236). That this part of the Eucharistic Prayer should be said by the priest(s) was restated by the 1980 Instruction *Inaestimabile Donum*, which says, "The doxology itself is reserved to the priest" (no. 4). Earlier in the document we read, "It is therefore an abuse to have some parts of the Eucharistic Prayer said by the deacon, by a lower minister or by the faithful." The *General Instruction* explicitly states the same prohibition (*GIRM* 236). In spite of these prohibitions, the faithful (sometimes at the priest's invitation) join the celebrant in reciting the Doxology. However, as Pecklers notes, this prohibition "is not an attempt at clericalism or to deny the lay faithful their right to participate, but rather a matter of good liturgical sense."[70] He draws attention to what Justin Martyr says in his *First Apology* (AD 150) about the importance of the people's great "Amen" as a grand assent to all that the presider had proclaimed in the Eucharistic Prayer. It is obvious that the "Amen" loses its vigor if there is no one to proclaim it.[71]

When the priest finishes saying the doxology, the congregation endorses and ratifies the ascription of praise to God by saying the *Amen*. For St. Paul, this ratification by the assembly was essential to the thanksgiving prayer (cf. 1 Cor 14:15–16), and early Christian writers put great emphasis on it as the people's confirmation of all that was proclaimed on their behalf by the priest. At the very least, the *Amen* should be sung or spoken loudly both at Sunday Masses and at simpler weekday Masses.

At the end of the Eucharistic Prayer, the priest should make a clear pause to show that the Eucharistic Prayer (the "thanksgiving") is over and that the Communion rite (the "breaking and sharing") is about to begin.

Communion Rite

Apart from what St. Paul says to the Corinthian Christian community about the need to refrain from eating and drinking before the communal celebration of the Lord's Supper, our earliest evidence for the Communion rite comes from Justin Martyr's *First Apology* (ca. 150). Describing the Eucharist that follows a baptism, he says,

> And when the presider has given thanks, and all the people have assented, those whom we call deacons give to each of those present a portion of the bread and wine and water over which thanks have been given, and take them to those who are not present.[72]

In the same *First Apology*, we find another description of the Eucharist that takes place on a Sunday:

> The elements over which thanks have been given are distributed, and everyone partakes; and they are sent through the deacons to those who are not present.[73]

The Communion rite in the Mass begins with the Lord's Prayer and ends with the Prayer after Communion.

THE LORD'S PRAYER

After the Doxology, the priest introduces the Lord's Prayer. The Missal offers only one option for this introduction and does not state that other similar words might be used. This means that the exact formula should be used.

The Lord's Prayer was not part of the Eucharistic liturgy before the middle of the fourth century at the earliest. Indeed, there is an echo of the exhortation introducing the Lord's Prayer ("At the savior's command and formed by divine teaching we dare to say") in Cyprian of Carthage's *Commentary on the Lord's Prayer* written in 258:

> Among the saving commandments and divine teaching that the Lord has left us for the salvation of his people, he has included a formula of prayer; he himself has taught us what we should ask for.

However, it is not certain that Cyprians's words refer to the Mass. The first clearly attested use of the prayer was in the late fourth-century *Mystagogical Catecheses* of Cyril of Jerusalem.[74] Since what took place in Jerusalem at this time was probably typical of the ancient Church as a whole, it is likely that the Lord's Prayer was a part of the Eucharistic liturgy and, together with the Creed, was one of the elements of instruction given to catechumens just before or immediately after their baptism.

Starting with John Chrysostom, liturgical commentators in the East spoke of praying the Lord's Prayer as a preparation for Communion. In the West, both Ambrose and Augustine also saw it as a preparation for Communion. From about 400 on, the Lord's Prayer has occupied a place in the Communion rites in Eucharistic celebrations.

The revised Roman Rite also sees this prayer as a preparation for Communion. In doing this, it affirms the link between daily bread and the Eucharistic bread received in holiness through the forgiveness of sin asked for in the Lord's Prayer. When Christians say this prayer, they affirm God's sovereignty and humankind's dependence on God's initiative. When believers say the Lord's Prayer, they admit their sin and the need for forgiveness from both

God and man. They express confidence in God's forgiveness in the face of evil, and express belief in the power of love that overcomes all evil.

The Lord's Prayer expresses confidence that the age of salvation is now being realized. This prayer contains the conviction that God's reign is already established, that God's presence breaks into human life in the present. Praying with childlike confidence and trusting that God will provide daily bread and forgive our sins is itself a manifestation of the kingdom of God for which believers pray.

In the Mass today, the whole congregation says or sings the Lord's Prayer after the priest introduces it, saying, "At the Savior's command and formed by divine teaching, we dare to say." During the recitation of the Lord's Prayer, the celebrant is required to extend his hands, as are concelebrants.[75] Members of the congregation may also extend their hands during the Lord's Prayer. Indeed, more and more lay people extend their hands during the recitation of the Lord's Prayer and it is probably time for Rome to authorize this gesture among the faithful. This would be in line with an early Christian custom. Frescoes in the Roman catacombs portray Christians with their hands raised in the *orantes* or *precantes* position.

There are two versions of the prayer in the New Testament. In Matthew (6:9–13), the prayer comes in the midst of the Sermon on the Mount, as one example of the authentic piety, along with almsgiving and fasting, that is to characterize the disciple of Jesus. In Luke (11:2–4), it introduces a longer instruction on prayer triggered by the disciples' request, "Lord, teach us to pray, as John taught his disciples" (11:1). Matthew's prayer is longer, consisting of the address ("Our Father in heaven") and seven petitions; Luke has the address ("Father") and five petitions.

In some manuscripts, Matthew's version, after the words "and do not subject us to the final test, but deliver us from the evil one," includes the doxology,[76] "For thine is the kingdom, the power and the glory for ever and ever, Amen." In the Catholic Church, the form of the Lord's Prayer that is used does not contain the doxology, whereas most Protestant churches use the form with the doxology. It is not found in Luke, in most of the early Church fathers, and in most modern texts and translations. It would be incorrect, however, to conclude from this that the Lord's Prayer was used without some concluding words of praise to God. Given the Jewish custom of concluding prayers with a doxology, it is unlikely that Jesus composed a prayer without one. The habit was already established in the Old Testament times (cf. Pss 41:13; 72:18–19). Nevertheless, the best and most important manuscripts do not have the doxology. Thus, judging by the weight of the textual evidence, "deliver us from the evil one" was the original conclusion of the Lord's Prayer in Matthew. This is confirmed by the Lucan text, which likewise has no doxology.

Perhaps the best solution is the suggestion that in Judaism there existed two ways of ending a prayer, a fixed conclusion and a conclusion composed freely by the supplicant called the "seal." According to this view, the Lord's Prayer originally was a prayer with a "seal," that is, with a freely formulated conclusion. It is possible that in early Church worship services, the leader formulated the doxology, and when, after some time, one doxology was accepted as the standard, it entered the textual tradition of Matthew. The doxology probably did not form part of the original prayer, but came to be added when the prayer was used liturgically in the various churches. It was added to the Lord's Prayer no later than the second century. The *Didache* adds a shorter doxology, "for thine is the power and the glory forever." The doxology is also found in the Byzantine, Anglican, and most Protestant rites of the Eucharist. Since in the Catholic Church the Lord's Prayer ends without the doxology, its addition to the Roman Rite (after the embolism) may have been inspired by ecumenical motives.[77]

It has been suggested that the doxology is based on 1 Chronicles 29:11, "Yours, O Lord, are the greatness, the power, the glory, the victory, and the majesty; for all that is in the heavens and on the earth is yours; yours is the kingdom, O Lord, and you are exalted as head above all."

In many places, members of the congregation hold hands during the recitation the Lord's Prayer during Mass. This gesture is not known to the Roman Rite. One objection to it is that it is not appropriate for prayer. Holding hands is not a traditional gesture of prayer. On the contrary, it is seen as a gesture of love and solidarity. It may be done by a young couple attending Mass together or by a group of people trying to establish unity.

If it seems necessary to include such a gesture, perhaps the *orans* posture, which has been used in Christian prayer for over two thousand years, should be used. It should be noted that in the revised Italian sacramentary, the whole congregation is allowed to extend their hands during the recitation of the Lord's Prayer in this ancient gesture.

THE EMBOLISM

The Lord's Prayer is followed by a prayer called the *embolism*, said by the priest alone. This is the English version of a Greek word meaning "insertion." It begins "Deliver us, Lord, we pray, from every evil...." It develops the final request of the Lord's Prayer, "...deliver us from evil," and petitions, in the name of the entire community, deliverance from the power of evil. The assembly concludes the embolism with the doxology to the Lord's Prayer, "For the kingdom, the power and the glory are yours...."

THE RITE OF PEACE

After the doxology to the Lord's Prayer, we have the Rite of Peace. On its meaning, DeGrocco says,

> First, the Church asks the Lord for peace and unity for herself and for the whole human family; second, the members of the assembly express their union of mutual charity to each other. Both aspects express important links to the Holy Communion which is about to occur – the Sacrament of unity cannot be worthily received if the recipient is not in loving communion with his or her brothers and sisters in the Body of Christ.[78]

The Rite of Peace was a universal practice in the early Church, one described in the *Apostolic Constitutions*:

> Let the bishop greet the congregation with the words: "May the peace of Christ be with all of you." And the entire congregation is to respond, "And with your spirit." The deacon then says to all: "Greet one another with a

holy kiss." Let the clergy then embrace the bishop, laymen, laywomen.[79]

In the Roman tradition, this practice eventually found its place after
the Lord's Prayer, whose themes of mutual forgiveness it echoes.

What is the biblical basis for this practice? In some of the
postresurrection appearances of Christ, the risen Lord greeted his
disciples with the words "Peace be with you" (John 20:19, 21, 26).
The Gospel of John records that the night before Christ died, he
prayed for unity (John 17:11) and gave his gift of peace to his disciples (John 14:27). Paul in his letters entreats Christians to greet
each other with "a holy kiss" (see Rom 16:16; 1 Cor 16:20; 2 Cor
13:12; 1 Thess 5:26). In 1 Peter 5:14, Christians are asked to greet
each other with "a holy kiss."

In most traditions, the ritual kiss takes place before the Presentation of the Gifts and is understood to point to that mutual
love and reconciliation that Jesus said was necessary before the
offering of sacrifice (see Matt 5:23).

The *General Instruction* specifies that the priest should
remain in the sanctuary in order not to disturb the celebration:
"The Priest may give the Sign of Peace to the ministers but always
remains within the sanctuary, so that the celebration is not dis-
rupted" (*GIRM* 154). In the dioceses of the United States, however, on special occasions, for example, in the case of a funeral, a
wedding, or when civic leaders are present, the priest may offer the
Sign of Peace to a few of the faithful near the sanctuary (*GIRM*
154). According to the *Ceremonial of Bishops* (no. 102), a deacon
or concelebrant at a Pontifical Mass goes and gives the Sign of
Peace to the Head of State, when he officially attends Mass.

According to the *General Instruction*, "It is appropriate that
each person, in a sober manner, offer the sign of peace only to
those who are nearest" (*GIRM* 82). In the light of this, it is not
proper for people to go and give the Sign of Peace to people in
faraway pews.

The *General Instruction* states that the priest "*may* give the
Sign of Peace to the ministers" (*GIRM* 154; my italics). This indicates that it is optional. However, it is strongly recommended to
have the Sign of Peace at every Mass. It is clear that it is to be given
during the solemn celebration of Mass by the bishop.[80] It may be

deduced from this that it is obligatory at all solemn Eucharistic celebrations.

The actual sign to be used during the Rite of Peace is left to the local bishops' conference to decide, since it will vary from place to place according to local customs and culture. In many places, the mode of giving the Sign of Peace is by shaking hands.

Regarding the placement of the Sign of Peace, we note that in 2005, members of the Synod of Bishops on the Eucharist adopted a formal proposition questioning whether the Sign of Peace might be better placed elsewhere in the Mass, for example, at the end of the Prayer of the Faithful and before the offering of the gifts. As we read in Pope Benedict XVI's post-synodal apostolic exhortation, *Sacramentum Caritatis,*

> Taking into account ancient and venerable customs and the wishes expressed by the Synod Fathers, I have asked the competent curial offices to study the possibility of moving the sign of peace to another place, such as before the presentation of the gifts at the altar.[81]

The pope said further, "During the Synod of Bishops there was discussion about the appropriateness of greater restraint in this gesture, which can be exaggerated and cause a certain distraction in the assembly just before the reception of Communion."[82]

An inspiration for the suggested change to the placement of the Sign of Peace was Christ's exhortation in Matthew 5:23–24, "So when you are offering your gift at the altar, if you remember that your brother or sister has something against you, leave your gift there before the altar and go; first be reconciled to your brother or sister, and then come and offer your gift." This suggested change would also have brought the Roman Rite into conformity, in that respect, with the Ambrosian Rite celebrated in Milan.

After studying the matter, the Congregation for Divine Worship and the Discipline of Sacraments in 2008 asked bishops' conferences around the world whether to keep the Sign of Peace where it is or move it to another place.

Finally, the *Circular Letter on the Ritual Expression of the Gift of Peace at Mass* published by the Congregation for Divine

Worship and the Discipline of Sacraments on July 12, 2014, made a definitive statement on this matter. The letter notes that in some Catholic liturgical traditions the exchange of peace occurs before the offering in response to Jesus' exhortation in Matthew 5:23–24 quoted above. It says, however, that in the Latin Rite, the exchange of peace comes after the consecration because it refers to "the 'Paschal kiss' of the risen Christ present on the altar." It comes just before the breaking of the bread during which "the Lamb of God is implored to give us his peace."

The letter adds, "After further reflection, it was considered appropriate to retain the Rite of Peace in its traditional place in the Roman liturgy and not to introduce structural changes in the Roman Missal." The letter says that this position "does not exclude the need for new or renewed efforts to explain the importance of the sign of peace so that the faithful understand it and participate in it correctly." The letter asked bishops to study whether it might be time to find "more appropriate gestures" to replace a Sign of Peace that use "familiar and profane gestures of greeting." It said that bishops should do everything possible to end "abuses" such as

- "The introduction of a 'song for peace', which is nonexistent in the Roman rite"
- "The movement of the faithful from their places to exchange the sign of peace amongst themselves"
- "The departure of the priest from the altar in order to give the sign of peace to some of the faithful"
- "People using the sign of peace in certain circumstances, such as at the Solemnity of Easter or of Christmas, or during ritual celebrations such as Baptism, First Communion, Confirmation, Matrimony, Sacred Ordinations, Religious Professions, and Funerals, to offer holiday greetings, congratulations or condolences"

The letter invites bishops' conferences to prepare liturgical catecheses on the meaning of the Rite of Peace in the Roman liturgy and its proper realization in the celebration of the Holy Mass.

THE RITE OF BREAKING THE BREAD (FRACTION)

After the Rite of Peace, the priest breaks the large host into several pieces. This is what Jesus did at the Last Supper, as we see in all the institution narratives. He took bread, said the prayer of thanks, broke the bread, and gave it to the disciples. For the early Church, this act was very symbolic. St. Paul gave a catechesis on the rite: "The bread that we break, is it not a sharing in the body of Christ? Because there is one bread, we who are many are one body, for we all partake of the one bread" (1 Cor 10:16b–17). The *General Instruction* speaks of this unity when it says, "The gesture of breaking bread done by Christ at the Last Supper, which in apostolic times gave the entire Eucharistic Action its name, signifies that the many faithful are made one body (1 Cor 10:17) by receiving Communion from the one Bread of Life, which is Christ, who for the salvation of the world died and rose again" (*GIRM* 83).

The act of breaking the Eucharistic bread is carried out by the presider, "with the assistance, if the case requires, of the Deacon or a concelebrant" (*GIRM* 83). The *General Instruction* reiterates that participation in the fraction "is reserved to the Priest and the Deacon" (*GIRM* 83).

However, when small hosts were introduced in the twelfth century, the practice of breaking of the bread virtually ended. The priest only broke the larger host into three unequal parts and put the smallest piece into the chalice. He consumed the two larger pieces in his own Communion. Because of this, the symbolism of the one bread was lost. The reform of the Mass carried out under Pope Paul VI tried to restore it by having the priest break one or more large hosts into small pieces and distribute them to at least a few of the faithful. This should be done especially in concelebrated Masses and in Masses for smaller groups, wedding Masses, and for confirmation. Then at least the newly confirmed should receive pieces of the broken bread.

ANTICIPATING THE FRACTION

Some celebrants break the host during the Eucharistic Prayer while saying the words, "He broke the bread, gave it to his disciples...". This is liturgically incorrect. It should be observed that in the Liturgy of the Eucharist, there are four distinct stages: (1) Jesus *took bread and wine* (the Preparation of the Gifts); (2) He *gave thanks* and so blessed the bread and wine (the Eucharistic Prayer); (3) He *broke the bread* that had become his Body (the fraction); (4) He *gave* his Body and Blood to the apostles (the Communion Rite). Breaking the host during the Eucharistic Prayer telescopes together two distinct actions in the Liturgy of the Eucharist— *blessing* and *breaking*. As Smolarski says, "In the liturgy of the Eucharist, we do not dramatically reenact the Last Supper scene but rather liturgically remember what occurs and incorporate the verbs into the structure of our worship."[83] It also damages the structure of the liturgy. Similarly, Ralph A. Kiefer says,

> Breaking the host at the institution narrative is an abuse because the narrative is mainly a recital of why we celebrate the Eucharist (because this is the way the Lord Jesus has given us to regularly share together and celebrate his presence and power to transform us), not a demonstration of what we do at Eucharist. If the narrative were a demonstration of what we do, it would be appropriate not only to break the bread, but also to eat it at that point, and, the words having been said over the cup, to share that at this point also. The institution narrative is not designed to be a liturgical show-and-tell. It is designed, rather, to say that we celebrate the Eucharist because it is the memorial of the Lord.[84]

THE *AGNUS DEI* (LAMB OF GOD)

The *Agnus Dei* is sung or said during the breaking of the bread. The singing of the *Agnus Dei* was introduced at the end of the seventh century by a Syrian pope, Sergius I (d. 701). It calls on Jesus as the Lamb of God (see John 1:29, 36) who has conquered sin and death (see 1 Peter 1:18; Rev 5:6; 13:18). The *Agnus Dei* is a litany-song intended to accompany the action of breaking and may therefore be prolonged by repetition. The breaking of the bread should not begin before the *Agnus Dei* has started. If it is necessary to have additional vessels for the distribution of Communion, they may be brought to the altar at this point. The consecrated bread is then divided among the plates or dishes. If special ministers are to assist at Communion, it is desirable that they come to the altar after the exchange of peace, in order to assist with the preparation of the vessels and the Eucharistic elements.

THE RITE OF COMMINGLING

During the breaking of the bread and the recitation or singing of the *Agnus Dei*, the priest puts a bit of the consecrated bread (called the *fermentum*) into the chalice. This is what is referred to as "commingling." This action has had various meanings.[85]

1. The Fermentum

At Rome and in other Episcopal churches in the West, the *fermentum*, a consecrated particle of the Eucharistic bread, was sent to surrounding presbyteral churches to be placed in the cup during their Eucharistic liturgies as a sign of the Communion of local churches with their bishop.[86] In the second century, popes sent the Eucharist to other bishops as a pledge of unity of faith, this being the origin of the expression to be *in communion* with each other. In Rome, priests were obliged on Sundays to celebrate Mass for their congregations in their own churches (the "titles") and therefore could not take part in the solemn papal Mass. A sign was used, however, to bring out the unity of the one Christian community. Pope Innocent I wrote of this in 416 in a letter to Bishop Decentius of Gubbio:

> With regard to the *fermentum* [literally: *leaven*] which we send on Sundays to the various "titles"....The priests of those churches cannot join us in celebrating on that day because they must take care of their own people; therefore acolytes bring them the *fermentum* which we have consecrated, so that on that day, of all days, they may not feel separated from communion with us.[87]

Bishops of other cities did something similar. The priests placed this piece of the host in the chalice during the next celebration of the Mass. This was a sign of brotherhood with the pope (or the bishop) and a symbol of oneness of Christ's sacrifice. However, we do not know just when this custom was introduced. Moreover, after the seventh century, it was retained only at the Easter Vigil.

2. *The* Sancta

After the Eucharistic liturgy was finished, some of the consecrated bread was kept in order to give Communion to the dying. This portion of bread was known as the *Sancta*. The bread was brought up and presented to the pope who "greeted" it at the beginning of the celebration and approved the quantity as adequate; the bread was then entrusted to a subdeacon and placed in the chalice after the Lord's Prayer. The action was thus seemingly the same as that performed by a priest who received the *fermentum* in his own church.

3. A Sign of Resurrection

These various testimonies applied only to Rome, and Innocent I expressly stated that there was no question of a *fermentum* for "rural parts of dioceses, since the sacraments should not be carried to distant places."[88] Yet the "commingling" took place almost everywhere.

Although no explanation of the rite is completely convincing, the most likely one, according to Cabie,[89] is found in the symbolism of the two species. In the Semitic mind, the separate giving of the Body and Blood by Christ at the Supper signified his death, since his life (his blood) was no longer in his body. In order, therefore, to signify that the Savior is now alive, it was natural to mix the bread and wine. This is the point that Theodore of Mopsuestia seems to be making with regard to the rite: "The entire human body is one with its blood; the blood mingles with every part.... That is how it was with the Lord's body before his passion."[90]

RECEPTION AND DISTRIBUTION OF COMMUNION

Private Preparation of the Priest

When the rite of the breaking of the bread and its accompanying song are finished, the priest says one of two prayers in preparation for Communion. Both prayers are taken from the

Gallican-Frankish liturgy of the ninth or tenth century. The first remembers Christ's redeeming death and attaches various petitions. The second, which is shorter, starts with a reference to Paul's warning against an unworthy reception of the Body of the Lord (1 Cor 11:27–29).

The prayer for the private preparation of the priest is "said quietly" (*GIRM* 84), but one often hears priests reciting it loud. Since it is the private preparation of the priest, the prayer is in the first person singular:

> ...free *me* by this, your most holy Body and Blood,
> from all *my* sins and from every evil;
> keep *me* always faithful to your commandments,
> and never let *me* be parted from you. [my italics]

There is an alternative prayer that is also in the first person singular:

> May the receiving of your Body and Blood,
> Lord Jesus Christ,
> not bring *me* to judgment and condemnation,
> but through your loving mercy
> be for *me* protection in mind and body
> and a healing remedy. [my italics]

However, some priests, in their desire to be inclusive, change the singular into the plural, that is, "...free *us*...keep *us*...and never let *us* be parted from you" or "May the receiving of your Body and Blood...not bring *us* to judgment...but through your loving mercy be for *us* protection...." This is incorrect, even though well intentioned. We should note that at this time the faithful are supposed to prepare themselves quietly and in their own way for Communion (*GIRM* 84; see *GIRM* 33). As DeGrocco says in this connection, "Priests who pray these prayers aloud and/or who change them into prayers said in the plural in order to include the assembly misunderstand not only the nature of the prayers but the nature of the liturgical act as a diversified action of the body in which not everyone has to do or be included in every action to fully participate."[91]

Some priests bow while reciting this prayer. However, it is

not stated anywhere that this prayer should be said in this manner. It is meant to be said with the priest standing upright, at the center of the altar.[92]

After saying the prayer in preparation for Communion, the priest is required to genuflect before taking up the host. The genuflection here is a sign of reverence before the reception of Holy Communion. After the genuflection, a custom that was still unknown at this point even in the late Middle Ages, the priest raises a piece of the broken host over the paten or the chalice and makes a statement based on John 1:29 and Revelation 19:9 respectively:

> Behold the Lamb of God,
> behold him who takes away the sins of the world.
> Blessed are those called to the supper of the Lamb.

The last line from the Book of Revelation refers to the eschatological fulfilment, for which the reception of Communion is a guarantee, based on Christ's promise (cf. John 6:51, 54).

Even though the *General Instruction* says that the Eucharistic bread can be raised slightly "over the paten or over the chalice" (*GIRM* 84), the latter seems more appropriate in the light of the *Instruction's* preference for Communion under both forms (for example, nos. 72, 85, 281). The significance of the broken bread suggests that a *single* broken piece of bread should be raised over the paten or chalice (*GIRM* 157). The presiding priest should not try to put together the two halves of the broken host, pretending as if it had not been broken. It is the broken bread that the people are invited to share, and this is what they should be shown. In other words, only one piece should be shown. If there are concelebrating priests and they have the hosts in their hands during the invitation to Communion, they should not elevate their hosts.[93] This ensures the clarity of the principal celebrant's presidential role.

Next the priest and the congregation speak words based on the words of the centurion of Capernaum (Matt 8:8). These words express humility and great trust:

> Lord, I am not worthy
> that you should enter under my roof,

but only say the word
and my soul shall be healed.

The Priest's Communion

The priest is the first to take the host and to drink from the chalice. If there are concelebrants, they do likewise, communicating themselves. These concelebrants come to the altar one after another or, if two chalices are used, two by two. They genuflect, partake of the Blood of Christ, wipe the rim of the chalice, and return to their seats. They may also partake of the Blood of the Lord while remaining in their places and drinking from the chalice presented to them by the deacon or by one of the concelebrants, or else passed from one to the other.

It is not necessary for the concelebrants to finish receiving Communion before the faithful are given Holy Communion. This will delay the Communion of the faithful. The *General Instruction* permits the principal celebrant, after his own Communion, to proceed with giving Communion to the faithful. If there is a deacon assisting at Mass, the presiding priest gives him Communion and offers him the chalice. If there are extraordinary ministers of Holy Communion, they are given Holy Communion and the chalice at this point.

It is not permitted for the extraordinary ministers and servers to receive Communion at the same time as the priest or to self-communicate. They are not concelebrants. Moreover, making a distinction between the Communion of the celebrant and the other ministers and laity is found in all the rites of the East and West. The present writer has observed the practice in some parishes in Europe where the presiding priest gives Communion to extraordinary ministers of Holy Communion and altar servers before he takes his own Communion! This practice is liturgically incorrect. Those who do this probably see the Mass primarily as a meal, in which case the priest celebrant is seen as a polite host who gives food to his guests first before taking his own. But this has never been the practice in the Eucharistic liturgies celebrated in the East or the West precisely because the Mass is primarily a sacrifice offered by the priest. As Elliot says,

When offering the Eucharistic Sacrifice, the celebrant first receives the Body and Blood of Christ, which completes the Sacrifice, and then he distributes the Eucharist to the faithful, drawing them into full communion with the Lord's Sacrifice.[94]

Distribution of Communion

Who is allowed to distribute Holy Communion during Mass? The only people permitted to open the tabernacle during Mass are those authorized to distribute Communion (1) by virtue of their sacred orders, a deacon, priest, or bishop; (2) an instituted acolyte who is an extraordinary minister of the Eucharist; (3) an authorized extraordinary minister of Holy Communion.

It is the duty of the presiding priest to distribute Communion to the faithful. The 1980 Instruction *Inaestimabile Donum* condemns the practice of priests sitting during Communion and leaving the distribution of Communion to laypeople. It says, "A reprehensible attitude is shown by those priests who, though present at the celebration, refrain from distributing Communion and leave this task to the laity" (no. 10).[95] The *General Instruction* explicitly notes that extraordinary ministers may assist in distributing Communion only when other priests are not present at Mass (*GIRM* 162).

According to the *General Instruction* (no. 245), "The Blood of the Lord may be consumed either by drinking from the chalice directly, or by intinction, or by means of a tube or a spoon." Drinking from the chalice is always the preferred option. When Communion is distributed under both kinds, the chalice is usually administered by a deacon or, when no deacon is present, by a priest, or even by a duly instituted acolyte or other extraordinary minister of Holy Communion, or by a member of the faithful who in case of necessity has been entrusted with this duty for a single occasion (*GIRM* 284). As the *General Instruction* says (160), "It is not permitted for the faithful to take the consecrated Bread or the sacred chalice by themselves and, still less, to hand them on from one to another among themselves." If Communion is carried out by intinction, it should be done by the priest, deacon, bishop, or the extraordinary minister of Holy Communion. Laypeople are not permitted to take the host themselves and dip it in the sacred Blood. The hosts should be neither too thin nor too small, but rather a little thicker than usual, so that after being dipped partly into the Blood of Christ they can still easily be distributed to each communicant (*GIRM* 285b).

Mode of Reception

Around the time unleavened bread was introduced, the custom arose of receiving Communion on the tongue, a custom already followed in exceptional cases, in particular in dealing with the sick. The new practice was sanctioned by a Council of Rouen in the reign of Louis the Pious: "The Eucharist is not to be placed in the hands of any layman or laywoman but only in their mouths."[96] This was understood as a mark of respect for the sacrament. In turn, the new practice probably led to the custom of the faithful kneeling to receive Communion, since this made it easier for the priest to put the host in their mouths.

Reception of the Precious Blood through intinction, that is, by wetting the consecrated host in the chalice, existed in the East, but the practice was rejected in the West by the Council of Braga in 675. The rule today is that the consecrated host may be received either on the tongue or in the hand, at the discretion of each communicant (*GIRM* 160). Can a priest refuse to give Holy Communion in the hand? A priest might do this on grounds of pastoral prudence in a few cases. Indeed, some priests have been known to have refused to give Communion in the hand to children who presented dirty hands at Communion time. Normally, where the options are permitted by the episcopal conference, people must be free to receive Communion either on the tongue or in the hand.

Communion under Both Kinds

In the Latin Rite of the Roman Catholic Church, Holy Communion can be given to the faithful in the form of bread alone or, when permitted, under both kinds, the bread and the wine; in case of necessity when a person cannot consume bread, it can be given under the form of wine alone (can. 925).

Communion under both kinds was the normal practice in the Western Church for about the first twelve centuries. Communion in the form of wine was given to infants, and in the form of bread to those who could not be present for the Eucharistic celebration. Beginning in the twelfth century and continuing in the thirteenth, Western churches gradually abandoned Communion in the form of wine for all except the presiding priest. Various factors led to this change. The Eucharistic piety of the time placed more emphasis on the adoration of the host than on the reception of Communion. At a time when people had a very strong belief that the consecrated wine was really the Blood of Christ, the widespread fear of spilling the consecrated wine contributed to the abandoning of the chalice. Another factor that contributed to this was the doctrine that the whole Christ is received under either species of bread or wine.

By the fourteenth century, the custom of giving Communion in the form of bread alone had become universal in the West, and Christians who returned to the original practice were condemned by the Church. In response to some who insisted on the right of the laity to receive the chalice, the Council of Constance in 1415 declared Communion under the species of bread alone to be the law of the Church. The Council of Trent in the sixteenth century attempted to respond to Protestant Reformers who had reintroduced the practice of giving the chalice to laypeople. However, it failed to achieve consensus, and referred the issue to the pope. To placate various civil rulers, especially Emperor Ferdinand I, Pope Pius IV in 1564 granted dispensations permitting Communion under both kinds in a number of states and dioceses in central Europe. However, subsequent popes withdrew all these dispensations, and from 1621 until 1965, Communion under both kinds was restricted to the presiding priest everywhere in the Latin Rite. No such development took place in Eastern Christianity, which remained faithful to the practice of the Lord's Supper and the early Church.

The issue of Communion under both kinds gave rise to a lively and prolonged debate at the Second Vatican Council and resulted in a text of the liturgy constitution that permitted Communion under both kinds, in the judgment of the bishops, to clerics, religious, and laity in cases to be defined by the Apostolic See. The 1965 *Rite for Distributing Communion under Both Kinds* listed several occasions when it could be given, and these were expanded in subsequent Church documents until the list of cases for the universal Church was finalized in the 1970 Roman Missal.

In 1970, the Apostolic See authorized episcopal conferences and ordinaries (bishops) to concede the faculty for Communion under both kinds in cases not determined by universal law. Although a complete restoration of Communion under both kinds is not yet practiced everywhere in the Church, the Holy See recognizes it as the ideal practice because of its symbolic value:

> Holy Communion has a fuller form as a sign when it takes place under both kinds. For in this form the sign of the Eucharistic banquet is more clearly evident and clearer expression is given to the divine will by which the new and eternal Covenant is ratified in the Blood of the Lord, as also the connection between the Eucharistic banquet and the eschatological banquet in the Kingdom of the Father. (*GIRM* 281)

While the tradition of offering the chalice to the faithful is an increasingly common practice in much of North America, the United Kingdom, and Oceania, it is not widely practiced in Italy, Portugal, Spain as well as Asia, Africa, and South America. The Church's requirement that the wine used must be from grapes poses a problem for many developing countries that do not produce such wine and have problems importing it from Europe or America because of foreign exchange constraints. If the chalice is not offered to the laity at Mass in some developing countries, the reason is simply economic. However, attempts should be made to offer the chalice, especially on certain feasts, for example, the Solemnity of Corpus Christi and others to be determined by the diocesan bishop or at the discretion of the parish priest. Communion can also be given by intinction, that is, dipping the host in the wine.

It needs to be stressed that the practice of giving Holy Communion under both species in no way diminishes the Church's teaching known as "concomitance." This is the belief that Christ is physically present in the Eucharistic elements of bread (which is his Body) and wine (which is his Blood). This means that the entire Christ is received in any one of the sacred species. It is the duty of pastors to ensure that the faithful are instructed on this matter to understand that those who receive under only one species are "in no way deprived of the fruits of the graces necessary for salvation or the fruits of the Eucharist."[97]

Who Can Receive Communion?

It is frequently asked whether non-Catholics can receive Communion at a Catholic Mass. This often comes up in the context of family events—weddings, baptisms, funerals—situations that put a great deal of pressure on families and ministers of Holy Communion, ordinary and extraordinary, to allow it. Some people believe that Catholics should extend Eucharistic hospitality to their non-Catholic brothers and sisters, either for the sake of kindness or for the sake of a sense of unity among the members of the congregation. While such motives may be good, intercommunion will have the effect of falsifying the sacramental meaning of the Eucharist as both a sign of communion with Christ and communion with the Catholic Church.

In order to safeguard the sacrament, and to ensure that Christ is received with the proper dispositions, the Church has enacted certain norms for determining those occasions when intercommunion is legitimate. In the 1983 *Code of Canon Law*, the following is prescribed:[98]

> Canon 844 §1. Catholic ministers administer the sacraments licitly to Catholic members of the Christian faithful alone, who likewise receive them licitly from Catholic ministers alone, without prejudice to the prescripts of §§2, 3, and 4 of this canon, and can. 861, §2.

> §2. Whenever necessity requires it or true spiritual advantage suggests it, and provided that danger of error or of indifferentism is avoided, the Christian faithful for whom it is physically or morally impossible to approach a Catholic minister are permitted to receive the sacraments of penance, Eucharist, and anointing of the sick from non-Catholic ministers in whose Churches these sacraments are valid.

§3. Catholic ministers administer the sacraments of penance, Eucharist, and anointing of the sick licitly to members of Eastern Churches which do not have full communion with the Catholic Church if they seek such on their own accord and are properly disposed. This is also valid for members of other Churches which in the judgment of the Apostolic See are in the same condition in regard to the sacraments as these Eastern Churches.

§4. If the danger of death is present or if, in the judgment of the diocesan bishop or conference of bishops, some other grave necessity urges it, Catholic ministers administer these same sacraments licitly also to other Christians not having full communion with the Catholic Church, who cannot approach a minister of their own community and who seek such on their own accord, provided that they manifest Catholic faith in respect to these sacraments and are properly disposed.

§5. For the cases mentioned in §§2, 3, and 4, the diocesan bishop or conference of bishops is not to issue general norms except after consultation at least with the local competent authority of the interested non-Catholic Church or community.

In keeping with the sacramental meaning of the Eucharist, this canon reserves the sacraments to Catholics, that is, those who are in communion with the Church. It then addresses the question of Catholics receiving the sacraments from non-Catholics. It sets the following strict conditions:

1. Necessity or genuine spiritual advantage
2. When the danger of error or indifferentism is avoided
3. When it is physically or morally impossible to approach a Catholic minister
4. When the recipient is a member of a church that has valid sacraments

This last condition is the key one, since it eliminates *all* the Reformation churches (Anglican, Episcopalian, Presbyterian, Methodist, Baptist, etc.), none of whom, in the eyes of the Catholic Church, have valid sacred orders, and therefore, a valid Eucharist. The possibility of a Catholic receiving from the minister of another church, when the first three conditions are fulfilled, is limited to the Orthodox Churches, other Eastern Churches, Old Catholics, Polish National, and others whose sacraments are recognized by the Holy See. As paragraph 3 notes, the members of those churches may likewise receive from a Catholic minister when they ask and are properly disposed.

Under what conditions, therefore, may non-Catholics from the Reformation churches receive Communion in the Catholic Church? Paragraph 4 addresses this matter and sets stricter conditions than for non-Catholics who belong to Churches that have a valid Eucharist, true Eucharistic faith, and valid penance. These conditions are as follows:

1. Danger of death, or other grave necessity
2. Compliance with the norms of the diocesan bishop, or the conference of bishops
3. The recipient cannot approach a minister of his or her own community
4. The recipient asks on his or her own for it
5. The recipient manifests Catholic faith in the sacraments
6. The recipient is properly disposed

These last two conditions are very important. When Catholics and Orthodox present themselves for Communion, either to their own minister or that of another church with valid sacraments, Eucharistic faith and proper disposition are assumed, given the introduction to both reconciliation and the Eucharist at an early age in churches that have a Catholic Eucharistic faith. However, when a non-Catholic presents himself, the norms presume an investigation to determine the person's faith, and to determine the necessary moral conditions for a proper reception of the Eucharist. A minister of Communion, ordinary or extraordinary, cannot determine that all these conditions, especially the last two, are met in the Communion line. This is why the guidelines of the United States Conference of Catholic Bishops (USCCB), which are published at the back of every worship aid, exclude weddings, funerals, and other such occasions as appropriate for intercommunion. The occasions would be individual, normally determined by a pastor after consultation with the bishop, or in accordance with norms drawn up based on this canon (see §5).

In this connection, we may quote the statement of guidelines for the reception of Communion offered by the United States Conference of Catholic Bishops. In the case of non-Catholic Christians, the guidelines say:

> We welcome our fellow Christians to this celebration of the Eucharist as our brothers and sisters. We pray that our common baptism and the action of the Holy Spirit in this Eucharist will draw us closer to one another and begin to dispel the sad divisions which separate us. We pray that these will lessen and finally disappear, in keeping with Christ's prayer for us "that they may all be one" (Jn 17:21).

In the case of those who are not Christians, the guidelines say:

> We also welcome to this celebration those who do not share our faith in Jesus Christ. While we cannot admit them to Holy Communion, we ask them to offer their prayers for the peace and the unity of the human family.

Purification of Vessels

Those who are allowed to purify the sacred vessels after Communion are: (1) a deacon, or in the absence of a deacon, a priest concelebrant or celebrant, or lacking all these, a bishop celebrant; (2) an instituted acolyte, whenever he assists at the altar. Servers or extraordinary ministers of Holy Communion are not allowed to purify the vessels after Communion. The present author has seen extraordinary ministers of Holy Communion purify the sacred vessels in some parishes in London, England. Extraordinary ministers may help to consume what remains of the Precious Blood, when Holy Communion has been given under both species, but they should leave the chalices at the credence table where the deacon(s), instituted acolyte(s), or the celebrant will see to the purification, which may be postponed until after Mass if this is more convenient. The extraordinary ministers should purify their fingers in a bowl of water before they return to their places.

Concluding Rites

After the post-Communion prayer, short announcements may be made. Announcements should not be made before the Prayer after Communion. The announcements are the first element of the Concluding Rites. If there is a deacon at the Mass, he makes them. Such announcements, which usually have to do with events outside the liturgy, already orient people's attention to the transition taking place as they are sent from the Mass to their everyday lives. The announcements should not be made from the ambo, which is reserved for the Word of God. After the announcements come the Concluding Rites, which comprise a greeting, blessing, and dismissal. The Concluding Rites are very short and have a functional character: the liturgy is over and the people and ministers depart.

THE GREETING

The greeting takes a very simple form: "The Lord be with you," followed by the usual response: "And with your spirit." The greeting at this point is the same one found at the beginning of Mass, the Gospel, and the dialogue introducing the Eucharistic Prayer, and it acknowledges that the assembly is constituted as the Body of Christ. "The dispersal thus becomes not just a dispersal of individuals but also an ecclesial act, sending forth the church as the Body of Christ to proclaim the Kingdom of God in the world."[99]

THE BLESSING

The Mass concludes by the invocation of the Trinity as it did at the beginning. If a deacon is present, he gives the invitation before the solemn blessing or prayer over the people. The priest blesses the congregation using the traditional biblical names of Father, Son, and Holy Spirit, and making the Sign of the Cross. Whereas the priest blesses with a single Sign of the Cross,[100] the bishop blesses with a threefold cross. What is the reason for this triple episcopal blessing? In the early Church, it was the bishop who mostly presided at the Eucharist and at all liturgies. With time, however, this became impossible in view of the many communities that came into existence. When priests began presiding at Eucharistic celebrations as delegates of the bishop, initially they were not allowed to give the blessing at the end of the liturgy. When that changed in the eighth or ninth century or perhaps even a bit earlier, the bishop then began giving the triple blessing in Trinitarian formula, to show the fullness of orders and to distinguish his blessing from that of the priest.

The Trinitarian formula for blessing used by the priest and the bishop "expresses the mystery of the Eucharist in which we participate: united in the communion of the Holy Spirit, the church is drawn into the saving event of the death and resurrection of the Son and joins the risen Christ in the eternal praise of the heavenly kingdom by which the Father is adored, praised and thanked."[101]

The formula for the blessing should be adhered to and not changed into something like: "May Almighty God bless *us*, the Father, the Son and the Holy Spirit." This tendency arises, for example, when a priest is celebrating Mass for fellow priests or if there are bishops present. There is no need for this change, because it is God who blesses, using the priest as a means. Neither should the formula for blessing be changed to something like this: "May Almighty God bless you, *in* the name of the Father and of the Son and of the Holy Spirit." Indeed, priests baptize in the name of the Trinity and in the sacrament of reconciliation forgive people their sins in the name of the Trinity. But when it comes to the blessing at the end of Mass, the scenario is different. It is not the priest who blesses but God, and God cannot bless in his own name. As Smolarski says in this connection, "When speaking words such as these, a priest is not bestowing a blessing (in his own name or in the name of anyone else). Rather, a priest is asking God that God (the Father, Son and Spirit) bestow divine blessings on the assembly."[102]

THE DISMISSAL

The dismissal comes after the blessing and concludes the celebration. The dismissal is given by the deacon, if one is present.

There are four formulas for the dismissal. The first alternative goes like this: "Go forth. The Mass is ended" (*Ite, missa est*). In this formula, the idea of being sent out on mission comes forth. One view holds that the *missa* in *Ite, missa est* is understood in the sense of mission, so that the faithful at the end of Mass are being sent on mission. However, according to Marcel Metzger, "This hypothesis is without foundation and the liturgical reform of Vatican II has rendered it useless, since it has allowed episcopal conferences to propose other formulas of dismissal."[103]

In spite of Metzger's contention, it would seem that the sense of "mission" should be included in the rite of dismissal. The name *Mass* (*missa*) can serve to remind us of the mission dimension of the Eucharist. The Eucharist strengthens Christians for service in the world. The *Catechism of the Catholic Church* sees the dismissal of Mass as sending forth (*missio*) of the faithful from their participation in the mystery of salvation, "so that they may fulfil God's will in their daily lives" (CCC 1332). Moreover, as Pope John Paul II reminds us, "The dismissal at the end of each Mass is *a charge* given to Christians, inviting them to work for the spread of the Gospel and the imbuing of society with Christian values" (*Mane Nobiscum Domine* 24).

The second alternative is "Go and announce the Gospel of the Lord." This is in line with the command given by the risen Christ to his disciples to go and to preach the good news to all creation (Mark 16:15; cf. Matt 28:19–20). The third and fourth alternatives use the familiar, "Go in peace," to which the third adds, "glorifying the Lord by your life."

CONCLUSION

If any liturgical action is to follow, for example, the final commendation at a funeral Mass, all of the concluding rites are omitted. The *General Instruction* summarizes the final procession by saying, "Then the Priest venerates the altar as usual with a kiss and, after making a profound bow with the lay ministers, he withdraws with them" (*GIRM* 169). The principal celebrant as a rule "venerates the altar by kissing it before he leaves, while the other concelebrants, particularly if there are a number of them, venerate the altar by bowing."[104] According to the *Ceremonial of Bishops*, those in the final procession should follow "the order in which they entered" (no. 170). According to Smolarski, "The final procession is mainly functional. It is an organized, dignified way to have the ministers leave the assembly and, in a sense, lead the rest of the assembly into the world from which they came."[105]

Chapter Eight

Conclusion

IN THE PREVIOUS CHAPTERS, WE ATTEMPTED A HISTORI-
cal, biblical, theological, and liturgical study of the Mass. From
the historical point of view, we had a look at the development of
the Christian Eucharist from the Last Supper to the present. We
looked at the history of the various parts of the Mass, drawing
attention to Jewish, Greco-Roman, and other influences on it.
From the biblical and theological perspectives, we looked at the
text of the Mass and discussed the various biblical and theological
sections in it, especially the *Gloria*, the Creed, the *Sanctus*, and
the Eucharistic Prayers. From the liturgical perspective, we
discussed the celebration of Mass, looking at the assembly and
its ministers, the things needed for the celebration of Mass, and
the various gestures used during Mass. We also drew attention to
what constitutes good liturgical practice and what does not. In
this concluding chapter, we will attempt to summarize the "dos"
and "don'ts" of good liturgical practice. It is my expectation that
this will be of help to deacons, priests, bishops, and the people of
God in general in celebrating the Eucharist in a liturgically correct
manner.

Dos and Don'ts of Good Liturgical Practice

1. The assembly should be able to see the altar as an altar
   table. For this reason, it is better to use altar cloths that
   cover only the top (*mensa*) of the altar.
2. If decorative cloths that hang down are used for the
   altar, these should not cover any symbols or artwork
   that is part of the design of the altar.

3. The uppermost cloth that covers the *top* of the altar should always be white in color, regardless of the liturgical season (*GIRM* 304).

4. Nothing should be put on the altar other than what is necessary, specifically the *Book of the Gospels* during the Liturgy of the Word, and the Missal, altar linens, bread, and wine during the Liturgy of the Eucharist (*GIRM* 306).

5. Concerning the use of candles, at least two can be used in any celebration, four or six for a Sunday Mass or holy day, and seven candles for celebrations at which the bishop presides.

6. Candles are to be placed on the altar or, better still, near or around it, so as not to distract from the sacred vessels or impede the view of participants (*GIRM* 307).

7. Floral decorations should always be done with moderation and placed around the altar rather than on its *mensa* (*GIRM* 305).

8. The tabernacle may be in the sanctuary, even on an old altar, but not on an altar on which Mass is being celebrated (*GIRM* 315).

9. The altar cross should have the image (*corpus*) of Christ on it (*GIRM* 117, 122, 308). A figure of the risen Christ behind an altar cannot be regarded as a substitute for the altar cross.

10. When the processional cross is used as the altar cross, it should have the image of Christ on it (*GIRM* 122).

11. If the tabernacle is in the sanctuary, the priest and ministers genuflect to it when arriving at the sanctuary and at the end of Mass, but not during Mass (*GIRM* 274).

12. If a processional cross is used during Mass, only that cross should be incensed.

13. The *Book of the Gospels* should be carried in both hands, slightly raised but without being held too high, and it is never waved from side to side (*GIRM* 120d, 133, 172 , 175).

14. The *Book of the Gospels*, but not the *Lectionary*, may be carried in the entrance procession (*GIRM* 120d, 172).

15. The vestment proper to the priest-celebrant at Mass and other sacred actions directly connected with Mass is, unless otherwise indicated, the chasuble, worn *over* the alb and stole (*GIRM* 337).

16. It is liturgically improper for celebrants to use vestments made from the special cloth designed to highlight a bishop, or priest, or even a Catholic community that is celebrating an anniversary or jubilee.

17. The entrance procession should include only those going to minister in the sanctuary, that is, the ministers of the altar, lectors, deacons, and priests.

18. A priest is not to enter into a concelebration or to be admitted as a concelebrant once the Mass has already begun.

19. Water for the *Asperges* should be blessed at the beginning of Sunday Mass, except on Easter Sunday, when the water would have been blessed the night before. It is blessed during the Opening Rite.

20. In the entrance procession, those who carry articles used in the celebration, for example, the cross, candlesticks, the *Book of the Gospels*, are not required to make a deep bow or to genuflect.

21. During the Easter season, the paschal candle is incensed. It is appropriate to do this throughout the Easter season as a way of stressing the importance of the great fifty days of Easter.

22. It is not good liturgical practice during a funeral Mass for the celebrant to incense the coffin/casket at the beginning of Mass when the altar is incensed. Incensation of the coffin/casket is done at the Presentation of the Gifts (when the faithful are also incensed) and during the Rite of Commendation.

23. The liturgical greeting *The Lord be with you* at the beginning of Mass should not be replaced by *The Lord is with you*, as is done by some priests. This is liturgically incorrect. The two are not the same.

24. The introduction to the Mass should be done *after* the initial greeting and not before the Sign of the Cross.

25. This introduction should be brief. It is not an occasion for one to give a short homily.

26. The Penitential Rite is omitted on certain occasions, such as on Passion Sunday, on the Feast of Presentation of the Lord, and on Ash Wednesday.

27. The custom found in some places of introducing each reading with a short commentary is incorrect and unnecessary. Any commentary on the readings should form part of the priest's homily.

28. Each reading is proclaimed by a single reader, but it is preferable that different readers proclaim different readings (*GIRM* 109).

29. It is not permitted for readers to go to the presider to receive a blessing before doing the first or second reading.

30. The Gospel should always be proclaimed either by a deacon or in his absence, a priest other than the priest celebrant. If, however, a deacon or another priest is not present, the priest celebrant himself should read the Gospel (*GIRM* 59).

31. The deacon who is to proclaim the gospel reading prepares himself by bowing before the priest or bishop celebrant and asking for a blessing.

32. At a Mass presided over by a bishop, a priest who reads the Gospel in the absence of a deacon asks for and receives the blessing in the same manner as would a deacon (*GIRM* 212).

33. In concelebrated Mass in which the presider is not a bishop, the concelebrant who proclaims the Gospel in the absence of a deacon neither requests nor receives the blessing of the presider (*GIRM* 212). Such a priest should bow toward the altar while reciting the following prayer: *Cleanse my heart and my lips....*

34. In preparing himself to read the Gospel by reciting the above prayer, the priest should bow toward the altar and not the tabernacle. During the liturgy, the altar is the primary architectural symbol of Christ (*GIRM* 298) and must be reverenced as such.

35. The giving of the homily should not be begun or concluded with the Sign of the Cross.

36. After the proclamation of the Gospel, when the deacon

is assisting the bishop, he carries the book to him to be kissed, or else kisses it himself, saying quietly, "May the words of the Gospel..." (*GIRM* 175).

37. After the proclamation of the Gospel, a bishop may bless the assembly with the *Book of the Gospels* (*GIRM* 175).

38. The homily can only be given by a deacon, priest, or bishop. Laypeople are not permitted to give the homily (cf. can. 767 §1).

39. The homily given during a funeral should not be turned into a eulogy or a tribute (*GIRM* 382).

40. In the Prayer of the Faithful, the petitions should not be addressed directly to God the Father or to Jesus. These intentions are invitations or biddings *to the faithful*, who then pray for the proposed intention silently and in a common petition.

41. During the Prayer of the Faithful, the presiding priest, as much as possible, should *not* offer the intentions unless there is no one who can do it.

42. It is not appropriate to include a prayer to Mary (e.g., the "Hail Mary") at the end of the intercessions. However, a prayer or a hymn to Mary at the end of Mass (for example, the "Salve Regina," "Regina Caeli," etc.) is permitted and this is sometimes done in papal Masses.

43. It is not liturgically correct for things such as the chalice, the purificators, the Missal, the water, and so forth, to be carried in procession during the Presentation of the Gifts.

44. The gifts should not be placed on the altar before the Presentation of the Gifts.

45. It is not required to make a Sign of the Cross to bless the water at the Presentation of the Gifts as was required in the Tridentine Mass.

46. It is liturgically incorrect for the priest to raise both the paten and chalice at the same time and offer the bread and wine together in a single action, adapting the words, *Blessed are you, Lord....*

47. For the incensation of the gifts, the presiding priest may either incense the gifts with *three swings* of the censer or

make a Sign of the Cross with the censer over the gifts (*GIRM* 277).

48. The elaborate triple crosswise and triple circular incensations are not permitted during the Preparation of the Gifts.

49. The people (including concelebrating priests) should stand after the priest's invitation to pray, *Pray, my brothers* and before the response, *May the Lord accept...* (*GIRM* 43).

50. According to the current missal, the assembly responds with *Amen* after the Prayer over the Offerings.

51. It is not liturgically proper for the priest to invite the members of the congregation (even when they are not many) to stand with him around the altar at the beginning of the Eucharistic Prayer.

52. Concelebrants are required to pronounce the words of consecration, but in a very low voice so that the principal celebrant's voice is heard clearly (*GIRM* 218).

53. At the consecration, it is not proper to leave the host on the paten at this elevation, for then the people cannot see it.

54. At the consecration, the priest must not replace the genuflection with a bow or some other gesture.

55. The memorial acclamation is for the people, and so the priest should not join in singing or saying the acclamation.

56. The deacon is not allowed to make the invitation to the memorial acclamation, as is sometimes done in some churches. These words are strictly meant to be said by the celebrant of the Mass.

57. During the Eucharistic Prayer, from the epiclesis until the priest shows the chalice, the deacon normally remains kneeling (*GIRM* 179; *Ceremonial of Bishops* 155).

58. At the elevation of the host during consecration, the gesture of elevation should be reverent but not prolonged, as it might affect the unity and continuity of the Eucharistic Prayer.

59. Musical accompaniment during the recitation of the Eucharistic Prayer is not proper and should not be done.

Silence is necessary for the words of institution to be clearly heard.

60. The Doxology of the Eucharistic Prayer still forms part of the presidential prayer, and thus should be said by the presiding priest *alone*, although at concelebrations, the concelebrants *may* join him, but are not obliged to do so. The faithful are not to say the concluding Doxology of the Eucharistic Prayer with the priest (*GIRM* 236).

61. During the recitation of the Doxology, only one chalice and the paten should be lifted up. Additional chalices and ciboria should remain on the altar even if there are deacons or concelebrants at the celebration.

62. During the recitation of the Doxology, the consecrated host should be *on* the paten and *must not be shown to the people*, as at the consecration. Thus, it is not liturgically proper to hold the host *vertically* over the chalice, as some celebrants do.

63. When Eucharistic Prayer IV is used, its special Preface must be used with it.

64. The priest should not leave the sanctuary at the Sign of Peace (*GIRM* 154).

65. The breaking of the bread is reserved for the priest and the deacon (*GIRM* 83).

66. The breaking of the bread should only be done at the Lamb of God, and not during the recitation of the institution narrative.

67. Before Communion, the priest prepares himself by a prayer, *said quietly*, that he may fruitfully receive Christ's Body and Blood. The faithful do the same, praying *silently* (*GIRM* 84). The priest should not "pluralize" this prayer to include the faithful.

68. The priest may hold the host over the chalice when inviting the assembly to Communion at the *Behold the Lamb of God...* (*GIRM* 157, 243, 268).

69. The significance of the broken bread suggests that a *single* broken piece of bread should be raised over the paten or chalice (*GIRM* 157). It is the broken bread that the people are invited to share, and this is what they should be shown. In other words, only one piece should

be shown. The presiding priest should not try to put together the two halves of the broken host, pretending as if it had not been broken.

70. The priest must hold a host consecrated *at that Mass* when inviting the assembly to Communion at the *Behold the Lamb of God...* (*GIRM* 157, 243).

71. The priest must receive Communion from what he consecrated at that Mass (*GIRM* 85).

72. Extraordinary ministers of Holy Communion approach the altar after the priest has received Communion and receive the vessels containing the Eucharistic species from the priest (*GIRM* 162). They are not allowed to take the Communion themselves.

73. Communicants should not pass the Eucharistic elements from one to another (*GIRM* 160).

74. The practice in some parishes in Europe where the presiding priest gives Communion to extraordinary ministers of Holy Communion and altar servers before he takes his own Communion is not liturgically correct.

75. The Precious Blood should be consumed at the altar after Communion. Excess consecrated hosts may be consumed or reserved in a tabernacle (*GIRM* 163).

76. The formula for the blessing should be adhered to and not changed into something like "May Almighty God bless *us*, the Father, the Son and the Holy Spirit" or "May Almighty God bless you, *in the name of* the Father and of the Son and of the Holy Spirit." It is not the priest who blesses but God, and God cannot bless in his own name.

Notes

Foreword

1. *Acta Sanctae Sedis* 36:28 [1904], 331.
2. Apostolic letter *Mane Nobiscum Domine*, October 7, 2004, no. 27.

Chapter One: The Evolution of the Christian Eucharist

1. I. H. Marshall, "Lord's Supper," in *Dictionary of Paul and His Letters*, ed. Gerald F. Hawthorne, Ralph P. Martin, and Daniel G. Reid (Downers Grove, IL: InterVarsity Press, 1993), 571.
2. J. Paul Sampley, "The First Letter to the Corinthians," in *New Interpreter's Bible*, ed. Leander Keck (Nashville: Abingdon Press, 2000), 10:934.
3. Jerome Murphy-O'Connor, "The First Letter to the Corinthians," in *The New Jerome Biblical Commentary*, ed. Raymond E. Brown, Joseph A. Fitzmyer, and Roland E. Murphy (Englewood Cliffs, NJ: Prentice Hall, 1990), 49:56.
4. Marshall, "Lord's Supper," 572.
5. Ibid.
6. R. H. Stein, "Last Supper," in *Dictionary of Jesus and the Gospels*, ed. Joel G. Green, Scot McKnight, and I. Howard Marshall (Downer's Grove, IL: InterVarsity Press, 1992), 444.
7. This addition to Luke and 1 Corinthians "may be an interpretative comment to help explain the meaning of the bread for the believer. Yet even if these are not authentic words of Jesus, this comment is certainly implied and makes explicit what was

implicit in Jesus' words" (Stein, "Last Supper," 447). For the view that the Marcan version of the institution narratives is older than the Pauline-Lucan form, see Stein, "Last Supper," 447.

8. J. A. Fitzmyer, *The Gospel according to Luke X–XXIV*, vol. 28A, Anchor Bible Series (Garden City, NY: Doubleday, 1985), 1401.

9. Paul F. Bradshaw, *Eucharistic Origins* (London: SPCK, 2004), 13.

10. See Stein, "Last Supper," 446.

11. 1 Pet 1:18–19 probably also refers to the Passover sacrifice.

12. I. H. Marshall, *Last Supper and Lord's Supper* (Exeter: Paternoster Press, 1980), 143.

13. Donald A. Hagner, *Matthew 14–28*, vol. 33B, *Word Biblical Commentary* (Dallas: Word Books, 1998), 773.

14. Daniel Harrington, "The Gospel according to Mark," in *The New Jerome Biblical Commentary*, 41:95.

15. Stein, "Last Supper," 448.

16. A. Vanhoye, "Non c'è contrapposizione dialecttica tra *pro multis* e *per tutti*," *30 Giorni* (2010): 4. See http://www.30giorni.it/articoli_id_22501_l1.htm.

17. Pheme Perkins, *The Gospel of Mark*, in *New Interpreter's Bible* (Nashville: Abingdon Press, 1995), 8:517.

18. Marshall, "The Lord's Supper," 573.

19. Bradshaw, *Eucharistic Origins*, 14.

20. Stein, "Last Supper," 449.

21. Ibid.

22. Ibid.

23. See, for example, Dennis Smith, *From Symposium to Eucharist: The Banquet in the Early Christian World* (Minneapolis: Fortress Press, 2003); Jan Michael Joncas, "Tasting the Kingdom of God: The Meal Ministry of Jesus and Its Implications for Contemporary Ministry and Life," *Worship* 74 (2000): 329–65.

24. The symposium in ancient Greece was a banquet at which men met to discuss philosophical and political issues and recite poetry. It began as a warrior feast. Rooms were designed specifically for the proceedings. The participants, all male aristocrats, wore garlands and leaned on the left elbow on couches, and there was much drinking of wine, served by slave boys. Prayers

opened and closed the meetings; sessions sometimes ended with a procession in the streets. Cf. *Encyclopedia Britannica. Encyclopedia Britannica Ultimate Reference Suite* (Chicago: Encyclopedia Britannica, 2013).

25. Joncas, "Tasting the Kingdom of God," 363. See also Joanne M. Pierce and John F. Romano, "The *Ordo Missae* of the Roman Rite: Historical Background," in *A Commentary on the Order of Mass of The Roman Missal*, ed. Edward Foley (Collegeville, MN: Liturgical Press, 2011), 11.

26. For this section, see Ibid., 12ff.

27. Justin Martyr wrote two *Apologies for the Christians*, which comprise an erudite defense of Christians against charges of atheism and sedition in the Roman state. Even though the *Apologies* were addressed to Emperor Antoninus Pius, they were intended primarily for the educated public of the provinces. Their central theme is the divine plan of salvation, fulfilled in Christ the Logos.

28. Bradshaw, *Eucharistic Origins*, 61. Cf. Justin, *First Apology*, 65:1–5, 66:1–4, and 67:1–7.

29. Pierce and Romano, "The *Ordo Missae* of the Roman Rite," 13.

30. Kurt Niederwimmer, *The Didache: A Commentary*, *Hermeneia* Series (Minneapolis: Augsburg Fortress, 1998), 161.

31. Ibid., 161. Eugene LaVerdiere, *The Eucharist in the New Testament and the Early Church* (Collegeville, MN: Liturgical Press, 1996), 128–47.

32. The *Didascalia Apostolorum* (i.e., the teaching of the apostles) is one of a number of undated (and perhaps undatable) documents that circulated early in Syriac-speaking areas.

33. The *Apostolic Constitutions* is a collection of eight books containing ecclesiastical directives supposed to have been composed by the twelve apostles and transmitted by them to Clement I of Rome. The books contain comprehensive rules for the Christian life. The content of the first six books is similar to a third-century work known as the *Didascalia Apostolorum*. Part of the seventh book contains material based on the Teaching of the Twelve Apostles, or *Didache*, written in the second century. The eighth book includes the eighty-five canons, considered the most valuable part of the Constitutions. All eight books were probably compiled and edited by one author, sometimes referred to as Pseudo-Clement,

probably of Syrian origin, and with Arian tendencies. Historians estimate the date of composition as between AD 340 and 400.

34. The *Apostolic Tradition* is an early Christian treatise that belongs to the genre of church orders. Rediscovered in the nineteenth century, it was given the name *Egyptian Church Order*. In the first half of the twentieth century, this text was unanimously identified with the lost *Apostolic Tradition* presumed to have been written by Hippolytus of Rome. Due to this attribution, this manual played a crucial role in the liturgical reforms of mainstream Christian bodies. Recent scholarship has highly contested this attribution. If the *Apostolic Tradition* was the work of Hippolytus, it could be dated about AD 215 and its origin would be Rome. On the contrary, recent scholars believe that it contains material of separate sources ranging from the middle second to the fourth century, being gathered and compiled about AD 375–400, probably in Egypt or even Syria.

35. See Matthieu Smyth, "The Anaphora of the So-Called 'Apostolic Tradition' and the Roman Eucharistic Prayer," in *Issues in Eucharistic Praying in East and West*, ed. Maxwell Johnson (Collegeville, MN: Liturgical Press, 2010), 71–97; John Baldovin, "History of the Latin Text and Rite," in *A Commentary on the Order of Mass of The Roman Missal*, 311.

36. Pierce and Romano, "The *Ordo Missae* of the Roman Rite," 14. See also John Baldovin, "Hippolytus and the Apostolic Tradition: Recent Research and Commentary," *Theological Studies* 64 (2003): 520–42.

37. Paul Bradshaw, Maxwell Johnson, and L. Edward Phillips, *The Apostolic Tradition: A Commentary*, ed. Harold W. Attridge, *Hermeneia* series (Minneapolis: Fortress Press, 2002), 160.

38. See Margaret Mary Kelleher, "Rites," in *The New Dictionary of Theology*, ed. J. A. Komonchak, M. Collins, and D. A. Lane (Wilmington, DE: Michael Glazier, 1987), 905.

39. For a history of the evolution of the Roman Rite, see Keith F. Pecklers, *The Genius of the Roman Rite—On the Reception and Implementation of the New Missal* (Collegeville, MN: Liturgical Press, 2009), 1–22.

40. Anthony D. Andreassi, "Roman Rite," in *The Modern Catholic Encyclopedia*, ed. M. Glazier and M. K. Hellwig (Collegeville, MN: Liturgical Press: 2004), 724.

41. Latin: "*Ego tamen mansi in munere missam facere coepi. Dum offero....*" *Epistola* 20, 4, *PL* 16, col. 995. See Marcel Metzger, "A Eucharistic Lexicon," in *Handbook for Liturgical Studies, III, The Eucharist,* ed. Anscar J. Chupungco (Collegeville, MN: Liturgical Press, 1999), 2. See also Cardinal Donald Wuerl and Mike Aquilina, *The Mass—the Glory, the Mystery, the Tradition* (New York: Image, 2013), 39.

Chapter Two: The Assembly and Its Ministers

1. The *General Instruction of the Roman Missal* is the detailed document governing the celebration of Mass of the ordinary form of the Roman Rite of the Catholic Church since 1969. It prefaces the Roman Missal and was updated for the Third Typical Edition. It contains a very thorough description of the rite, along with important theological and canonical explanations. The version cited in this book is the *General Instruction of the Roman Missal,* Including Adaptations for the Dioceses of the United States of America, English translation of the *General Instruction of the Roman Missal* (Third Typical Edition) © 2010, International Committee on English in the Liturgy, Inc. It is henceforth cited as *General Instruction* or *GIRM.* For a discussion of the 2002 translation of the *General Instruction of the Roman Missal,* see Keith F. Pecklers, *The Genius of the Roman Rite: On the Reception and Implementation of the New Missal* (Collegeville, MN: Liturgical Press, 2009), 69–92.

2. *Lumen Gentium,* Vatican II's Dogmatic Constitution on the Church.

3. Francis Cardinal Arinze, *Celebrating the Holy Eucharist* (San Francisco: Ignatius Press, 2005), 43.

4. *Directory on the Pastoral Ministry of Bishops* (Washington, DC: National Conference of Catholic Bishops, 1973), no. 78.

5. *Promoting Liturgical Renewal: Guidelines for Diocesan Liturgical Commissions and Offices of Worship* (Washington, DC: National Conference of Catholic Bishops, 1988), no. 5.

6. *Ceremonial of Bishops, Revised by Decree of the Second Vatican Ecumenical Council and Published by Authority of Pope John Paul II* (Collegeville, MN: Liturgical Press, 1989).

7. John Paul II, *Ecclesia de Eucharistia* ("Church from the Eucharist"), encyclical published on April 17, 2003, on the Eucharist and its relationship to the world.

8. Cf. *Instruction on Certain Questions regarding the Collaboration of the Non-Ordained Faithful in the Sacred Ministry of Priest* (Practical Provisions, Article 6 § 2). This document was released on November 13, 1997, by a group of eight dicasteries of the Holy See and was intended to answer certain questions and respond to complaints of abuses that the Holy See had received. Cf. also canon 907: "In the celebration of the Eucharist it is not licit for deacons and lay persons to say prayers, in particular the Eucharistic prayer, or to perform actions which are proper to the celebrating priest."

9. John D. Laurance, "Liturgical Vestments," in *The New Dictionary of Sacramental Worship*, ed. Peter E. Fink (Collegeville, MN: Liturgical Press, 2000), 1305–14.

10. Anthony D. Andreassi, "Liturgical Vestments," in *The Modern Catholic Encyclopedia*, ed. M. Glazier and M. K. Hellwig (Collegeville, MN: Liturgical Press: 2004), 864.

11. Although the *General Instruction* (no. 336) specifies the alb as a garment common to ordained and instituted ministers, it may also be worn by "acolytes, altar servers, lectors and other ministers" if approved by the local conference of bishops (*GIRM* 339). The alb, however, is not required by the ministers listed here, who may also wear other vesture or clothing which is to be "appropriate and dignified" (*GIRM* 339).

12. Cf. *Ceremonial of Bishops*, nos. 66, 126.

13. Congregation for Divine Worship and the Discipline of the Sacraments, *Redemptionis Sacramentum: On Certain Matters to Be Observed or to Be Avoided regarding the Most Holy Eucharist*, March 25, 2004.

14. On the chasuble, see Keith F. Pecklers, "On Papal Vestments," *The Tablet*, July 14, 2007.

15. Richard E. McCarron and Anne C. McGuire, "Requisites for the Celebration of Mass," in *A Commentary on the General Instruction of the Roman Missal*, ed. Edward Foley, Nathan Mitchell, and Joanne M. Pierce (Collegeville, MN: Liturgical Press, 2007), 398.

16. Pecklers, "On Papal Vestments."

17. *Ceremonial of Bishops*, no. 61.

18. Ibid., no. 58.

19. A tonsure is a patch shaved from the crown of the heads of priests and monks in some religious orders.

20. Leonard Doohan, "Crosier (Crozier)," in *The Modern Catholic Encyclopedia*, ed. M. Glazier and M. K. Hellwig (Collegeville, MN: Liturgical Press: 2004), 204.

21. Pope Paul VI, *Motu proprio Ministeria quaedam*, August 15, 1972, no. 6.

22. See Ibid.

23. Cf. *Ceremonial of Bishops*, no. 31, p. 25.

24. Sacred Congregation of the Sacraments, *Immensae Caritatis: On Facilitating Reception of Communion in Certain Circumstances* (January 29, 1973).

25. Ibid., no. 1

26. See https://en.wikipedia.org/wiki/Female_altar_servers.

27. Sacred Congregation for Divine Worship, *Liturgicae Instaurationes: Instruction on the Orderly Carrying Out of the Constitution on the Liturgy* (September 5, 1970).

Chapter Three: Liturgical Furnishings

1. On this, see Joseph Quinn, "Altar," in *The Modern Catholic Encyclopedia*, ed. M. Glazier and M. K. Hellwig (Collegeville, MN: Liturgical Press, 2004), 20–21.

2. Enrico Mazza, *The Celebration of the Eucharist: The Origin of the Rite and the Development of Its Interpretation* (Collegeville, MN: Liturgical Press, 1999), 225.

3. Dedication of an Altar, no. 22a, in *The Rites of the Catholic Church*, 2 vols. (Collegeville, MN: Liturgical Press, 1991), 2:411.

4. See also Mark E. Wedig and Richard S. Vosko, eds., "The Arrangement and Furnishings of Churches for the Celebration of the Eucharist," in *A Commentary on the General Instruction of the Roman Missal*, ed. Edward Foley, Nathan Mitchell, Joanne M. Pierce (Collegeville, MN: Liturgical Press, 2007), 365–66.

5. T. Jerome Overbeck, "Cross," in *The New Dictionary of Sacramental Worship*, ed. Peter E. Fink (Collegeville, MN: Liturgical Press, 2000), 306.

6. Peter J. Elliot, *Ceremonies of the Modern Roman Rite* (San Francisco: Ignatius, 1995), 64.

7. International Committee on English in the Liturgy, *Book of Blessings: Approved for Use in the Dioceses of the United States of America by the National Conference of Catholic Bishops and Confirmed by the Apostolic See* (Collegeville, MN: Liturgical Press, 1989); cf. James Akin, *Mass Confusion: The Do's and Don'ts of Catholic Worship* (San Diego: Catholic Answers, 1999), 187.

8. Mark E. Wedig and Richard S. Vosko, "The Arrangement and Furnishings of Churches for the Celebration of the Eucharist," in *A Commentary on the General Instruction of the Roman Missal*, 367.

9. Joseph DeGrocco, *A Pastoral Commentary on the General Instruction of the Roman Missal* (Chicago: Liturgy Training Publications, 2011), 101.

10. Martin Connell and Sharon McMillan, "The Different Forms of Celebrating Mass," in *A Commentary on the General Instruction of the Roman Missal*, 230.

11. Ibid.

12. *Environment and Art in Catholic Worship*, 67. *Environment and Art in Catholic Worship* is a 1978 statement of the Bishops' Committee on the Liturgy of the United States Conference of Catholic Bishops. The purpose of the document is to provide principles for those involved in preparing liturgical space.

13. See "missal," in *Encyclopedia Britannica Ultimate Reference Suite* (Chicago: Encyclopedia Britannica, 2011).

14. DeGrocco, *A Pastoral Commentary on the General Instruction of the Roman Missal*, 39.

15. Connell and McMillan, "The Different Forms of Celebrating Mass," 230.

16. See Wedig and Vosko, "The Arrangement and Furnishings of Churches," 376.

17. T. Jerome Overbeck, "Sacred Vessels," in *The New Dictionary of Sacramental Worship*, 1300–1305.

18. Joseph Quinn, "Ciborium," in *The Modern Catholic Encyclopedia*, 167.

19. Richard N. Fragomeni, "Uses of Incense," in *The New Dictionary of Sacramental Worship*, 593–94.

20. Nicholas Halligan, *The Sacraments and Their Celebration* (New York: Alba House, 1986), 66–67.

21. See ibid.

22. See Congregation for Worship and the Discipline of the Sacraments, *Redemptionis Sacramentum* (2004), no. 50.

23. See Pierre-Marie Gy, "Le vin rouge, est-il preferable pour l'Eucharistie?" in *Liturgia et Unitas: In honorem Bruno Bürki*, ed. Martin Klöckener and Arnaud Join-Lambert (Geneva: Labor and Fides, 2001), 178–84.

Chapter Four: Liturgical Postures and Actions

1. See Robert Vereecke, "Liturgical Gestures," in *The New Dictionary of Sacramental Worship*, 503–13.

2. Edward Sri, *A Biblical Walk through the Mass—Understanding What We Say and Do in the Liturgy* (West Chester, PA: Ascension Press, 2011), 65.

3. *De Oratione* 23, CCL, 1:271–72.

4. *De Corona Militis* 3, CCL, 2:1043.

5. *Epist. ad Ephes.* pro. PL 26:472.

6. *Questions to the Orthodox* 115; PG 6:1363.

7. *Fragment* 7 of a treatise on Easter; PG 7:1234.

8. *De Oratione*, 23; CCL, 1:272.

9. *Peri Euxus* 31; PG 11:552.

10. *Ceremonial of Bishops*, no. 68.

11. Ibid., 70.

12. *Peri Euxus* 31; PG 11:552.

13. *De Oratione* 14; CCL, 1:265.

14. Ibid., 18; CCL, 1:267.

15. It should be noted that the *General Instruction* provides for no Sign of the Cross during the formula following the Penitential Act.

16. Tertullian, *De Corona*, no. 30, cited by Sri, *A Biblical Walk*, 17–18.

17. St. John Chrysostom, *Instructions to Catechumens*, 2, 5, in Andrew Arnold Lambing, *The Sacramentals of the Holy Catholic Church* (New York: Benziger Brothers, 1892), 70.

Chapter Five: The Introductory Rites

1. DeGrocco, *A Pastoral Commentary on the General Instruction of the Roman Missal*, 33.

2. Ibid.

3. Donald A. Withey, *Catholic Worship: An Introduction to Liturgy* (Rattlesden, Bury St. Edmunds: Kevin Mayhew Ltd, 1990), 120.

4. Ibid.

5. *Ceremonial of Bishops*, no. 131.

6. Ibid., no. 70.

7. Dominic E. Serra, "Theology of the Latin Text and Rite," in *A Commentary on the Order of Mass of The Roman Missal*, 128.

8. Cf. DeGrocco, *A Pastoral Commentary on the General Instruction of the Roman Missal*, 101.

9. Adolf Adam, *The Eucharistic Celebration: The Source and Summit of Faith*, trans. Robert C. Schultz (Collegeville, MN: Liturgical Press, 1994), 19–20.

10. My emphasis.

11. See Dennis C. Smolarski, *How Not to Say Mass: A Guidebook on Liturgical Principles and the Roman Missal* (New York/Mahwah, NJ: Paulist Press, 2002), 49.

12. Cf. Dennis C. Smolarski, *Q&A: The Mass* (Chicago: Liturgy Training Publications, 2002), 3.

13. DeGrocco, *A Pastoral Commentary on the General Instruction of the Roman Missal*, 102.

14. Josef A. Jungmann, *The Mass: An Historical, Theological and Pastoral Survey* (Collegeville, MN: Liturgical Press, 1976), 166.

15. It should be noted that the original Greek has no verb.

16. Thomas A. Krosnicki, "Grace and Peace: Greeting the Assembly," in *Shaping English Liturgy: Studies in Honor of Archbishop Denis Hurley*, ed. Peter C. Finn, James M. Schellman (Washington, DC: Pastoral Press, 1990), 93–106, at 96–97.

17. Bernard Botte, "Dominus Vobiscum," *Bible et vie Chretienne* 62 (1965): 34.

18. Cf. Finn and Schellman, *Shaping English Liturgy*, 97.

19. Thomas A. Krosnicki, "Grace and Peace," in *Shaping English Liturgy*, 104; see also Smolarski, *How Not to Say Mass*, 51–52.

20. DeGrocco, *A Pastoral Commentary on the General Instruction of the Roman Missal*, 35.

21. Theodore of Mopsuestia, *Hom. cat.* XV, 37–8, T-D, 519–21. See J. Lecuyer, *Le sacrement de l'ordination* (Paris, 1983), 106.

22. Cf. R. Cabié, *The Eucharist*, ed. A. G. Martimort, vol. 2, *The Church at Prayer* (Collegeville, MN: Liturgical Press, 1986), 50–51, quoting Narsai of Nisibis, *Hom.* 17, ed. R. H. Connolly, *The Liturgical Homilies of Narsai*, TS 8/1 (Cambridge: Cambridge University Press, 1909), 8.

23. Henry Ashworth, "*Et cum spiritu tuo*," *The Clergy Review* 51 (1966): 128.

24. Anscar J. Chupungco, "The Introductory Rites: The ICEL2010 Translation," in *A Commentary on the Order of Mass of The Roman Missal*, 137–38.

25. Ibid., 138.

26. Dominic E. Serra, "The Introductory Rites: Theology of the Latin Text and Rite," in *A Commentary on the Order of Mass of The Roman Missal*, 129.

27. Ibid.

28. Joseph Quinn, "Confiteor," in *The Modern Catholic Encyclopedia*, 183.

29. Adam, *The Eucharistic Celebration*, 23.

30. Cf. Sri, *A Biblical Walk*, 33–34.

31. Latin: *peccavi nimis*.

32. Johannes H. Emminghaus, *The Eucharist: Essence, Form, Celebration*, trans. Matthew J. O'Connell (Collegeville, MN: Liturgical Press, 1978), 119–20.

33. United States Conference of Catholic Bishops, *Sing to the Lord: Music in Divine Worship* (Washington, DC: USCCB, 2008), 147.

34. *Kyrie* comes from the Greek word *kurios* (*kyrios*), which means "Lord." It is the vocative form of the word.

35. Josef A. Jungmann, *The Mass of the Roman Rite*, trans. Francis Brunner, 2 vols. (New York: Benziger, 1951 & 1955; reprinted Westminster, MD: Christian Classics, 1986), 168.

36. Pecklers, *The Genius of the Roman Rite*, 9.

37. "Matins" refers to the first of the daily prayer services in Roman Catholic and Anglican churches. In the Roman Catholic tradition, matins consists of readings from the Bible, lessons about

the lives of the saints, and sermons. The term *matins* is derived from a Latin word meaning "of the morning."

38. Sri, *A Biblical Walk*, 43.

39. Greek: *huios* (son).

40. Greek: *tekna* (children).

41. Greek: *monogenēs*.

42. M. M. Thompson, "Gospel of John," in *Dictionary of Jesus and the Gospels*, ed. Joel G. Green, Scot McKnight, I. Howard Marshall (Downers Grove, IL: InterVarsity Press, 1992), 377.

43. Sri, *A Biblical Walk*, 45.

44. DeGrocco, *A Pastoral Commentary on the General Instruction of the Roman Missal*, 33.

45. Ibid., 37.

46. See Pecklers, *The Genius of the Roman Rite*, 11.

47. It is to be noted in this connection that the other presidential prayers, that is, Prayer over the Gifts and the Post-Communion Prayer, do not end in this fashion. Rather, the shorter ending should be used, for example, "Through Christ our Lord."

48. Smolarski, *How Not to Say Mass*, 55.

Chapter Six: The Liturgy of the Word

1. Paul F. Bradshaw, *The Search for the Origins of Christian Worship: Sources and Methods for the Study of Early Liturgy*, 2nd ed. (New York: Oxford University Press, 2002), esp. 21–72.

2. Cf. *Introduction to the Lectionary of the Mass*, no. 52.

3. Smolarski, *Q&A: The Mass*, 18.

4. Pecklers, *The Genius of the Roman Rite*, 88.

5. Cf. Joanne M. Pierce and John F. Romano, "Ordo Missae," in *A Commentary on the Order of Mass of The Roman Missal*, 16. See Peter Jeffery, "The Introduction of the Psalmody into the Roman Mass by Pope Celestine I (422–32): Reinterpreting a Passage in the *Liber Pontificalis*," *Archiv für Liturgiewissenschaft* 26 (1984): 147–55.

6. DeGrocco, *A Pastoral Commentary on the General Instruction of the Roman Missal*, 44.

7. *Ceremonial of Bishops* (Collegeville, Minnesota: Liturgical Press, 1989), no. 90, p. 40.

8. Cf. Smolarski, *How Not to Say Mass*, 67.

9. DeGrocco, *A Pastoral Commentary on the General Instruction of the Roman Missal*, 106.

10. Cf. *Ceremonial of Bishops*, no. 74, p. 38. *GIRM* 277: "The following are incensed with three swings of the thurible...the *Book of the Gospels*."

11. *Ceremonial of Bishops*, no. 74, p. 38.

12. DeGrocco, *A Pastoral Commentary on the General Instruction of the Roman Missal*, 107.

13. On this, see Robert P. Waznak, "Homily" in *The New Dictionary of Sacramental Worship*, 552–58.

14. Kevin W. Irwin, *Responses to 101 Questions on the Mass* (New York/Mahwah, NJ: Paulist Press, 1999), 64.

15. Edward Foley, "The Structure of the Mass, Its Elements and Its Parts," in *A Commentary on the General Instruction of the Roman Missal*, ed. Edward Foley, Nathan Mitchell, Joanne M. Pierce (Collegeville, MN: Liturgical Press, 2007), 156.

16. Smolarski, *How Not to Say Mass*, 69.

17. *Instruction on Certain Questions regarding the Collaboration of the Non-Ordained Faithful in the Sacred Ministry of Priest* (Vatican City: Libreria Editrice Vaticana, 1997).

18. Under special circumstances, a layperson or a male or female religious may read a prepared address or message, after a brief homily given by the celebrant or deacon or before the final blessing. The bishop may authorize this, for example, during a Sunday set aside for a special appeal or to promote a good cause. Laypersons, such as catechists, or religious may also be permitted to read a homily when they are authorized to lead a Sunday Communion service in the absence of a priest. The text is usually prepared beforehand by or in consultation with a priest.

19. Jeremy Driscoll, *What Happens at Mass?* (Chicago: Liturgy Training Publications, 2005), 51.

20. DeGrocco, *A Pastoral Commentary of the General Instruction of the Roman Missal*, 205.

21. *Ceremonial of Bishops*, no. 142. See DeGrocco, *A Pastoral Commentary on the General Instruction of the Roman Missal*, 108.

22. See Robert P. Waznak, "Homily," in *The New Dictionary of Sacramental Worship*, 556.

23. Ibid., 553.

24. See the Reply to Query 42, Official Interpretations of the *GIRM*, in the *Notices of the Sacred Congregation for Divine Worship and the Discipline of the Sacraments [1969–1981]*.

25. Arianism was a Christian heresy of the fourth century that denied the full divinity of Jesus Christ. It was named for its author, Arius, a Christian priest of Alexandria (d. 336). The teaching of Arius was condemned in 325 at the first ecumenical council at Nicaea.

26. B. Demarest, "Creeds," in *New Dictionary of Theology*, ed. Sinclair B. Ferguson and J. I. Packer (Downers Grove, IL: InterVarsity Press: 2000), 179–80.

27. Cf. Adam, *The Eucharistic Celebration*, 47.

28. For a detailed study of the Creed, see Luke Timothy Johnson, *The Creed: What Christians Believe and Why It Matters* (New York: Image, 2003).

29. Johnson, *The Creed*, 122.

30. Ibid., 122–23.

31. See Murray J. Harris, *Jesus as God: The New Testament Use of Theos in Reference to Jesus* (Grand Rapids, MI: Baker, 1992) for a detailed study of sixteen New Testament passages that refer to Jesus as God.

32. J. A. Komonchak, M. Collins, and D. A. Lane in *The New Dictionary of Theology* (Collegeville, MN: Liturgical Press, 2000), 489.

33. Johnson, *The Creed*, 155.

34. Sri, *A Biblical Walk*, 78.

35. Adam, *The Eucharistic Celebration*, 49.

36. Johnson, *The Creed*, 235.

37. M. K. Hellwig, "Marks (or Notes) of the Church," in *The Modern Catholic Encyclopedia*, 522.

38. Avery Dulles, "Catholicity," in *The New Dictionary of Theology*, 172–74.

39. International Commission on English in the Liturgy (ICEL) 2010. This is the ICEL translation of the *Missale Romanum* 2002 with the 2008 emendations, given the *recognitio* by Rome.

40. Anscar J. Chupungco, "The ICEL 2010 Translation," in

A Commentary on the General Instruction of the Roman Missal,
184.

41. ICEL 1973. This was the original English translation of
the *Missale Romanum, editio typica* done by ICEL, proposed for a
five-year period of use *ad experimentum.*

42. Chupungco, "The ICEL 2010 Translation," 185.

43. Justin Martyr, *First Apology,* 67, as quoted in *CCC* 1345.

44. Withey, *Catholic Worship,* 133.

Chapter Seven: The Liturgy of the Eucharist and the Concluding Rites

1. U.S. Conference of Catholic Bishops, Bishops' Committee on the Liturgy, *Introduction to the Order of Mass* (Washington, DC: USCCB, 2003).

2. *Traditio Apostolica* 4 and 21; cf. R. Cabié, *The Eucharist,* 77.

3. St. Cyprian, *Liber de opera et eleemosinis,* 15, ed. G. Hartel (CSEL3, Vienna, 1868), cited by R. Cabie, *The Eucharist,* 77.

4. St. Augustine, *Confessions,* V, 9 (CCL 27:66).

5. Council of Carthage, canon 23 (according to the *Breviarium Hipponense*), ed. C. Munier, *Concilia Africae* (CCL 149), 39–40. Cf. Cabié, *The Eucharist,* 83.

6. Ibid.

7. Dennis C. Smolarski, *Q&A: The Mass* (Chicago: Liturgy Training Publications, 2002), 50.

8. *Notitiae* 17 (1981): 61. *Notitiae* is the publication of the Holy See's Congregation for Divine Worship and the Discipline of the Sacraments.

9. Smolarski, *Q&A: The Mass,* 51.

10. The *Instruction* says that the priest *must* receive Communion from what he consecrated at that Mass (*GIRM* 157).

11. Patrick Regan, "The Preparation of the Gifts: Theology of the Latin Text and Rite," in *A Commentary on the Order of Mass of the Roman Rite,* 216.

12. Cf. Adam, *The Eucharistic Celebration,* 59.

13. Reply to Query 51, Official Interpretations of the *General Instruction* in the Notices of The Sacred Congregation for Divine

Worship and the Discipline of the Sacraments (1969–1981). My emphasis.

14. Martin Connell and Sharon McMillan, "The Different Forms of Celebrating Mass," in *A Commentary on the General Instruction of the Roman Missal*, 248.

15. In fact, in the German Missal, the simple "Let us pray" is given as one of three options to introduce the prayer over the offerings.

16. Anscar J. Chupungco, "The Preparation of the Gifts: The ICEL 2010 Translation," in *A Commentary on the Order of Mass of the Roman Missal*, 220.

17. According to Chupungco, "The Latin conjunction *atque* (*ac* before a consonant) is different from *et*, although both are translated in English with the conjunction 'and'. In Latin lexical usage *et* enumerates, while *atque* or *ac* joins together nouns, pronouns, and verbs. The Latin text does not say *meum et vestrum sacrificium* ('my sacrifice and your sacrifice'). Rather, it carefully chooses *ac*: 'my sacrifice, which is also your sacrifice'..." (Ibid.).

18. Ibid.

19. Baldovin, "History of the Latin Text and Rite," 247.

20. Enrico Mazza, *The Eucharistic Prayers of the Roman Rite* (Collegeville, MN: Liturgical Press, 2004), 56.

21. John Barry Ryan, "Theology of the Eucharistic Prayer," in Fink, ed., *The New Dictionary of Sacramental Worship*, 451–58.

22. DeGrocco, *A Pastoral Commentary on the General Instruction of the Roman Missal*, 63.

23. David Power, "Eucharistic Prayer I: Theology of the Latin Text and Rite," in *A Commentary on the Order of Mass of the Roman Missal*, 261.

24. Latin: *dignum*.

25. Power, "Eucharistic Prayer I: Theology of the Latin Text and Rite," 262.

26. Latin: *iustum*.

27. Bernard Botte and Christine Mohrmann, *L'Ordinaire de la Messe. Texte critique, traduction et études* (Paris: Cerf. 1955), 74n1.

28. Latin: *aequum et salutare*.

29. *Deus Sabaoth*.

30. Barry Hudock, *The Eucharistic Prayer: A User's Guide* (Collegeville, MN: Liturgical Press, 2010), 50.

31. Power, "Eucharistic Prayer I," 265.

32. Latin: *clementissime*.

33. Enrico Mazza, *The Eucharistic Prayers of the Roman Rite* (Collegeville, MN: Liturgical Press, 2004), 59.

34. Ibid., 60–61.

35. Jungmann, *The Mass of the Roman Rite*, 2:150–51.

36. Mazza, *Eucharistic Prayers*, 59.

37. Cf. Ibid., 62.

38. Cf. Ibid., 63.

39. Ibid.

40. Gilbert Ostdiek, "Eucharistic Prayer I: The ICEL2010 Translation," in *A Commentary on the Order of Mass of the Roman Missal*, 278.

41. Mazza, *Eucharistic Prayers*, 65.

42. Latin: *salus*.

43. Latin: *incolumitas*.

44. It should, however, be noted that the ancient Anaphora of Addai and Mari does not have an institution narrative. It should also be pointed out that the Catholic Church formally acknowledges that it is possible to validly confect the Eucharist in a liturgy that does not include the words of consecration. This is exemplified in the permission, given by Pope John Paul II in 2001, for Chaldean Catholics to participate in the liturgy of the Assyrian Church of the East, even though that rite's Eucharistic Prayer, the ancient Anaphora of Addai and Mari, as we have stated above, lacks an institution narrative. Cf. The Pontifical Council for the Promotion of Christian Unity, "Guidelines for Admission to the Eucharist between the Chaldean and the Assyrian Church of the East." See also Robert Taft, "Mass without a Consecration? The Historic Agreement on the Eucharist between the Catholic Church and the Assyrian Church of the East Promulgated 26 October 2001," *Worship* 77 (2003): 482–509.

45. Latin: *tradetur*, from *tradere*, "give up," "betray," "hand over."

46. Latin: *ex hoc*.

47. See Charlton T. Lewis and Charles Short, *A Latin Dictionary* (Oxford: Clarendon Press, 1998) who give the same range of meaning for *poculum*.

48. Greek: *poterion*; Latin: *calix*.

49. Latin: *testamentum*.

50. Prot. N. 467/05/L, in *Notitiae* 481–82 (2006): 444–46.

51. *Statuts synodaux de Paris*, no. 80, cited by Cabié, *The Eucharist*, 137–38.

52. See the Reply to Query 12 in *Not*. 13 (1977) 94–95, no. 2.

53. This third acclamation is said to be a blend of phrases from Rev 5:9 ("You are worthy to take the scroll and to open its seals, for you were slaughtered and by your blood you ransomed for God saints from every tribe and language and people and nation." and 1 Pet 1:18–19 ("You know that you were ransomed from the futile ways inherited from your ancestors, not with perishable things like silver or gold, but with the precious blood of Christ, like that of a lamb without defect or blemish"). See Michael Witczak, "Eucharistic Prayer III: History of the Latin Text and Rite," in *A Commentary on the Order of Mass of the Roman Missal*, 358.

54. DeGrocco, *A Pastoral Commentary on the General Instruction of the Roman Missal*, 115.

55. Hudock, *The Eucharistic Prayer: A User's Guide*, 54–55.

56. Ibid., 58.

57. Edward Foley, "The Structure of the Mass, Its Elements and Its Parts," in *A Commentary on the General Instruction of the Roman Missal*, 175.

58. R. C. D. Jasper and G. J. Cuming, *Prayers of the Eucharist: Early and Reformed*, 3rd ed. (Collegeville, MN: Liturgical Press, 1990), 24.

59. Ibid., 35.

60. Mazza, *Eucharistic Prayers*, 82.

61. Cf. Basil of Caesarea, *Contra Eunomium* (III, 5), who says, "Baptism is the seal [*sphragis*] of faith and faith is an assent to God" (*PG* 29:665).

62. Cf. Mazza, *Eucharistic Prayers*, 85.

63. David Power, "Eucharistic Prayer II: Theology of the Latin Text and Rite," in *A Commentary on the Order of Mass of The Roman Missal*, 322. See also Mark 1:10; Luke 3:22; Matt 3:16.

64. Latin: *ministrare*.

65. Power, "Eucharistic Prayer II," 316.

66. *Lumen Gentium*, nos. 6–7; Eph 5:23–32. See also Tom Elich, "Eucharistic Prayer II: The ICEL 2010 Translation," in *A Commentary on the Order of Mass of the Roman Missal*, 333.

67. Witczak, "Eucharistic Prayer III: History of the Latin Text and Rite," 369.

68. Latin: *pertubatio*.

69. Witczak, "Eucharistic Prayer III: History of the Latin Text and Rite," 372.

70. Pecklers, *The Genius of the Roman Rite*, 84.

71. Ibid.

72. Justin Martyr, *First Apology*, 65:1. See John Baldovin, "The Communion Rite: History of the Latin Text and Rite," in *A Commentary on the Order of Mass of the Roman Missal*, 593.

73. Martyr, *First Apology*, 67:1.

74. Cyril of Jerusalem, *Mystagogical Catechesis* V:11, in *The Awe-Inspiring Rites of Initiation*, ed. Edward Yarnold, 2nd ed. (Collegeville, MN: Liturgical Press, 1994), 94.

75. *Ceremonial of Bishops*, no. 159.

76. A liturgical expression of praise to God.

77. Cf. Baldovin, "The Communion Rite," 598.

78. DeGrocco, *A Pastoral Commentary on the General Instruction of the Roman Missal*, 67.

79. *Apostolic Constitutions*, VIII, 11, 8–9. See Cabié, *The Eucharist*, 113–14.

80. Cf. *Ceremonial of Bishops*, nos. 99–103.

81. *Sacramentum Caritatis*, no. 50n150.

82. Ibid., no. 49.

83. Smolarski, *How Not to Say Mass*, 73.

84. Ralph A. Kiefer, *To Give Thanks and Praise* (Washington, DC: National Association of Pastoral Musicians, 1980), 140.

85. For the following, see R. Cabié, *The Eucharist*, 111–13.

86. Allan Bouley, "Eucharistic Reservation," in *The New Dictionary of Theology*, ed. J. A. Komonchak, M. Collins, D. A. Lane (Collegeville, MN: Liturgical Press, 2000), 878.

87. Innocent I, *Ep. 25 ad Decentium*, quoted by Cabié, *The Eucharist*, 111.

88. Innocent I, *Ep. 25 ad Decentium*. Cf. Cabié, *The Eucharist*, 112.

89. See Cabié, *The Eucharist*, 113.

90. Theodore of Mopsuestia, *Homiliae catecheticae*, 16, 15. See Cabié, *The Eucharist*, 113.

91. DeGrocco, *A Pastoral Commentary on the General Instruction of the Roman Missal*, 25.

92. Ibid, 118.

93. United States Conference of Catholic Bishops, *Guidelines for Concelebration of the Eucharist* (Washington, DC: USCCB, 2003).

94. Peter J. Elliot, *Liturgical Question Box: Answers to Common Questions about the Modern Liturgy* (San Francisco: Ignatius Press, 1998), 107.

95. Sacred Congregation for the Sacraments and Divine Worship, *Inaestimabile Donum: Instruction Concerning Worship of the Eucharistic Mystery* (April 17, 1980).

96. Council of Rouen, canon 2; cf. Cabié, *The Eucharist*, 135.

97. DeGrocco, *A Pastoral Commentary on the General Instruction of the Roman Missal*, 156.

98. See can. 671 in the *Code of Canons of the Eastern Churches*.

99. Tom Elich, "The Concluding Rites: The ICEL2010 Translation," in *A Commentary on the Order of Mass of the Roman Missal*, 640.

100. It should be noted that in the 1570 Missal, the priest could also bless three times. However, according to the present Roman Missal, the priest blesses only once.

101. Elich, "The Concluding Rites: The ICEL2010 Translation," 640.

102. Smolarski, *How Not to Say Mass*, 95.

103. Metzger, "A Eucharistic Lexicon," 3.

104. *Ceremonial of Bishops*, no. 73.

105. Smolarski, *Q & A: The Mass*, 82.

Select Bibliography

Adam, Adolf. *The Eucharistic Celebration: The Source and Summit of Faith*. Translated by Robert C. Schultz. Collegeville, MN: Liturgical Press, 1994.

Akin, James. *Mass Confusion: The Dos and Don'ts of Catholic Worship*. San Diego: Catholic Answers, 1999.

Arinze, Francis Cardinal. *Celebrating the Holy Eucharist*. San Francisco: Ignatius Press, 2005.

Ashworth, Henry. "Et cum spiritu tuo," *The Clergy Review* 51 (1966).

Botte, Bernard. "Dominus Vobiscum," *Bible et vie Chretienne* 62 (1965).

Bradshaw, Paul F. *Eucharistic Origins*. London: S.P.CK., 2004.

———. *The Search for the Origins of Christian Worship: Sources and Methods for the Study of Early Liturgy*. 2nd ed. Oxford and New York: Oxford University Press, 2002.

Bradshaw, Paul, Maxwell Johnson, and L. Edward Phillips. *The Apostolic Tradition: A Commentary*. Edited by Harold W. Attridge, Hermeneia series. Minneapolis: Fortress Press, 2002.

Cabié, R. *The Eucharist*. Vol. 2 of *The Church at Prayer*. Edited by A. G. Martimort. Collegeville, MN: Liturgical Press, 1986.

Chupungco, Anscar J., ed. *The Eucharist*. Vol. 3 in *Handbook for Liturgical Studies*. Collegeville, MN: Liturgical Press, 1999.

DeGrocco, Joseph. *A Pastoral Commentary on the General Instruction of the Roman Missal*. Chicago: Liturgy Training Publications, 2011.

Driscoll, Jeremy. *What Happens at Mass?* Chicago: Liturgy Training Publications, 2005.

Elliot, Peter J. *Ceremonies of the Modern Roman Rite*. San Francisco: Ignatius, 1995.

Emminghaus, Johannes H. *The Eucharist: Essence, Form, Celebration*. Translated by Matthew J. O'Connell. Collegeville, MN: Liturgical Press, 1978.

Finn, Peter C., and James M. Schellman, eds. *Shaping English Liturgy: Studies in Honor of Archbishop Denis Hurley*. Washington, DC: Pastoral Press, 1990.

Fitzmyer, J. A. *The Gospel According to Luke X–XXIV*. Anchor Bible Series, vol. 28A. Garden City, NY: Doubleday, 1985.

Foley, Edward, Nathan D. Mitchell, and Joanne M. Pierce, ed. *A Commentary on the Order of Mass of The Roman Missal*. Collegeville, MN: Liturgical Press, 2011.

Halligan, Nicholas. *The Sacraments and their Celebration*. New York: Alba House, 1986.

Harrington, Daniel. "The Gospel according to Mark." In *The New Jerome Biblical Commentary*, 41:95. Englewood Cliffs, NJ: Prentice Hall, 1990.

Irwin, Kevin W. *Responses to 101 Questions on the Mass*. New York/Mahwah, NJ: Paulist Press, 1999.

Johnson, Luke Timothy. *The Creed: What Christians Believe and Why It Matters*. New York: Image, 2003.

Joncas, Jan Michael. "Tasting the Kingdom of God: The Meal Ministry of Jesus and Its Implications for Contemporary Ministry and Life," *Worship* 74 (2000): 329–65.

Jungmann, Josef A. *The Mass of the Roman Rite*. Translated by Francis Brunner. 2 vols. Westminster, MD: Christian Classics, 1986.

———. *The Mass: An Historical, Theological and Pastoral Survey*. Collegeville, MN: Liturgical Press, 1976.

Kiefer, Ralph A. *To Give Thanks and Praise*. Washington, DC: National Association of Pastoral Musicians, 1980.

LaVerdiere, Eugene. *The Eucharist in the New Testament and the Early Church*. Collegeville, MN: Liturgical Press, 1996.

Marshall, I. H. *Last Supper and Lord's Supper*. Exeter: Paternoster Press, 1980.

———. "The Lord's Supper." In *Dictionary of Paul and His Letters*, edited by Gerald F. Hawthorne, Ralph P. Martin, and (assoc. editor) Daniel G. Reid. Downers Grove, IL: Intervarsity Press, 1993.

Matthieu, Smyth. "The Anaphora of the So-Called 'Apostolic Tradition' and the Roman Eucharistic Prayer." In *Issues in Eucharistic Praying in East and West*, edited by Maxwell Johnson. Collegeville, MN: Liturgical Press, 2010.

Mazza, Enrico. *The Celebration of the Eucharist: The Origin of the Rite and the Development of Its Interpretation*. Collegeville, MN: Liturgical Press, 1999.

———. *The Eucharistic Prayers of the Roman Rite*. Collegeville, MN: Liturgical Press, 2004.

Murphy-O'Connor, Jerome. "The First Letter to the Corinthians." In *The New Jerome Biblical Commentary*, edited by Raymond E. Brown, Joseph A. Fitzmyer, and Roland E. Murphy. Englewood Cliffs, NJ: Prentice Hall, 1990.

Pecklers, Keith F. *The Genius of the Roman Rite: On the Reception and Implementation of the New Missal*. Collegeville, MN: Liturgical Press, 2009.

Perkins, Pheme. "The Gospel of Mark." In *New Interpreter's Bible*, 8:517. Nashville: Abingdon Press, 1995.

Pierce, Joanne M., and John F. Romano. "The Ordo Missae of the Roman Rite: Historical Background." In *A Commentary on the Order of Mass of the Roman Missal*, edited by Edward Foley. Collegeville, MN Liturgical Press, 2011.

Sampley, J. Paul. "The First Letter to the Corinthians." In *New Interpreter's Bible*, edited by Leander Keck, 10:934. Nashville: Abingdon Press, 2000.

Smith, Dennis. *From Symposium to Eucharist: The Banquet in the Early Christian World*. Minneapolis: Fortress Press, 2003.

Smolarski, Dennis C. *How Not to Say Mass: A Guidebook on Liturgical Principles and the Roman Missal*. New York: Paulist Press, 2002.

———. *Q&A: The Mass*. Chicago: Liturgy Training Publications, 2002.

Sri, Edward. *A Biblical Walk through the Mass—Understanding What We Say and Do in the Liturgy*. West Chester, PA: Ascension Press, 2011.

Stein, R. H. "Last Supper." In *Dictionary of Jesus and the Gospels,* edited by Joel G. Green, Scot McKnight, and I. Howard Marshall, 444. Downer's Grove, IL: InterVarsity Press, 1998.

Withey, Donald A. *Catholic Worship: An Introduction to Liturgy.* Rattlesden, Bury St. Edmunds, UK: Kevin Mayhew Ltd, 1990.

Wuerl, Cardinal Donald, and Mike Aquilina. *The Mass—the Glory, the Mystery, the Tradition.* New York: Image, 2013.

Index